DOUGLAS GOLF CLUB
GALF-CHUMANN NA DÚGHLAISE

Centenary History 1909–2009

DOUGLAS GOLF CLUB

Centenary History 1909–2009

Diarmuid Ó Drisceoil

FIRST PUBLISHED IN 2009 BY
Douglas Golf Club,
Cork

ISBN: 978-0-9564411-0-2

Design and typesetting by Stuart Coughlan at edit+
Cover design by Stuart Coughlan at edit+
Typeset in Sabon
Printed in Cork by City Print Ltd

Contents

The Royal and Ancient Golf Club of St Andrews
Fife KY16 9JD
Telephone (01334) 460000

July 2009

Mr Tom Collins
Captain
Douglas Golf Club
Douglas
Co.Cork
Ireland

Dear Mr Captain

On behalf of the Members of The Royal and Ancient Golf Club, I send you our warmest congratulations on your Centenary.

We trust that your Members both present and future will enjoy their golf and the friendships made and renewed during your celebrations.

With all good wishes for your continued success.

Yours sincerely

H.M.J. RITCHIE
Captain

Hamish M J Ritchie,
captain of Royal and Ancient
Golf Club of St Andrews

Foreword

For me, writing this foreword meant taking a long journey down 'memory lane' – a journey of seventy-seven years – because it was in 1932 that I found my way up Maryborough Hill to first try my hand at the game of golf. I discovered, like many others, that it was not as easy as it looked. It took a fair share of practice to move out of the 'hit and miss' stage, and still more work to achieve any measure of consistency. I discovered that a humble approach to the game was very important, because when you thought you had found the secret, your game would go to pieces and you could do nothing right!

But those years of striving at Douglas Golf Club brought me much in return. They brought me the friendship of so many kind people – the members, both ladies and men. When I had to leave Douglas and golf over sixty years ago, I took my memories with me. They were to help later in difficult times.

Let this foreword be my 'Thank You' for that.

Dan Fitzgerald

Officers' Introduction

Being the Douglas Golf Club officers during the celebrations of our centenary year was a special honour and a great privilege. The three of us have had parents who were committee members and officers in the past, and this continuity and tradition typifies the family ethos of the club, of which members are rightly proud.

The various events that marked the passage of centenary year were the product of dedicated planning by the centenary year committee established in 2007, enthusiastically supported by the other committees and by hundreds of members. As this book shows, the club has passed through many exciting and often difficult times. We are certain that the spirit and enthusiasm of the members over all those years will be just as willingly harnessed to carry the club forward to even greater achievements in the future.

As a great year draws to a close, our fondest wish is that the members of Douglas Golf Club will look back in another 100 years as proudly as we look back at our first century.

We wish all our members, present and future, many years of enjoyment at Douglas Golf Club.

Seán McHenry
President

Deirdre Buckley
Lady Captain

Tom Collins
Captain

Author's Preface

As Douglas Golf Club planned its centenary-year celebrations for 2009, it was thought appropriate that a history of the club should be written to record its origins, growth and development through its first hundred years. I was honoured to be asked to undertake the task, and in over two years of research and writing I have got to know not only many of the current members but also many of those who were part of the club in its early years. The latter have long gone to their eternal rewards, but they are very much alive in the handwritten minute books, old photographs, memories and traditions of the club.

Though founded in 1909, the records of the club survive only from 1921, as in May of that year the clubhouse was destroyed in an arson attack. All the minute books, account ledgers, photographs and other documents were lost, and the history of the first twelve years of the club had to be sourced elsewhere. For the years from 1921, the sources within the club are more complete, and the task of research was made somewhat easier through having access to the recorded details of club meetings, accounts, and so on.

The story of Douglas Golf Club is more than a story about golf: it is the story of men and women who have created a tradition of participation, competition, enjoyment and success that has survived 100 years. The story has its memorable characters – some who rallied the members when the club faced imminent extinction, others who achieved the very highest honours on the field of play, and still more who drove change at significant stages to ensure the club's future. There are also memorable events: the destruction of the clubhouse in May 1921, the course redesign by the great Alister Mackenzie, the exhibition matches by George Duncan and Arthur Havers at Douglas in 1926, the twelve Senior Cup victories by the ladies of the club, Bill Kelleher's wonderful international debut in 1962, John McHenry's participation in the Walker Cup of 1987, and many more.

I have endeavoured to do justice to the history of the club, and to capture the spirit that has sustained and driven its members through its first century. I could not have completed the task without the help of many people both within and outside the club. The members of the centenary year committee under its chairman Val O'Mahony were always available and supportive through the two and a half years of the project. Centenary year president, Seán McHenry, was particularly helpful in sourcing photographs and other memorabilia, as well as sharing his memories of over sixty years at the club. Secretary/manager, Ronan Burke, and Deirdre McAuliffe and Caroline McCarthy at the club office were always patient and accommodating, and made my work there a pleasure.

A number of people at the club consented to being interviewed and greatly helped my understanding of the club and its traditions: Frank Bowen, Con and Grace Buckley, Dave Canty, Fr Daniel Fitzgerald, Oonagh Fitzpatrick, Ann Hegarty, Helen Hennessy, Ann Heskin, Eavan Higgins, John McHenry, Éamonn McSweeney, Peter Morris, Gary Nicholson, Tadgh O'Halloran and Geoff Thompson. A number of others also assisted me in my work by sharing their memories, providing photographs, answering numerous questions about the rules and etiquette of golf, lending books and albums, offering helpful suggestions, and correcting my errors: Margaret Barry, the family of the late John Brett, Bob Casey, Seán Cody, Tom Collins, Dan Daly, Wendy Daly, Pat Desmond, Kitty Dillon, Maria Dorgan, Pauline Downey, Declan Farmer, Tony Floyd, Jennifer Flynn, Barry Galvin & Co. Solicitors, Fr James Good, Phyllis Harrington, Donal Hurley, John Keating, Seán Kelly, Ed Kenny, Richard Lonergan, Phyllis Martin, Frank McGrath, Jim McKenna, Ogie O'Callaghan, Barry Oliver, the family of the late Piaras Ó Dálaigh, Teddy O'Donovan, Pádraig Ó Drisceoil, Colman O'Mahony, John O'Shaughnessy, Kevin N O'Sullivan, Sinéad O'Sullivan, Tim O'Sullivan, Ray Quinn, Clare Roseingrave, Andrew Scanlan, Eamonn Scanlon, John Sheehan, Máiréad Thomas, Helen Bennett Whelan and Hilda Whelehan.

A special 'thank you' to Éamonn McSweeney, Hilary Herbert and Úna Kindlon, who were very generous in providing photographs from their own collections. I am also very grateful to Tim O'Brien of the *Irish Examiner*, who very kindly allowed me access to his as yet unpublished work, *Golf in Cork*, which proved to be an invaluable source.

I would particularly like to acknowledge the help of Douglas member Liam Connolly in connection with this project – he made his unique golf library available to me, made many valuable suggestions, and pointed me in worthwhile directions. I am also grateful to him for writing the feature on Redmond Simcox.

The National Library of Ireland and the British Newspapers Library at Collindale, London, facilitated aspects of the research, and the staff of the Local Studies Department of Cork City Library were, as ever, most helpful.

I thank Stuart Coughlan at edit+ for his creative and professional work on the design and typesetting, and Dominic Carroll for copy-editing, proofreading and indexing the text. Finally, I thank my family, Miriam, Méabh and Aonghus, for their support and understanding throughout the project.

Diarmuid Ó Drisceoil
December 2009

1 *Origins*

It is not possible to say precisely when or where golf was first played. Games using a club and ball are common to many places, peoples and periods of history. Indeed, it has been suggested, somewhat tongue-in-cheek, that Cú Chulainn, the great hero of ancient Irish literature, played a form of golf, although he is more commonly associated with the sport of hurling. The part of the saga *Táin Bó Cúalnge* that recounts the boyhood deeds of Cú Chulainn has the following description of a game played by young warriors:

> When they played the hole-game – a game which was played on the green of Emain – and when it was their turn to cast the ball and his to defend, he would catch the thrice fifty balls outside the hole and none would go past him into the hole. When it was their turn to keep goal and his to hurl, he would put the thrice fifty balls unerringly into the hole ...[1]

While many interpret this as a description of a form of hurling, it is interesting that the object of the game was to put the ball in a hole. One could not, however, use a reference such as this to suggest an Irish origin for the game!

Sports like hurling, shinty, lacrosse, hockey, croquet and cricket are all variations on basic club-and-ball games that were common in many European countries in the medieval and later periods. These games are depicted in illustrated manuscripts and paintings as team games with much physical contact, and are more reminiscent of hockey, lacrosse or hurling rather than golf. In thirteenth-century France, returning crusaders adapted the Persian game of *chawgán*, or polo, that they had seen in the Middle East, and created a game called *pallemail*. This was a target ball-and-club game and involved no physical opposition. This later developed into a multi-club driving-and-putting game. By the fifteenth century two target games had evolved from *pallemail*: one was played cross-country or along malls with wooden mallets and balls; the other, called *colf*, developed in Flanders and was played with a small ball and a wooden club with a curved heel. By the mid-1500s a Dutch variant called *kolf* had developed; it was played with more sophisticated equipment. At that time, sports were not codified as they are today, and the rules and

Facing page, clockwise from top:

Charles I on the links at Leith in 1641 as he receives news of an outbreak of rebellion in Ireland.

A seventeenth-century Dutch tile depicting *kolf*.

A club-and-ball game as depicted in a fifteenth-century manuscript.

procedures no doubt varied greatly from place to place. Dutch and Flemish artists often depicted these games, or versions of them, being played on land and on ice.

It is from these origins that the game of golf developed in Scotland, a fusion of *pallemail*, *colf* and *kolf* that evolved over time as players experimented with multiple clubs and different balls until a satisfying long target game was established in the late seventeenth/ early eighteenth century. An early version of golf was being played on the eastern Scottish coast as early as the 1400s, following the introduction of variants of the game from the Low Countries across the North Sea, probably through contacts in trade and fishing. This process of outside influence and local evolution happened over a considerable time, and eventually the game grew and strengthened in Scotland, and took on the characteristics that have made it one of the most widely played games in the world today.

Early Golf in Ireland

Golf, or 'goff', as it was originally known, is first mentioned in an Irish context in the early seventeenth century in connection with the acquisition of lands in the Ards Peninsula of County Down in 1606 by two Scottish adventurers, James Hamilton and Hugh Montgomery. Amongst other things, Montgomery had a school built in the vicinity of what is now Newtownards, with a green 'for recreation at goff, football and archery'.[2] The first documented mention of a golf club in Ireland appears in an advertisement in *Faulkner's Dublin Journal* of 23 October 1762 concerning the meeting of a 'Goff Club' in Bray, County Wicklow. Golf was played on common ground on the seafront in Bray at the time, as evidenced by an advertisement for the letting of a property adjacent to the town in 1773 that mentions that it is 'bounded on the East by a Common, famous for that manly Exercise called GOFF'.[3] References such as these are rare, and while they do suggest that golf was known and played by some in Ireland as early as the seventeenth and eighteenth centuries, it was not until the second half of the nineteenth century that golf took firm root in this country.

Up to the nineteenth century, golf was essentially a Scottish game, and was not widely played outside that country. Before the game became organised by clubs and played on courses specifically designed or laid out for the purpose, golf was played on commons or on links – undulating sandy ground near the sea. At this time, and into the twentieth century, golf was mostly played in the winter months when grass growth was slow or at a standstill, and seaside links were particularly favoured as grass growth was coarse and sparse, and more suitable to the playing of the game. People of all classes played, and they shared their 'courses' with other users of the commons and links, including animals – especially sheep – that grazed those lands. As golf developed in eighteenth-century Scotland, it came more under the control of those with money and leisure time. As Geoffrey Cousins explains in *Golf in Britain: A Social History from the Beginnings to the Present Day*, 'Everybody continued to play on the links but there were tacitly accepted distinctions. The gentlemen became exclusive, the artisans and tradesmen knew their places, and a third class, composed of club- and ball-makers, caddies and professional players made golf their livelihood'.[4]

The idea of a golf club (sometimes called a 'company' or 'society') grew out of the custom that developed whereby players adjourned after a match to a local inn, tavern or private residence to socialise, review play and plan future matches. Many such clubs required members to wear a uniform – usually a red coat – when playing so as to distinguish them from other people on the links, and members were required to wear the uniform not only on the course but also at club meetings and dinners. This led to the game becoming more expensive, and the cost of equipment, balls, uniforms and club membership gradually made golf the preserve of those with money, while the rules of admission to golf clubs and societies ensured that members came from the higher strata of society.

The first clubs became established in Scotland from the 1730s onwards, and by 1800 there were only seven clubs in existence, all of them in that country. Even in the first fifty years or so of the nineteenth century only sixteen further clubs came into being, and fourteen of these were again in Scotland. In the second half of the century things changed, and golf rapidly grew from being a somewhat peculiar Scottish pastime to a sport and leisure activity beloved of many in the rest of Britain and in Ireland. One factor that contributed significantly to this growth and spread was the development of a new type of golf ball: the 'guttie', or gutta-percha ball.

Up until the mid-nineteenth century, golfers played with a ball known as a 'feathery', so-called as it consisted of a leather outer skin tightly filled

A uniformed golfer, watched by his caddie, on an early links course.

Top:
Feathery balls were used up until the mid-nineteenth century and were so-called as they consisted of a leather outer skin tightly filled with feathers.

Below:
The gutta-percha, or 'guttie' ball, replaced the feathery, and became the standard ball of the second half of the nineteenth century.

with feathers. Traditionally, the fill of a top hat of feathers was needed, the feathers being boiled to make them more manageable. The work of manufacture was delicate and time-consuming as the hand-stitched finished ball had to be as near to spherical as the skill of the maker could achieve, so as to give the ball an adequate level of aerodynamism. These balls were expensive, and could cost from a half-crown to four or five shillings each – the equivalent of an artisan's weekly wage in the eighteenth century.

The gutta-percha ball was invented in the 1840s by Dr Adam Peterson, a Scottish clergyman. He found that gutta-percha – a tough plastic substance derived from the latex of various Malayan trees – could be softened by heat and moulded, after which it hardened again. This was ideal for moulding into golf balls, and Dr Peterson took out a patent on his invention. He negotiated a manufacturing deal with a firm in London, and the new ball was in commercial production by 1848. The early versions of the ball were smooth and did not fly well. It was observed that wear and tear, resulting in numerous cuts and striations, improved their aerodynamic quality, and this resulted in such markings being incorporated into the moulding process, leading eventually to the development of the characteristic dimpled surface of the ball. These balls were much less expensive than the old featheries, and greatly reduced the cost of playing golf. They became the standard ball for the next fifty years or so until they were superseded at the beginning of the twentieth century by the Haskell ball. This consisted of a rubber core with elastic wound around it at tension enclosed within a dimpled outer 'jacket'. When Sandy Herd won the Open in 1902 using a Haskell ball, the guttie very quickly went out of use.

The latter half of the nineteenth century saw other changes in Britain and Ireland that impacted on society and the economy in general, and which facilitated the growth and spread of golf. In this period, changes in Britain were usually closely mirrored in Ireland. The Industrial Revolution in Britain, and to a lesser extent in Ireland, created employment for many, and wealth and leisure time for the few. The traditional Ascendency sports of hunting, shooting, fishing and the like may have attracted some, but the landed gentry, high-ranking military men and clergy tended to see these sports and their attendant social gatherings as their own preserve. It was difficult for 'outsiders', wealthy though they may have been, to join in and be accepted as equals. A 'new' sport like golf did not have centuries of established exclusivity behind it, and clubs formed by the new men of money and leisure could cater very satisfactorily to the sporting and social needs of the not-so-highly born, although many of the earlier golf clubs had a distinctly upper-class membership. A growing middle class of professionals, businessmen, bankers, academics and higher civil servants became established in Britain and Ireland in the second half of the nineteenth century, and they had the leisure time, the interest and the means to play golf. As Geoffrey Cousins notes:

> The game of social self-importance was now in full swing among the middle classes and the modes of Mayfair were followed by worldly men and their ambitious wives. To such people golf seemed to be a pastime peculiarly suitable for inclusion in the daily whirl, and membership of a golf club a useful addition to one's self-importance … In various parts of the country residents of equal standing combined to form clubs from which they hoped to derive not only health-giving exercise but also the right kind of social intercourse.[5]

Four of the seven men who founded Douglas Golf Club in 1909, for instance, were merchants, and the others a stockbroker, a solicitor and an academic. Men such as these typified the new middle class that grew and prospered in the latter part of the nineteenth century, and which made up the bulk of the membership of golf clubs.

The growth of the railway network in the second half of the nineteenth century was a significant influence on the growth and spread of golf on both sides of the Irish sea. The railways gave a cheap and efficient means of transport to golf courses within easy reach of the cities. As William Gibson wrote:

> Uppermost in the minds of the golfing pioneers at this time [1880s and 1890s] was the proximity of a railway station, close to their intended golfing venture, and the railway companies were most willing to assist. Train timetables were altered to suit the golfing public, reduced fares were agreed with the golf clubs and in some instances the railway companies decided to build their own golf courses.[6]

Proximity to rail and tram
lines was key to the siting
of early golf courses. The
course at Douglas was
a relatively short walk
from the terminus of the
Blackpool–Douglas tram.
A young H H Nalder,
club president in 1919, is
seated on the upper deck.

Proximity to rail and tram lines was key to the siting of early golf courses. The course at Douglas was a relatively short walk from the terminus of the Blackpool–Douglas tram. A young H H Nalder, club president in 1919, is seated on the upper deck.

The Douglas course was purposely sited near the terminus of the tram from Cork's city centre. Elsewhere in County Cork, the golf course at Muskerry was served by the Muskerry Light Railway, Monkstown could be reached on the Cork–Blackrock–Passage rail line, while Cork Golf Club and Rushbrooke also had rail connections to the city as well as to Youghal and Queenstown. The railway companies valued their golfing customers, and supported clubs financially as well as donating trophies. Douglas Golf Club's earliest trophy, for example, is the Tramway Cup, donated by the Cork Electric Lighting and Tramways Company.

Hotel development in the later decades of the nineteenth century also helped the growth and spread of golf, and in some cases these hotels were owned by railway companies. Holidays were strongly promoted that combined golf on a seaside links with comfortable hotel accommodation, all accessed by rail. Golf courses at Spanish Point, Ballybunion, Lahinch, Portrush and elsewhere benefitted from this combination of development.

The British military presence in Ireland was a very significant factor in the growth of golf here. This was particularly noticeable in the case of Scottish regiments, whose officers, drawn from the upper classes of Scotland, were often committed golfers. The golf clubs in many so-called 'garrison towns' owe their origin to the presence of regiments such as these.

A growing interest in sport in general in the later nineteenth century assisted the popularisation of golf, amongst many other sports. A growing affluence, free time and cheap rail transport enabled not only players but also spectators of sport to travel to play

LAKES OF KILLARNEY.
ROYAL VICTORIA HOTEL.

(Exquisitely situated directly on the Lake Shore).

The Home of Royalties and other Distinguished Personages when Touring in Ireland.

The Royal Victoria Hotel is the ONLY Hotel in Killarney at which the late King Edward VII. ever stayed, and where His Majesty's signature can be seen. Under the distinguished Patronage of T.R.H. The Duke and Duchess of Connaught, Prince Arthur, Princess Margaret, and Princess Victoria Patricia of Connaught ; the Countess of Aberdeen, the Royal Families of France and Belgium, the Nobility and Gentry of Great Britain and Ireland, and the leading German and American Families.

Lighted throughout, including all Bedrooms, by Electricity. Moderate charges.

Telegraph and Telephone Offices in Hotel.

Visitors to this Hotel have free access to the Killarney Golf Links, the finest inland 18 hole course in Ireland. A small charge is made for Green Fees.

This Hotel, containing over 100 Rooms, is situated on the Shore of the Lower Lake, facing Innisfallen Island, and commands the most exquisite views in Killarney. It is ten minutes from the Railway, and a short distance from the far-famed Gap of Dunloe.

MOTOR GARAGE.

The Official Hotel of the A. Club of G. B. and I., the I.A.C., the A.A., the Touring Club of America, and the A. C. de France.

Accumulators charged off Hotel Electric Plant. Petrol. All Motor Oils stocked. Experienced Mechanic on Premises.

For beautifully Illustrated Brochure apply

THE PROPRIETOR,

GOLF LINKS HOTEL,
GREENLANDS, ROSSES POINT, SLIGO.

This Hotel is beautifully situated on the Golf Links overlooking Sligo Bay.

Splendid Sea Bathing, Boating, Fishing.

Post Cars on the Premises will attend Trains when required.

Terms, which are moderate, apply to

T. J. EWING, Proprietor.

E*

WEST CLARE RAILWAY
(IRELAND).

Health and Pleasure Resorts
OF WEST CLARE
Served by the West and South Clare Railways.

LAHINCH.—An increasingly popular Tourist resort, about 20 miles from Ennis, occupies a fine position on the shores of the Atlantic, with magnificent coast scenery. The village is quaint, and nestles in the corner of Liscannor Bay. There is a fine walk to Hag's Head and the celebrated Cliffs of Moher, which extend for about 3 miles along the coast, and rise perpendicularly in places to about 700 feet. A tower on top gives superb views of the coast from Loop Head to Galway Bay and Arran Isles. The Lahinch Golf Links are highly spoken of, as is also the Golf Links Hotel.

LISDOONVARNA.—Famous for its Mineral Wells, is reached from Ennistymon Station. There is also a 9 holes Golf Course, made under the instructions of Harry Vardon, who speaks favourably of it.

KILKEE.—Is a most delightful Watering-place, and possesses very romantic cliff scenery. The town is built in a semi-circle, and protected from the boisterous waves of the

---

In the late nineteenth century, many hotels were developed to cater for the needs of the golfing tourists who used the developing railway network.

In the later 1800s, ladies were somewhat restricted in their golf by the fashions of the time.

and watch their favourite sports. During the late Victorian period, a number of sports were codified and organised on a footing that has survived to the present. In Ireland the GAA was founded in 1884 and grew to become the strongest amateur sporting organisation in the country. The Irish Rugby Football Union was formed in 1879, and had seventy-seven affiliated clubs at its foundation, while cricket, tennis and soccer were also organised. Golf in Ireland was also growing at this time, and was organised on a national basis with the founding of the Golfing Union of Ireland (GUI) in 1891, the first such national golfing body in the world. The Irish Ladies' Golf Union was founded only two years later.

By the later decades of the nineteenth century, ladies had become quite active in golf. Earlier taboos about female involvement in sport had relaxed somewhat, and middle and upper-class ladies could now be active and play golf without the fear of being regarded as immodest. Ladies were also helped greatly by changes in fashions that enabled them to play in clothes that were less restrictive and less voluminous than had been the norm. Male and female were able to compete together on the golf course on more or less equal terms in the popular mixed foursomes and the like, and the wives and daughters of the respectable men of golf could also enjoy the social benefits of what had become a very fashionable and desirable pastime. Gender equality in other aspects of the game and its administration, however, was still very much in the future.

Ireland in the 1890s, the decade of most growth in golf, was a more settled country, politically and socially, than it had been for a considerable time. The agrarian unrest and attendant upheavals of the 1880s had abated, and following the death of Charles Stuart Parnell in 1891 the political scene was somewhat quieter. These settled conditions, the affluence of the middle class, the development of the concept of leisure time, a growing interest in sport, the steady emancipation of women, the expanding railway network and advances in golf-ball design all combined to facilitate the growth of golf. However, these factors would have had little relevance or impact had the game of golf itself, as a game, not been as attractive and appealing as it undoubtedly is.

Ireland's First Clubs

From the 1850s onwards, golfing activity in Ireland began to gain momentum, and there was invariably a strong Scottish or military connection. There is good evidence that a David Ritchie from Scotland laid out a course on the Curragh in 1852, and in 1858 John Gourlay – a famous feathery-ball maker and golf professional from Musselburgh in Scotland – came to the Curragh and also laid out a course, possibly an improvement on or expansion of the earlier one. There is no documentary evidence of a golf club being founded at that time, though there is no doubt that golf was played there regularly, especially by military men, prior to the foundation of a garrison golf club there in 1883. There is also evidence of golf being played at Portmarnock and Phoenix Park in Dublin, and at Laytown, County Meath, in the 1850s.

Royal Belfast Golf Club, founded in 1881, is regarded as Ireland's oldest properly documented golf club, and a Scottish connection was significant in its foundation: one of the co-founders, G L Baillie, was a Scotsman from Musselburgh, the home of one of Scotland's oldest golf clubs.

Ireland's second golf club was founded in 1883 at the Curragh in County Kildare. In 1882 the 71st Highland Light Infantry had arrived at the Curragh, and in March of the following year the *Irish Times* carried a report that the formation of a garrison golf club there had been sanctioned by the commanding officer of the Curragh Brigade, and that 'The rules of the club will be the same as those of the Royal and Ancient [Golf] Club of St Andrews'.[7]

In the 1880s, golfing activity in Ireland tended to be concentrated in Ulster and around Dublin. However, there is very clear documentary evidence of golf being played in County Cork in the early 1880s. In his account of the golf clubs of County Cork, Tim O'Brien quotes from an edition of the *Belfast Newsletter* from February 1883 that mentions the playing of golf on a course at Fota Island, and that the game 'had been initiated with great success'.[8] This would suggest that golf was being played there from as early as February 1883, a month before the military club was formed at the Curragh. There is no mention of a club being formed at Fota, the course in all likelihood being a private one developed on the Barrymore estate at Fota for private use. The early date for golf at Fota is confirmed by another report in the *Belfast Newsletter* of 1 November 1886 that states: 'Since November 1881 when the Belfast Golf Club was instituted

... no less than three additional courses have been laid down in different parts of the country. The second was at Fota Island ... one of our contemporaries noticing an opening game there in 1883'.[9] Golf continued to be played there until 1909 at least, when it is reported that in October of that year Lady Barrymore had presented a cup for competition between members of the Cork and Rushbrooke clubs to be played on the course at Fota.[10]

County Cork was also the location of another of Ireland's early golf clubs. In April 1883 the King's Own Borderers (later the King's Own Scottish Borderers) arrived at Kinsale and spent the following eighteen months stationed there. An account in *The Field* of 16 June 1883 reports that the regiment 'resuscitated their old golf club' at Kinsale, and had an eight-hole course near Prehane Point on ground formerly used for horse racing. After the regiment's departure, the course continued to be marked on military maps, suggesting that golf continued to be played there for some time.[11]

Royal Dublin Golf Club was founded in 1885 by a Scotsman, John Lumsden, and its first course at the Phoenix Park was Ireland's first eighteen-hole course. In all, eight clubs were formed in the 1880s. In the following decade, there was an explosion in the number of golf clubs founded: between 1890 and 1899 103 new clubs came into being, a number not equalled in any decade since, and golf took a firm and solid root in Ireland. The Golfing Union of Ireland was formed in 1891 and the Irish Ladies' Golf Union in 1893. The first Irish Amateur Close Championship was played at Royal Portrush in 1892, and the first Interprovincial was played in 1896, also at Portrush. This latter competition saw Leinster take the title, an indication that Ulster's initial primacy in Irish golf was broken. In the 1890s golf spread from its early strongholds in the north and east of Ireland to all four provinces, and some of the country's more famous clubs were established in that decade: Lahinch in 1892, Killarney and Ballybunion in 1893, Rosse's Point and Cork Golf Club in 1894, and Bundoran in 1896.

Golf in County Cork Pre-1909

Golf in County Cork followed the pattern of unprecedented growth in the rest of the country. Between 1890 and 1909, the year Douglas Golf Club was founded, over twenty clubs were formed in the county, though not all have survived. As noted above, golf was being played on Fota Island from as early as 1883, but there is as yet no documentary evidence for a club there. Similarly, golf was being played by a British regiment near Kinsale in 1884, though the first Kinsale Golf Club was not formed until 1897. The playing of golf in County Cork in the 1880s and 1890s, as elsewhere in the country, was very often due to the stationing of regiments of the British army in the region, especially Scottish regiments.

According to a directory published in 1892, a thirteen-hole golf course was attached to St Ann's Hydro near Blarney, and it was noted that the course was available to visitors and officers of the army, navy and Royal Irish Constabulary.[12] Fermoy Golf Club, for example, was founded in 1893, golf having been played there from 1892 at least, the impetus coming from the army presence in the nearby town.[13] Similarly, the Queenstown and Rushbrooke club, founded in 1892 or 1893, was located close to the major British naval base at Queenstown (as it was then known). Personnel based there frequently played on the Queenstown and Rushbrooke course, and also at Cork Golf Club on Little Island and, later, at Monkstown. The British military presence at Berehaven in west Cork led to the formation of the Channel Fleet Golf Club in 1906, with a nine-hole course on Bere Island and another on the nearby mainland. This later became the Atlantic Fleet Golf Club and, later still, the Royal Naval Club.

Mallow had a golf club as early as 1892, and a club was in existence at Bandon in 1893, though the latter has 1909 as its official foundation date. Cork Golf Club was instituted in 1894, and though there are claims that the club was founded many years earlier, there is no definite documentary evidence to support those claims. The *Golfing Annual* for 1895–96 states that the club was founded in November 1894, and Tim O'Brien quotes an article in the *Cork Constitution* from September 1895 that supports this foundation date.[14] The club's original course was at Lotamore, nearer the city, but a new nine-hole course was laid out at Killahora, near Queenstown Junction, in 1895. This served the club for only three years, after which a nine-hole course was laid out at the present location on Little Island. This course was extended to eighteen holes in 1910. A golf club was also founded in Coachford in 1894, and seems to have lasted until 1899.[15] In the 1890s clubs were also formed in a number of other places in County Cork: Clonakilty (1895), Midleton College and Trabolgan (1896), and Youghal (1898). There is also some documentary evidence for clubs in Newmarket and Courtmacsherry at this time.[16]

The growth of golf and golf clubs in County Cork in the 1890s mirrored developments in the rest of Ireland and in Britain also, and while the pace of this growth slowed a little in the first decade of the twentieth century, new clubs continued to be formed. Between 1900 and 1909 sixty-eight new clubs were formed in Ireland, compared to 103 in the previous decade. In County Cork, new clubs were formed in Bantry and at St Anne's Hill, Blarney in 1901, in Kilbrittain in

1902, and the Skibbereen and West Carbery club was founded in 1905. Closer to the city, there was a club in Rathcooney in the 1890s and a club called the Southern Club, based at Kilbarry, was functioning in 1904.[17] The demand for golf in Cork city and in its growing and increasingly prosperous hinterland led to the formation of three new clubs in the second half of that decade: Muskerry in 1907, Monkstown in 1908 and Douglas in 1909. These clubs, along with Cork Golf Club, have formed the core of golf in Cork for over a century.

An Earlier Douglas Golf Club?

The *Golfing Annual 1895–96* lists a Blackrock Golf Club, instituted in 1895. While the entry appears with clubs in the Dublin district, it is clear from the details that the club was in County Cork: 'The course is situated at Mounthovel, Rochestown. The club days are Tuesday, Thursday, and Saturday'.[18] The honorary treasurer was H Humphreys of Ballintemple, and the honorary secretary was Miss L E Parke of Ballinlough. The committee was J Murphy, C E B Mayne, G R Mahony, Colonel Seymour, G Stokes, R H Torkington, R O'Grady, J McNamara, Mrs Stopford, Mrs Seymour, Miss Smyth. No president or captain is named.

It is most likely that the course was a private one, laid out on the demesne of Mount Hovel, a large house a short distance east of the present Douglas Golf Club. Members of the club had access on only three days a week, which suggests that the club did not have a formal lease on the lands – rather, that the owners facilitated play on those named days. It is probable that the club was called the Blackrock Golf Club because most of its members came from the Blackrock area, the growing residential suburb much favoured by the affluent of the city. The honorary treasurer and honorary secretary were from Ballintemple and Ballinlough respectively, areas in the vicinity of Blackrock. It is noteworthy that three of the committee were female, as was the honorary secretary, a level of gender equality not seen in other clubs at the time, nor for many years afterwards.

Blackrock Golf Club is listed each year in the *Golfing Annual* from 1895–96 to 1908–09, but apart from the first listing, no details as to officers and committee are given. The club was not affiliated to the Golfing Union of Ireland.[19]

Guy's Cork Almanac and Directory 1903 lists a Douglas Golf Club with a links at Douglas. There is no information as to the precise location of the course, but the club officers are listed as J Barry, president; T C Butterfield, captain; Harrison E Keane, honorary treasurer; Arthur B Fitzgerald, honorary secretary. The committee members were J F McMullen, W J Dunlea, James G Crosbie, N F Barton, D A Kenealy and R H Marsh. The entry appears only for 1903, and no further information on this club has as yet come to light. Club president T C Butterfield was later a member of the Douglas Golf Club founded in 1909, as was committee member J F McMullen.

It is not possible to establish if this 1903 Douglas club was a later incarnation of that which functioned at Mount Hovel from 1895, or if it was a completely different entity. Neither can it be established if this later club was a precursor of the 1909 Douglas Golf Club. However, the names of T C Butterfield and J F McMullen represent a connection between the 1903 and 1909 Douglas clubs. The *Golfing Annual* entry for the Blackrock club at Mount Hovel appears annually from 1895 to 1909, the year Douglas Golf Club was founded, suggesting that Douglas Golf Club 'succeeded' the earlier club. Was the need for the Mount Hovel club, with its restricted playing days, removed with the formation of Douglas Golf Club in 1909? Whatever the precise succession of events and possible connection between the three clubs, the information is a clear indicator of an interest in golf in the Douglas area at the time.

2 *Beginnings: 1909–1911*

Douglas Golf Links Ltd

On 15 September 1909, in the offices of Barry C Galvin, Solicitors, at 36 South Mall, Cork, the memorandum and articles of association of Douglas Golf Links Ltd[1] were signed by seven men, the founding fathers of Douglas Golf Club. This act established the company that ran the affairs of the club in its early years. Four of these men described themselves as merchants: John J O'Brien of Clermont, Douglas; John G Green of Carrigduve, Blackrock Road; Francis Lyons of 4 Ashton Place, Blackrock Road; Arthur Mahony of 21 Dyke Parade. Another, Walter Morrogh, was a partner in the stockbroking firm of W & R Morrogh, 74 South Mall, and lived at Rosetta near Blackrock Castle. William Beamish Barrington, of Glanseskin, Douglas, was a solicitor with offices at 58 South Mall, and the seventh signatory was John P Molohan, professor of Latin at University College, Cork, who lived at Glenavon, College Road. The occupations and professions of these seven men are typical of the occupational background of the majority of golf-club members at the time.

It can be suggested that John J O'Brien was the leader of this group of seven. His is the first signature to both the memorandum and articles of association, and some months earlier he had negotiated an agreement with Patrick McAuliffe, a farmer and landowner in the townland of Maryborough, to take a lease on approximately ninety-six acres of land for the purpose of laying out a golf course. They signed this agreement on 15 May, giving Mr O'Brien the option of taking a lease on the land. In the memorandum of association signed on 15 September, Douglas Golf Links Ltd acquired this option, 'carrying into effect the said Agreement of the 15th day of May, 1909, to become Lessees of the Lease therein mentioned'. The lease proper was signed on 9 October 1909 by John J O'Brien and William Guest Lane as directors of the company, and by M W Litton as secretary. This ninety-six-acre plot included two fields located across the Carrigaline Road to the south-west. The lease was for a period of sixty years at an annual rent of £160, and allowed for the lands to be used for 'the playing of Golf, Lawn Tennis, Badminton, Cricket or

Facing page:
John G Green of Carrigduve, Blackrock Road, one of the seven founders of Douglas Golf Club.

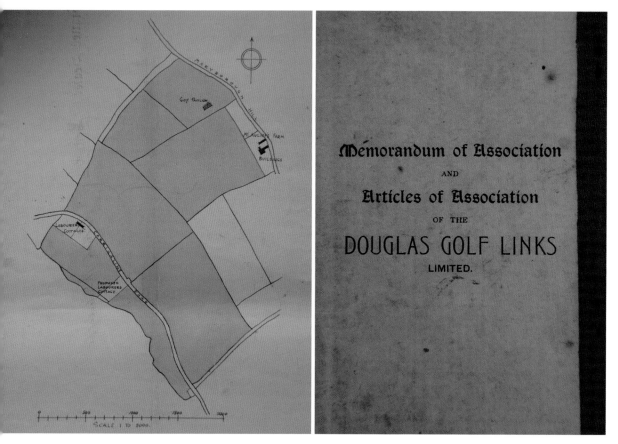

Left:
1909 lease map showing
the lands leased from
Patrick McAuliffe. Note
the two fields south of
the Carrigaline road that
were part of the original
course.

Right:
Cover of the
Memorandum of
Association and Articles
of Association of
Douglas Golf Links Ltd.

other similar games'. The directors of Douglas Golf Links Ltd were obliged 'within twelve months … to erect … a pavilion according to the design already approved of … and expend in the erection thereof a sum of seven hundred pounds at the least'.

The memorandum of association runs to four printed pages and details the twenty-six objectives of the company. These relate to the erection of a pavilion, the acquisition of a licence for a bar, the employment of a professional and caddies, the maintenance and future development of the course, as well as issues of finance, insurance, employment and other matters relevant to the effective running of a golf club in a businesslike fashion. The founders were open to the potential use of the course for activities other than golf: paragraph 3(a) of the document allows for the possible use of the newly acquired lands 'for Outdoor Sports, Recreations and Amusements, and other purposes which may seem to the Company capable of being carried on upon said lands'.

Paragraph 3(j) permits the company 'To enter into arrangements with Tramway Companies or Carriers for the conveyance of persons to said Links on such terms as may be deemed expedient by the Company'. The tramline that connected Douglas village to the city centre was a significant factor in the siting of the new golf course about a kilometre away on Maryborough Hill. Many members relied on the tram, and the minutes of the general committee for 7 March 1922 note: 'Proposed that Tramway Company be approached re some reduction of fares for members from Parnell Br to Douglas'. It is not noted if members got such a reduction or if they had one at any time prior to this, but the members' reliance on the Douglas tram and the contribution they made to the finances of the Cork Electric Tramways and Lighting Company are reflected in that company's presentation of the Tramway Cup to the club in November 1910.

The share capital of the Douglas Golf Links Ltd was £100, divided into fifty shares of £2 each, and the company had the power to increase its capital by the issue of new shares as it deemed necessary. Each of the seven founders took one £2 share. A further twenty mortgage-debenture shares of £100 each were also issued and taken up. The articles of association state that the total membership of the company shall not exceed fifty. This does not imply that the golf-club membership was restricted to fifty but that the company, Douglas Golf Links Ltd, owners of the club and course, would have a maximum of fifty shareholders. It is clear from an article in the *Irish Field* of 18 December 1909 that the club had more than fifty members: 'The club has been growing rapidly; over 250 men have applied for membership, and the limit for ladies has almost been reached'. The articles of association also lay down the very strict rules governing the ownership and transfer of shares. The public would not be invited to subscribe for any shares or debentures. Any proposed transfer of shares, whether by sale, inheritance or otherwise, had to be approved by the directors, ensuring a continuing control of membership of the company.

The signing of the memorandum and articles of association in September gave a legal standing to the company behind the new golf club, and was the culmination of much preparatory work by this group of seven men. Numerous meetings and discussions would have taken place over the previous months, potential sites in the vicinity of the city would have been visited, discussions with landowners undertaken, and members for the new club canvassed. As noted above, John J O'Brien had negotiated an agreement on leasing land for the course four months prior to the official coming into being of the company. The *Irish Times* of 26 June 1909 noted that 'a company has been formed to open a fine clubhouse and course at the end of the tramline near Douglas'. In July 1909 Harry Vardon was brought to Cork by the promoters of the club to mark out the new course. The decision to develop the new course had clearly been taken many months before Douglas Golf Links Ltd came into being.

This was to be the first eighteen-hole course in the Cork area – another indicator of the self-confidence of the club's promoters and their belief in the potential for golf. They were in no doubt that they would attract a membership of sufficient size to enable the project to prosper. The other courses in the area – at Little Island, Rushbrooke, Muskerry and Monkstown – were at this stage nine-hole courses. It was felt that Douglas Golf Club would bring golf in the south of Ireland to a new level. The golf correspondent of the *Irish Times* wrote that

> with few exceptions, the courses [in the south] are decidedly second class. To begin with all of them are nine holes courses, which speaks for itself. Now this inferiority is about to cease ... and in Cork we have in the process of rapid formation an eighteen holes course at Douglas.
>
> Littleisland [*sic*] has been a grand nursery ... but to really get on their game these players have to make for Lahinch or elsewhere. Monkstown and Rushbrooke are pleasant small courses, offering a good test of the game; but at best they can only prove to be nurseries.
>
> [Douglas] is a step in the right direction, and must prove a successful venture.[2]

Harry Vardon at Douglas

The ambition of the founders of Douglas Golf Club is evidenced by their invitation to Harry Vardon to mark out the new course. Harry Vardon was the most famous golfer in Britain at the time, and his visit was sure to give the new club and its course some added cachet. The *Cork Examiner* of 21 July 1909 reports on the visit of the great golfer, calling him 'one of the best exponents of the game in the world'. Vardon visited the site of the new course on 20 July, and some days later that newspaper quoted some extracts from his report:

> Gentlemen, – After walking over the land of the proposed golf course I saw that a splendid course could be laid out, and after staking same out I was able to get the length without crossing or in any way getting too near one and other in playing there. Heaps of room; and I am sure, if done well in the first place, a splendid 18-hole course can be made.
>
> For view, I hardly know any to beat it; the turf is quite suitable, and a fair number of natural hazards are already on the ground.[3]

The lengths of the proposed holes as given later in the above account were incorrect, and were corrected in the *Cork Examiner* of 28 July: first, 330 yards; second, 350 yards; third, 330 yards; fourth,

300 yards; fifth, 550 yards; sixth, 270 yards; seventh, 240 yards; eighth, 360 yards; ninth, 330 yards; tenth, 540 yards; eleventh, 160 yards; twelfth, 210 yards; thirteenth, 350 yards; fourteenth, 250 yards; fifteenth, 400 yards; sixteenth, 300 yards; seventeenth, 210 yards; eighteenth, 500 yards. This plan would give the course a total length of 5,980 yards.

Following on his work at Douglas, Vardon played a series of exhibition matches at the Little Island course of Cork Golf Club. The prospect of seeing Vardon play in Cork created much interest, and the *Cork Examiner* reported that 'such an opportunity to see first-class golf rarely occurs in these parts, and we have no doubt all followers of the game will assemble in large numbers to witness one of the most interesting matches that has ever taken place in the South of Ireland'.[4] The public were invited to attend at a charge of one shilling. Over 300 spectators turned out for the spectacle, and watched Vardon play two rounds – the first, a threeball with Brown and McNamara, the respective professionals at Cork and Muskerry, and the second, a foursome, in which Vardon and McNamara played against Brown and Le Follet of Midleton. In the first match, Vardon and Brown finished all square, having gone round in 78, and in the second Vardon and McNamara won on the last green. According to the report in the *Cork Examiner,* the best feature of the match was Vardon's drive on the eighth: 'It was the biggest drive ever seen on these links … the ball travelled over three hundred yards'.[5]

Rapid Progress

Work on the course and the pavilion got underway very quickly after the marking out of the holes in July and the formalities of the foundation of Douglas Golf Links Ltd in September. The developments at Douglas attracted much favourable comment in the sporting columns of the newspapers in the second half of 1909. The *Irish Field* reported on 25 September 1909 that 'very satis-

GOLF.

HARRY VARDON IN CORK.

The above ex-champion and one of the best exponents of the game in the world, arrived in Cork yesterday, and went to Douglas to select a site for a new golf course.

He has kindly consented to play Brown (Little Island) and McNamara (Muskerry) the best of their balls, for a prize given by the Cork Golf Club, at the Little Island Links, on to-day (Wednesday) on the arrival of the 1.15 p.m. train from Cork. Such an opportunity to see first-class golf rarely occurs in these parts, and we have no doubt all followers of the game will assemble in large numbers to witness one of the most interesting matches that has ever taken place in the South of Ireland. The public are invited to attend, and a nominal charge of 1s (field money) will have to be paid by each visitor who is not a member of the Cork Golf Club.

Top: Harry Vardon, six-time winner of the Open, who laid out the first Douglas course.

Below: Report of Vardon's visit in the *Cork Examiner*, 21 July 1909.

factory progress is being made with the new links and clubhouse of the Douglas (County Cork) Golf Club'. The report also noted that the foundations for the pavilion had been laid, and that the contractor hoped to have the work completed by Christmas. The first nine holes of the course were to be 'in full working order for the Christmas holidays, and the full eighteen holes will be ready by the spring'.

The *Irish Times* of 20 November 1909 differed a little, and suggested that the second nine holes would not be ready for play until summer 1910. This report went on:

> The promoters have gone the right way about the club and a fine clubhouse, with capital accommodation, is now nearly completed. The Douglas tram line runs to within ten minutes' walk of the clubhouse. The membership list is nearly full, and those who are anxious to join without an entrance fee should communicate with Mr M W Litton, the Secretary, at 21 Cook street, Cork. Everyone will wish the venture – though there ought to be nothing venturesome about an eighteen holes course near Cork – all success, and will congratulate the promoters on having filled a void that was most unmistakably felt.

Messrs Denis Duggan & Sons of Douglas, the contractors for the building of the new pavilion, were clearly making very good progress only two months into the build.

Open for Play

Play on the first nine holes began, as planned, during the Christmas holiday period at the end of 1909. The first mention in the local press of a competition on the new course at Douglas, however, does not appear until 9 April 1910, when the *Cork Examiner* notes: 'An open mixed foursome competition against bogey for prizes presented by the club will take place on the Douglas Golf Links on Thursday, 14th inst. Post entries. Players to make up their own matches'. *Douglas Golf Club 1910–1985*, produced to mark the seventy-fifth anniversary of the club, quotes the following, attributed to the *Cork Examiner* of 7 January 1910:

> The prettily situated links of the Douglas Golf Club will be open for play from today onwards. Members have been permitted to play on the course during the holidays and everyone who has gone around the links has been delighted with the excellence of the turf and charming situation. Today the club will be formally opened and in the last few weeks the membership has been greatly augmented ... The inauguration of the Douglas Golf Club is

doing much for the popularity of the game in Cork and within a brief period it can be safely predicted it will be one of the most flourishing institutions in the country.[6]

The Clubhouse

No account of the formal opening appeared in the local press, but on 5 February the *Cork Examiner* published a lengthy piece about the new club, devoting over half the article to a glowing description of the new clubhouse, or pavilion. The article notes that golf clubs of the time usually functioned for a number of years with modest clubhouse accommodation before investing in buildings of the standard with which Douglas was starting:

> The most striking artificial feature is the clubhouse. If the success of a links depended on a large, well-designed, comfortable, excellently furnished, substantially built pavilion, then those at Douglas would beyond question be successful to an extent not anticipated by the promoters. Indeed it would be safe to assert that no golf club in this country was ever started with such expensive quarters for its members. Usually a very modest shanty has to do duty in the early days of a new club, and not until the institution has reached a prosperous stage, does the old building give way to a more luxurious one. So the members of the Douglas Club are very lucky in this respect. Indeed they have started with comforts, unknown for years, to the members of the best clubs.

The professional's workshop and caddie shed were not at that stage complete.

It is unfortunate that no photograph of the clubhouse has come to light. However, a photograph published in the *Cork Examiner* on 30 May 1921 of the remains of the building following the arson attack of four days previously gives a very good impression of the size and extent of the clubhouse (see p. 60). This photograph suggests a substantially built, long, two-storey building with high chimneys at each gable. The clubhouse was enclosed by a low wall. The census returns for 1911 include a form filled by the resident caretaker at Douglas Golf Club. The brief details include the information that there were ten rooms in the building with twelve windows to the front, and one outbuilding, described as a store. The resident caretaker, John Graily, was born in England and was aged thirty-seven in 1911. He lived in rooms at the clubhouse with his wife, Maria, and their only child, Mary Louisa.

The New Course

The situation of the course is described in the *Cork Examiner* article of 5 February as 'superb, commanding, as it does from the pavilion, a panoramic view of Cork and the River Lee that at once arrests the attention of the visitor'.

The course was at that time, February 1910, still confined to nine holes. The turf was said to be 'excellent, being of mossy nature, which invariably gives good lies'. The holes had not yet been bunkered and, in consequence, the course presented few difficulties.[7] The *Irish Field* noted that 'natural fences, hummocks, quarries, and trees form the chief hazards. Accuracy will be essential, and good driving an advantage'.[8] A month later, the same publication assessed the course as follows:

> The course is not only beautifully situated, but also possessed of fine natural golfing turf providing good lies but so close as to call for accurate use of the club. Wisely the planners of the course have sought to give the holes character in preference to undue length, and while the hazards call for good driving, the feature of many of the holes will be the difficulty of the second shot.[9]

The lengths of the nine holes differ somewhat from the proposed layout marked out by Harry Vardon in July 1909. The *Cork Examiner* report of 5 February 1910 gives the lengths as follows (Vardon's proposed lengths are given in brackets): first hole, 300 yards (330); second hole, 326 yards (350); third hole, 416 yards (330); fourth hole, 200 yards (300); fifth hole, 520 yards (550); sixth hole, 296 yards (270); seventh hole, 400 yards (240); eighth hole, 120 yards (360); ninth hole, 300 yards (330); totalling 2,908 yards, 152 yards shorter than Vardon's proposed first nine. It also remarked that the eighth hole, the shortest of the nine, was the most sporting, 'a fence and a quarry, the latter close to the green, making an accurately played pitch shot from the tee essential, if trouble is to be avoided'.

First Professional

John McNamara was Douglas Golf Club's first professional. The *Irish Field* of 27 November 1909 notes that he was appointed in November, and had left the Muskerry club, where he had served as professional since its opening in 1907. Muskerry Golf Club's centenary publication, however, states that he left in December of that year. McNamara came from a well-known Lahinch golfing family, and had previously served at the Rushbrooke and Tramore clubs. In the absence of records at Douglas for this period, it can be assumed that McNamara was coming to Douglas, an eighteen-hole course, for

John McNamara, the first professional at Douglas.

a higher wage and better conditions than he received at Muskerry, a nine-hole course. McNamara's replacement at Muskerry, Sidney Humphreys, received £1 per week and the profit on clubs and balls sold. In addition, he received one shilling per hour for lessons.[10] The *Cork Examiner* of 5 February 1910, in its account of the new club, noted that McNamara had played the nine holes at Douglas in 38, two under 'bogie', and remarked that he had little time for play

> as he is almost constantly giving lessons, there being quite a big proportion of beginners amongst the members. He takes a keen interest in his pupils, and he really enjoys his work. McNamara, who is a fine player, has had extensive experience of different courses, both in England and Ireland. Prior to taking up his present position, he was at Muskerry ... McNamara spent two years at Tramore, where his best round was 36, while he has done the Lahinch course in 74 and Hoylake in 78. At the last named links he often played with John Ball and H H Hilton [both of whom won the Open Championship and Amateur Championship]. It will certainly not be his fault if his pupils' handicaps are not reduced quickly.

First Groundsman

There is some confusion regarding the first groundsman or greenkeeper at Douglas. The *Irish Field* of 25 September 1909 wrote that the new Douglas club had received over twenty applications for the position of groundsman, and that John Henry of the Fordham Golf Club in Surrey was appointed, 'a very competent man ... [who] has given very ample evidence of his experience and thorough knowledge of his work'. The records do not show a club of that name in Surrey at that time. The *Irish Times* of 20 November 1909, however, noted that George Henry of the Farnham Golf Club in Surrey had been appointed to the post. This golf club did exist at the time, but the confusion continues in that the *Irish Golfer's Guide* for 1910 names the groundsman as George Hurry! T M Healy in his centenary history of Portmarnock Golf Club notes that a 'Mr Henry of Troon who had earlier worked at Douglas in Co. Cork' became greenkeeper at Portmarnock in 1910.[11] This supports the case of a John or George Henry having been Douglas' first greenkeeper from September 1909 to sometime in 1910. The *Irish Golfer's Guide* for 1911 and 1912 gives the groundsman as Maurice S Harris. No groundsman is named in the entry for Douglas Golf Club in this guide after 1912. The extant records of Douglas Golf Club begin in 1921, and at that stage William Magee is named as groundsman, later greenkeeper.

W C Pickeman, the founding father of Portmarnock Golf Club, who suggested alterations to the new course at Douglas in 1910.

Problems with the Course

After less than three months of play on the new course at Douglas, it seems that there was serious dissatisfaction with certain aspects of the new course. In March of 1910 the *Cork Examiner* published a piece about 'Douglas Golf Links' that had appeared in Dublin's *Evening Herald* a short time earlier; it was written by 'a well-known Irish amateur, a very strong player, and a sound judge of the game'.[12] The criticisms of the course were quite strong. This correspondent wrote that the new eighteen-hole course at Douglas 'did not provide a test of the game or give any indications that it would do other than provide … featureless golf'. He went on to say that it was 'completely without character, and could not even be termed "sporting". The holes for the most part were long and flat, and grouped so close together, that made it positively dangerous to play there when there were many players on the course'. The article suggests that these faults were pointed out to the committee at Douglas, but that there was some reluctance on its part to accept the criticisms. Eventually, the committee sought outside advice as to how the course might be improved and altered. W C Pickeman was invited to come to Douglas so as to inspect the course. Pickeman was the founding father of Portmarnock Golf Club in 1894, and its honorary secretary from that date to 1917. He was also one of the founders of Milltown Golf Club in 1907. He accepted the invitation 'and went carefully over the course, spending the greater part of a day there'. He proposed 'a very large number of alterations', and the *Evening Herald*'s correspondent felt that 'in the course of a year or so a really good 18-hole course will be at the disposal of the Cork players'. His comments on the proposed alterations continue:

> There will be three very fine short holes – all of the difficult and sporting order – where a slip means drastic punishment. The other holes will vary from the drive and pitch to two drives and a pitch. The ground for the most part is very suitable, but some spots will require draining. The course is a long one, about 6,000 yards all told, if anything, over this mark, is undulating, but not unduly so, and the views from the course are magnificent.

The piece finishes with this comment: 'The Douglas course ought to be a favourite resort for the business and professional men of Cork, particularly during the "dog" days, when the city becomes unbearable'.

In the absence of any other sources of information as to these alterations, it is not possible to say how extensive the improvement works were. Play does not seem to have been much interrupted, as the local press carried regular reports of men's and ladies' competitions on the course from early April 1910 onwards.

A year later, in March 1911, work on the course was still not complete. An article in the *Evening Herald* gives 'A Visitor's Impressions' of the course. The piece was written by 'WCP', presumably the William Chalmers Pickeman who had suggested changes to the layout a year before. He makes no reference to his input, and not surprisingly is generally happy with the course:

> The course ... has undergone several alterations from the original plan, and ... is by no means finished yet, new greens are being made, and several new holes are not yet completed. The ground, though standing on a hill, is rather on the flat side, and many of the holes in consequence resemble each other. Judicious bunkering, however, should do much to put character into some of the holes, which at the present time appear quite characterless. The turf is excellent, but some draining at one or two places may be found necessary. However, for three quarters of the year there ought to be excellent golf found at Douglas. The greens, if the worm killer is used with effect, will be very good greens indeed; in fact, even though there exists every evidence of a plentiful supply of worms, they are by no means bad. The Committee have erected a handsome and picturesque club-house, which commands beautiful views of Cork and district.[13]

The language of Pickeman's article and the aspects of the course he comments on suggest that he was also the author of the first, highly critical *Evening Herald* piece.

Eighteen Holes?

In its first months Douglas Golf Club had a nine-hole course. The original plan was to have the first nine holes in play by Christmas 1909, and the full eighteen by spring or summer 1910. The entry for Douglas in the *Irish Golfer's Guide* for 1910 states: 'An eighteen holes inland course ... The full eighteen holes will be ready in June'. The entry also says: 'The course will be a fine one when completed, and should do much to advance golf in the South of Ireland, where 18 holes courses are few and far between'. This latter comment is repeated in this annual publication each year until 1914. The proviso 'when completed' may refer to ongoing course improvements rather than implying a course of less than eighteen holes. The entry in the *Irish Golfer's Guide* for 1911 notes that 'Twenty additional acres

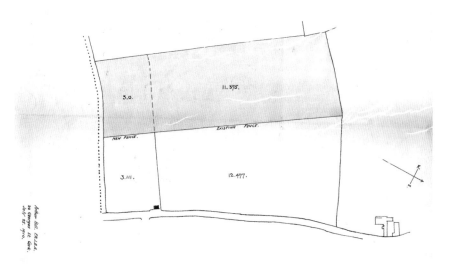

Lease map showing the fourteen acres added to the course in 1911 (see 1909 map, p. 28).

have been added, in which three holes will be placed; an amount of bunkering has been done, and this will be continued as speedily as possible'. A 1911 lease may explain that entry. On 14 February of that year, Patrick McAuliffe leased an additional fourteen-and-a-half acres to Douglas Golf Links Ltd at an annual rent of £35 for 59½ years; this land was made up of two fields where the fourth, fifth and sixth holes are now located. It should also be borne in mind that guides such as this, though valuable in many respects, tended not to be thoroughly updated in every detail from year to year. Very often, the accuracy of the entries depended on the thoroughness of the individual clubs in submitting or correcting their details. The eighteen holes of the course were certainly in play from July 1910, at the latest, when the *Cork Examiner* of 27 July noted in a short piece on Douglas Golf Club: 'The eighteen hole course will be open for play on Saturday next, the 30th July. On that day the usual competition for the Gentlemen's Monthly Medal will take place.'

The First Competitions
While play on the course began in January 1910, the first published report of a competition at the club did not appear in the local press until 23 April. This first report, headed 'Douglas Golf Club: Mixed Foursomes', gives details of a competition held on 21 April.[14] Twenty-six couples competed, and the best scores were:

> Mr O'Callaghan and Miss Waggett .... 1 down.
> Mr Cove and Miss Cramer .... 2 down.
> Mr and Miss McMullen .... 3 down.
> Mr Blackham and Miss Ashlin .... 3 down.
> Captain and Mrs Annesley .... 4 down.
> Mr Winder and Miss Gregg .... 5 down.
> Mr D Galvin and Mrs Galvin .... 5 down.

Five days later, the first report of the Ladies' Monthly Medal appeared in the *Cork Examiner*. Twelve ladies played, and the following is the published result:

	Gross	H'cap	Net
Miss P McMullen	128	27	101
Miss Sugrue	128	27	101
Miss M Morrogh	129	27	102

The tie between the Misses P McMullen and Sugrue had to be played off before 7 May. It was subsequently reported that Miss McMullen won the tie with a net score of 88.[15]

The first account of the Men's Monthly Medal appeared on 3 May 1910, again in the *Cork Examiner*. Twenty-two entered the competition, which was played on Saturday 30 April.[16] The *Examiner* published the best seven scores:

	Gross	H'cap	Net
J O'Brien jun.	99	26	73
J B Coughlan	104	27	77
W Pericho	107	23	84
D Galvin	103	18	85
R Simcox	108	22	86
G Ogilvie	104	18	86
M English	111	22	89

The *Cork Examiner* continued to publish the results of competitions at Douglas, and from 23 April 1910 to the end of April 1911, sixty different reports on the activities at Douglas Golf Club appeared.

First President's and Captain's Prizes

The winner of Douglas Golf Club's first President's Prize is not known, but the *Cork Examiner* for 24 October 1910 lists those who went forward to the second round of the competition, having played their first round on 21 October:

> The following qualified for the second round for President's Prize – J J McLure, 69; Dr W Magner, 71; R Simcox, 75; W V Pericho, 80; Dr Wm Keatinge, 81; J Murphy, 82; M English, 82; D Kelleher, 84; M J Conron, 84; Professor Moore, 85; W Morrogh, junr, 86; J J Cashman, 86; J O'Callaghan, 86; R 'Richards', 86. D 'Tee', J B Coghlan, A Murphy, R A Galwey, D O'Connor tied for the last two places with 87, and play off (medal play) by Wednesday evening.[17]

The next round was to be completed by 30 October, and the match-play pairings were listed as follows:

W V Pericho v J O'Callaghan, J Murphy v W Morrogh, junr,

The first published report of a competition at Douglas, from the *Cork Examiner*, 23 April 1910.

> M J Conron v J J McLure, Professor Moore v R Simcox,
> M English v Dr Wm Keatinge, Dr W Magner v D Kelleher,
> J J Cashman v best score of tie, R Richards v second best score
> of tie.

No reports of the subsequent stages of the competition were published.

The qualifying round for the first Captain's Prize was played on 14 and 18 December 1910. On 16 January 1911, under the heading 'Captain's Prize Semi-finals', the *Cork Examiner* published a very short but incomplete report of the semi-finals:

> R Crosbie beat D T Barry, 1 up.
> In the finals J J O'Brien retired.

This seems to imply that R Crosbie won the prize, J J O'Brien having retired in the final.

The qualifying round for the first President's Prize for Ladies at Douglas was played on 3 November 1910,[18] and eight went forward to play the final rounds. The *Cork Examiner* of 25 November 1910 reported that Miss P McMullen won the prize, having beaten Miss Guest Lane by 6 and 5 in the final. The runner-up was the daughter of William Guest Lane, the first president of Douglas Golf Club.

The Tramway Cup

The Tramway Challenge Cup was the first major trophy to be presented to Douglas Golf Club. The cup is named for the Cork Electric Tramways and Lighting Co. Ltd, the firm that operated the three cross-city tramlines from 1898 until the lines were closed in 1931. One of these three lines ran from Blackpool to Douglas by way of the 'Statue' on St Patrick Street. In the early decades of the club, many members relied on the tram to travel from the city to Douglas. Hubert H Nalder came from Newcastle to Cork to work as an engineer for the tram company around 1900, and was a member of Douglas from its foundation. He was club president for 1919. Whether through the good offices of Nalder or otherwise, the cup was presented, and marked the interdependence of the club and the company.

The cup is first mentioned in a newspaper article of 3 October 1910 that announces: 'November 15th – Qualifying Round for Challenge Cup Presented by the Cork Electric Tramways and Lighting Co. Ltd, open to members of recognised golf clubs in Co. Cork.'[19] The cup was valued at twenty guineas, over five times the annual club subscription of the time. Eight were to advance from the qualifying round, and the competition was confined to members of 'recognised golf clubs in County of Cork' of 18 handicap or better, who would pay an entrance fee of 2s 6d.[20] The cup was put on display in the window of the jewellers Messrs Egan & Sons on St Patrick Street, and

Details of the Tramway Cup, presented to Douglas in 1910 by the Cork Electric Tramways and Lighting Co. Ltd.

was said to be 'a fine example of old Irish plate'. The cup would be won outright if won three times, not necessarily in succession.[21]

Fifty-six players played in the qualifying round on 15 November, and four of the eight who qualified for the next stage were Douglas members – W Keatinge, J B Coghlan, W Morrogh junior, and H O'Keeffe. The final was played over thirty-six holes, and took place on 26 November between two Douglas players, W Keatinge and J B Coghlan. Keatinge won the match 5 and 1. The *Cork Examiner* of 28 November published a full account of the final, and remarked:

> It was a splendid struggle. Coghlan had very hard luck, having played three severe matches during the week … The strain of this would have been bad enough on any seasoned player, but to a comparative beginner it was terrific, and one could see plainly in the second round of the final that Coghlan was beaten out, and had he been fresh, the match would certainly not have been won so easily.
>
> The Douglas Golf Club may well be proud of the result. The flower of Cork county golf competed in the qualifying round, four of the eight qualifying were Douglas men, and the final round found two Douglas men competing.

Dr W Keatinge and J B Coghlan, the two finalists, had only been playing golf eleven months, having started when they joined the new club in January 1910. John McNamara, the Douglas professional, won much praise for his teaching of these two players, and their success in 'the biggest competition in the county speaks volumes for the teaching', the *Cork Examiner* concluded. (The *Irish Times* of 3 December reported the result incorrectly, noting that 'the Tramway Cup final at the Douglas Club, Cork, was won by Mr J B Coghlan, Dr W Keatinge being beaten by 3 and 1 over 36 holes'.)

The Lord Mayor's Cup and Other Early Trophies

In 1911 the lord mayor of Cork, Alderman James Simcox, presented the club with its second silver trophy, which is officially titled the Lord Mayor's Cup but is now better known by Douglas members as the Simcox Cup. James Simcox was the proprietor of a well-known Cork bakery, and lived at Bloomfield House on the Rochestown road. He was the father of Richard and Redmond, the former a founder member of Douglas Golf Club, while the latter, born in 1904, would later become a very successful amateur golfer and winner of the South of Ireland Championship on two occasions (representing Douglas), an Irish international, and the president of the Golfing Union of Ireland. The cup was first played for in July 1911, and its first winner was John Murphy. The *Cork Sportsman* weekly newspaper gave an account of the first competition for the cup, and said that it

Details of early club trophies:

Top: Ladies' Open Challenge Cup, 1911.

Bottom: Lord Mayor's Cup (also called the Simcox Cup), 1911.

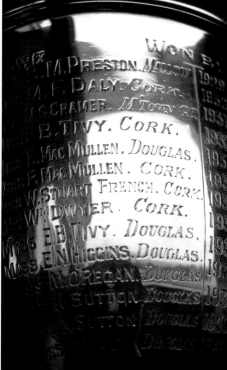

Details of the Maryboro Challenge Cup, presented by Alfred Blake in 1911.

excited the greatest possible interest, and proved the most successful event yet promoted by this young club. No less than seventy-one members entered for the competition, and the results of the earlier rounds were followed with the deepest interest. Many of the long handicap men revealed remarkably good form, and completely upset calculations, as several of the 'fancied' ones received the knock early in the competition. When the contest closed the Handicapping Committee were very busy with the pruning knife. The trophy eventually went to Mr John Murphy, who showed consistent form throughout and played really good golf in all his games.[22]

The first major trophy of the Ladies' Branch at Douglas was the Ladies' Open Challenge Cup, which was presented in 1911. Its first winner was Miss B M Preston of Mallow. At Christmas 1911 Alfred Blake presented the club with the Maryboro Cup, which was first contested in 1912 and won by Mick English, club captain in 1920, and honorary secretary from 1916 to 1922, and from 1925 to 1928.

Officers and Members

The entry for Douglas Golf Club in the *Irish Golfer's Guide* for 1910 does not name the president, captain or committee of the club, though contact details are given for the honorary secretary, M W Litton. The information in annual guides such as these is generally a year in arrears, the published details often being those from the previous year. The *Irish Golfer's Guide* for 1911 and subsequent years *does* give the names of club officers, committee members and so on.

The first president of Douglas Golf Club was William Guest Lane, a solicitor who lived on Blackrock Road. He served as president for 1910 and 1911. The first captain, R A Galwey, also served two years, as did the committee. Five of the original seven founders of the club served on the first committee, J J O'Brien, J P Molohan, W Morrogh, J G Green and F Lyons, and were joined by three others – A Winder, Dr R Crosbie and H O'Keeffe.

The first honorary secretary of the club was M W Litton, who worked at 21 Cook Street, Cork, and this address was used for all club correspondence in the first years. His full name was Marshal William Litton, and according to the census returns for 1911 he resided at Douglas Golf Club, where he was a boarder with John Graily, the resident caretaker, and his family. Litton was born in County Antrim in 1871, and his occupation is given as 'Insurance Inspector and Secretary Golf Club'. The *Irish Golfer's Guide* for 1913 names Lieutenant-Colonel M J Carpendale as honorary secretary, in succession to Litton, and the edition for 1914 has Mr S G James holding the position. According to a short history of the club published in the *Irish Field* of 1 May 1926, Carpendale took up the position of honorary secretary some time in 1912, having been 'some years ago secretary of the Kingstown Club'. The piece continues: 'Later on the secretarial duties were undertaken by Mr L A D'Obree and Mr S G James'. The 1913 edition of *Guy's Commercial Directory* names J D Hilliard as secretary, with an address at 13 Marlboro Street. This suggests the succession of the holders of that office to be M W Litton, Lieutenant-Colonel M J Carpendale, J D Hilliard, L A D'Obree and S G James. James, in turn, was succeeded by O C Barry, as indicated in the *Irish Golfing Guide* (as it came to be known from 1915) for 1915 and 1916.

Members paid an annual subscription of £4, while the entrance fee was £4 4s. The *Irish Times* of 26 June 1909 felt that these rates were high, 'but, owing to the scarcity of golf clubs in Cork, this will not militate much against the new club'. A report on developments at the new club in that newspaper on 20 November suggests that early applicants for membership would not have to pay the entrance fee. In these early years, there were between 250 and 300 gentlemen members. The *Irish Field* of 18 December 1909 noted that 'over 250 men have applied for membership, and the limit for ladies has almost been reached'.

As all club records for the period 1909 to 1921 were lost in the burning of the clubhouse on 27 May 1921, there is no extant 'official' list of members for that period. In an effort to establish as many members' names as possible for the first year of the club's history, all the Douglas members' names mentioned in golf reports in the *Cork Examiner* for the period 23 April 1910 (the date of the first report to name Douglas players) to 30 April 1911 are listed here. It has been possible to collect the names of 129 men and 31 ladies for that period.

Members mentioned in golf reports in the Cork Examiner *for the period 23 April 1910–30 April 1911*

MEN

A number after a name indicates the number of times the name is mentioned in reports. No number indicates one mention. These members are those reported to have played in, been placed in, or to have won competitions, and are the better golfers of the membership.

A number of the names are pseudonyms – e.g. A J Brassie, A Driver, A Drover, J Mashie, D Tee – and were probably used by players who did not want their names published in the local press. Many clergymen used this tactic to avoid the accusation that they were neglecting their flocks by spending time on the golf course!

Capt. Annesley	W B Barrington 2	Prof D T Barry 3
R J Bell	J Bell	A Beale
F Blake	A Blake	Mr Blackham
A J 'Brassie'	W W Brew	M P Buckley jun
Dr Cagney 2	J Callanan	J J Cashman 4
J Cleary	T Clery	J Collins
Mr Cove	M J Conron	J B Coghlan 9
Henry Cronin 2	Dr R Crosbie 4	M Cullinane 2
G H Dennehy	H A Denton 5	F Denton
'A Driver'	'A Drover'	M English 18
? Ewen	C H Exham	J S Fitzpatrick
D Galvin 4	W Gardiner 5	R A Galwey 8
H Gillespie 3	? Gorgan	J G Green
J Griffin 2	G Griffin	W Guest Lane 3
J Harding	L Harrington	? Heale
H H Hill 2	E C Hitchmough 3	H Hitchmough
W M Keatinge LLD 6	D Kelleher 2	'Jay Pay'
J B Kelleher 2	J Keller 3	? Kirk
J S Kirkpatrick 3	C J Lane 4	C T Lane
C Y Lane	G E Litton	M W Litton 6
F Lyons 2	Dr W Magner 4	R M Magrath 3
R Marmion	H H 'Mashie'	'J Mashie'
Dr J L McKee 5	G L McKie	J J McLure 2
Mr McMullen	G Meyers 2	Prof Molohan
Prof A E Moore 7	Dr H R Moorehead 2	D Morrogh 2
Walter Morrogh 9	W Morrogh jun 4	Wm Morrogh 2
A Murphy 3	John Murphy 4	N Murphy
R Murphy 2	Father Murray	Major Noblett 3

H Nalder	D O'Brien	Father O'Brien
J J O'Brien jun 8	J J O'Brien 7	J R O'Brien 3
J O'Callaghan 7	S O'Callaghan	D J O'Connor
Dr J T O'Connor 2	J J O'Connor	D M O'Connor 4
W F O'Connor	G H Ogilvie 2	R Ogilvie
S H Ogilvie	W R Ogilvie 4	H O'Keeffe 3
Dr O'Riordan	J O'Riordan	T O'Sullivan
W T O'Sullivan 4	'J P'	J Pericho
W V Pericho 13	S Punch 2	J Rearden 5
R 'Richards' 2	? Richardson	H Riordan
R S Russell 2	R Simcox 6	C A Slicer 2
B 'Spalding' 2	D Spalding	D J Sullivan
F Sullivan	B Sutton	D 'Tee' 6
'J Thomas'	Col. S Townsend	A W Winder 6
A Wood	E D Wrixon	A Young 2

Two clergyman, Fr O'Brien and Fr Murray, did not feel the need to disguise their names. The R Simcox who is mentioned six times in the above list is Richard Simcox, the older brother, by fifteen years, of Redmond Simcox, who later became a member of Douglas Golf Club, and who represented his club and country many times during an illustrious amateur golfing career.

LADIES

These are the thirty-one ladies' names similarly gleaned. Again, a number after a name indicates the number of times the name is mentioned in reports. No number indicates one mention.

Mrs Annesley	Miss Ashlin	Mrs Beadon
Miss Buckley 2	Miss Cramer	Mrs Henry Cronin
Miss Daly	Mrs Denton 2	Miss Exham
Mrs Galvin 2	Miss A Gregg 5	Miss Guest Lane 6
Miss Guy	Miss N Kelleher	Miss Magner
Miss F McMullen	Miss P McMullen 7	Mrs W J McMullen
Mrs Montgomery 5	Miss M Morrogh 7	Mrs Walter Morrogh 2
Miss Ogilvie	Mrs O'Keeffe	Miss O'Reilly
Miss Pearson	Miss Sugrue 7	Mrs Sugrue
Miss Sergeant 2	Miss Tivy 2	Miss B Tivy
Miss Wagget		

Harry Vardon

Harry Vardon, who first marked out the course at Douglas in July 1909, was one of the so-called Great Triumvirate of Golf (along with John Henry Taylor and James Braid) that dominated the international professional golf scene from the end of the nineteenth century into the early decades of the twentieth. These three golfers won fifteen Open titles between them. Vardon was born on 9 May 1870 in Jersey in the Channel Islands. He became an apprentice gardener at the age of thirteen, and began to play golf in his later teens. His older brother Tom was an accomplished golfer, and was enjoying some success, having turned professional. Harry followed in his footsteps, entering the professional ranks in 1890 when he was twenty. Having worked for short periods at a number of golf clubs in England, he eventually settled at South Hertfordshire Golf Club, near London, where he remained for thirty-four years.

Harry Vardon won his first Open in 1896 – the first Englishman to win the event – and won the title another five times, in 1898, 1899, 1903, 1911 and 1914. In 1900, with three Open titles to his credit and a huge international reputation, he travelled to the US and played more than eighty exhibition matches. He also won the US Open that year, and became golf's first international superstar.

In 1903 – the year he won his fourth Open – Harry Vardon contracted tuberculosis and played little competitive golf over the succeeding seven years. During this time, he did some work as a golf-course architect, and it was towards the end of this period that he came to mark out the new course at Douglas, in 1909. He resumed his competitive playing career in 1911, and won the Open that year and again in 1914. He travelled to the US a number of times, and was runner-up in the US Open in 1913 and again in 1920, when he was fifty years of age.

Vardon popularised the overlapping grip that now bears his name and which is used by the vast majority of professionals today. He was the first professional player to play in knickerbockers and fancy-topped stockings, and is said to have had 'enormous hands that melted perfectly around the club', and to have had 'a sweet, peaceful temperament'. Harry Vardon died on 20 March 1937.

3 *War, Turbulence & Change: 1912–1920*

Douglas Golf Club continued to prosper through 1912 and 1913. The eighteen-hole course was now complete and maturing after the initial construction work and subsequent additions, changes and improvements. Competitions continued to be played and reported upon in the local press. Professor J P Molohan was president for 1912 and 1913, and a number of others of the original seven founders of the club continued to serve on the committee. Miss A Gregg of Ballinlough House was secretary of the Ladies' Branch at Douglas, a position she held for many years. The annual subscription continued to be £4 for gentlemen and £2 for ladies. According to the *Irish Golfer's Guide* for these years, visitors were welcome to play the course at a charge of one shilling per day or five shillings per week. These rates were raised to two shillings and seven-shillings-sixpence respectively in 1913.

This pre-war period saw increasing middle-class prosperity and a consequent growth in leisure-time activities such as outdoor sports. Golf was flourishing in Ireland in the decade up to 1914, and by that year there were 190 clubs in the country, with many thousands of members.[1] The members of Douglas and, indeed, of other golf clubs could have been forgiven for thinking that this heyday, so comfortable for the more privileged, would continue into the future.

The Years of the First World War

Things changed with the outbreak of war in 1914, and as many millions suffered death, destruction and upheaval as a direct result of the hostilities in Europe, the effects of the war were felt in Ireland also. In the first year of the war, over 75,000 Irishmen enlisted in the British army, and men from Ireland continued to enlist in large numbers in the following years. The class divisions of pre-war Britain and Ireland were replicated in the army, and while working-class men made up the bulk of those who enlisted as ordinary soldiers, it was from the middle classes that most of the officers were drawn. Many golf clubs saw their membership numbers fall during the war years (1914–18) as men enlisted, members mostly joining the officer corps while the

Facing page:
Back cover of the
Irish Golfer's Guide,
1911.

49

caddies, groundsmen and other club employees joined the ordinary ranks. Golf clubs in so-called garrison towns were particularly affected in this way. At Douglas, the professional John McNamara left the club at the outbreak of war and enlisted in the British army. There is no record of him returning to any golf club in Ireland or Britain as a professional after the war. He may have survived and followed a different career path after 1918, he may have been killed, or he may have been wounded to such an extent that he could not resume life as a professional. The records of the Commonwealth War Graves Commission list three soldiers named John McNamara of the Royal Munster Fusiliers (the regiment he most likely joined) who were killed during the war, but it cannot be ascertained if any of these was the John McNamara of Douglas Golf Club.

Golf clubs were also affected by restrictions on travel, fuel rationing, food shortages and a range of government orders that resulted in some golf courses becoming rifle ranges,[2] for example, while the Tillage (Ireland) Racecourses and Golf Links Order required golf courses to devote a minimum of ten per cent of their land to tillage. In the absence of records for the period, it is not possible to say how this order affected Douglas Golf Club, but at the nearby club at Monkstown the order was observed, with a portion of the course being fenced and ploughed for tillage.[3]

The pro-war hysteria that gripped so many in the early stages, and which led to such numbers enlisting, also gave rise to an attitude that golf and other sports were wasteful and shameful pastimes at a time when many were making great sacrifices, directly and indirectly, for the war effort. William Gibson, in his *Early Irish Golf: The First Courses, Clubs and Pioneers*, quotes a piece from a 1916 edition of *Irish Life* that captures the guilt felt by some golfers during the war years: 'No man feels exactly comfortable walking through the city with a big bag of clubs slung across his shoulder'.[4]

The competitive side of the game also suffered as many championships at various levels were not played during the war years: the Irish Amateur Open and Close Championships were suspended for the war years, as were the Senior and Junior Cup, and the various provincial championships. The Irish Ladies' Golf Union (ILGU) at its AGM in 1914 passed a motion 'That the ILGU shall not organise any competitions until the War is over'. All meetings of the ILGU other than AGMs were also suspended for the duration of the war.[5] The number of golf clubs founded during the war years and after dropped significantly after a decade of vigorous pre-war growth. In the ten years from 1904 to 1913, ninety clubs were founded in Ireland, whereas in the following decade, 1914–23, only twenty-seven new clubs came into being.

A New Douglas Golf Club

In many clubs, the annual subscription was reduced and entrance fees were suspended in an effort to attract members, as falling numbers were putting the viability of those clubs at risk. In 1914 Douglas Golf Club was 'in a flourishing condition', according to a short history of the club published in the *Irish Field* of 1 May 1926, but within two years membership had fallen drastically to only seventy-seven men and forty ladies. These numbers could not sustain the club. Clubs that were owned by their membership had different options open to them if they were facing financial difficulties: levies on members, and loans or guarantees by members could, in some cases, relieve potentially fatal financial situations. Douglas Golf Club was not, however, owned by its members; it was owned by a limited company, Douglas Golf Links Ltd, and – faced with severe financial difficulties in 1916 – the company voluntarily liquidated. The difficulties had come to a head by June 1916; a surviving draft copy of the surrender of the lands of the course to the lessor, Patrick McAuliffe, is dated 8 June 1916. The surrender was effected on 20 December of that year. After much discussion and acrimonious debate, it was agreed that a new body, Douglas Golf Club – owned by its members – would be formed.[6] A number of members gave personal guarantees for the loan taken out to facilitate the transfer of assets and the other financial arrangements associated with the formation of the new club. The generosity of these guarantors was recognised in 1925 when they were given – after the officers of the club – first choice of lockers in the new clubhouse opened that year. The assets – principally the clubhouse and the lease on the club lands – passed to the new Douglas Golf Club, and in December 1916 a new lease was agreed with Patrick McAuliffe, the owner of the land on which the course stood.

The original lease on the course, agreed in May 1909, was for a period of sixty years at a yearly rent of £160, with an additional fourteen-and-a-half acres added in 1911 at an annual rent

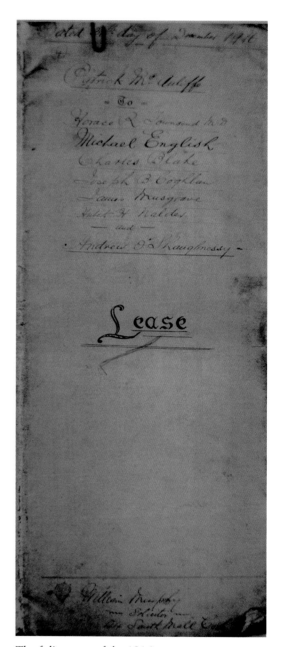

The folio cover of the 1916 lease, with the signatures of the seven trustees of the club at the time: Horace R Townsend, Michael English, Charles Blake, Joseph B Coghlan, James Musgrave, Hubert H Nalder and Andrew O'Shaughnessy.

of £35. The new lease was for a term of thirty-one years at an annual rent of £100 for the first three years, and £120 for the remaining period for the full 110½ acres. The reduced cost of the lease was due either to the generosity of Patrick McAuliffe or, as is more likely, the straitened circumstances of the time. McAuliffe, faced with the prospect of the club winding up completely and the loss of his yearly payment, may have been glad to compromise on price and accept a less-rewarding lease. Seven named trustees of the new Douglas Golf Club signed the lease on 30 December 1916. Their names, addresses and occupations are given as follows: Horace Townsend, Sidney Place, medical doctor; Michael English, Hazelmere, Cross Douglas Road, electrical engineer; Charles Blake, Chiplee Villas, Ballintemple, stockbroker; Joseph B Coghlan, Ballygarvan House, gentleman; James Musgrave, Bellevue, Cross Douglas Road, merchant; Hubert H Nalder, Albert Road, engineer; Andrew O'Shaughnessy, Montpellier, Douglas, merchant.

Douglas Golf Club was now owned by its members, and its future prospects were in their hands. The club had survived the restrictions and difficulties caused by the First World War, and managed to reorganise itself following the collapse of Douglas Golf Links Ltd. Having shown such resilience and determination over such a short period of years, the members could have reasonably expected that better times lay ahead.

On 20 November 1918 – just nine days after the Armistice – Lionel Hewson of the *Irish Field,* in a mood no doubt felt by many golfers, delighted in the prospects for the game:

> it seems too wonderful to be true that once more we can, with a clear conscience, indulge in all the varied pleasures (and griefs) of the links. Thousands of golfers, who were not quite sure if they were doing all they could for the Empire, will now feel a light heart in their game.[7]

One hopes that the correspondent and those thousands of light-hearted golfers also shared a thought for the millions of soldiers and civilians killed and maimed during the war. By the beginning of 1919, golf was getting back to normal again, and the various championships that were suspended during the war were again played from that year. Douglas golfers enjoyed two relatively peaceful years before the hostilities of Ireland's War of Independence brought the unpleasant effects of conflict literally to their own doorstep.

Caddies

The word 'caddie' was first used in Scotland, and comes from the French word *cadet*, meaning a young person, a young sportsman or the youngest child in a family. In golf's early years, caddies were usually young boys, and their primary duty was to carry clubs. Before golf bags came into general use in the 1880s, caddies carried the golfer's clubs in the crook of the arm, and this is depicted in many paintings and prints of golf scenes from the nineteenth century. Caddies were very familiar with their courses, and assisted players in tracking the driven ball, replacing divots, cleaning clubs, searching for lost balls, and in dispensing advice to those unfamiliar with the course. A good caddie often progressed to becoming a club professional, having learned the trade of club repair and manufacture – the essentials of the early professional's work. Caddies were not usually invited to become members of golf clubs, but they learned the game and sometimes became quite proficient through using their masters' clubs, which were often left in their care.

As golf spread and grew in the late nineteenth century, caddies became an essential part of clubs, and those who caddied on a full-time basis were able to earn a regular, if modest, income. At Douglas, for example, a class-A caddie earned

1*s* 6*d* per round in 1922, while a class-B caddie earned 1*s* 2*d*. The class-B, or junior, caddie lacked the experience and golfing knowledge of the former. It was also customary to tip the caddie, and in 1931 the committee at Douglas had notices put up in the locker room alerting members to the limit of sixpence for a caddie's tip.[1] By 1947 the rates for caddies had risen to 2*s* 6*d* per round for senior caddies, and 2*s* for juniors. Five years later, the respective rates were 3*s* and 2*s* 6*d*, while in 1965 – the last time that the minutes of the general committee record an increase – the rates were 7*s* and 4*s* 6*d*. Regular caddies were also included in the list of employees who received a Christmas gratuity, although the amount they received was a fraction of that given to the other employees. At Christmas 1936 the caddies received five shillings each, while regular employees at the club were given between £2 and £8.[2]

A caddie house or shed was also provided by clubs, where the caddies were obliged to wait until called upon to accompany a player. The caddies – mostly boys and young men, though they also numbered more mature men amongst their ranks – were under the control of the caddie-master, another golf-club employee whose job, once essential to the efficient running of a club, progress has since made redundant. At Douglas, Victor Morecroft took up duty as caddie-master in 1926, the post having been advertised in October 1925, and he served the club in that and other capacities until his retirement in 1964. The available records do not mention a caddie-master at Douglas prior to 1925. Morecroft was born in Maidenhead, England, in 1897, and fought in the First World War with the Royal Berkshire Regiment. After the war, he was stationed at Victoria Barracks, and was in Cork at the time of the burning of the city in December 1920. After his demobilisation, he returned to Cork, and eventually found employment at Douglas Golf Club, where he worked for thirty-eight years. As caddie-master at Douglas, Victor Morecroft worked from 10am until the end of play on weekdays, and from 9am until the end of play on Sundays. He had Thursdays free, and he was initially paid thirty-five shillings per week. Victor Morecroft died in 1972.

The procedure for employing a caddie changed from time to time. In the 1920s, caddies had to be taken in rotation, and the committee decided that 'no player can book a caddie in advance. Preferential treatment must not be allowed'.[3] Caddies could only be engaged through the caddie-master, and in the early 1920s they were given a badge that was handed in to the steward at the end of a day's play, after which they were paid. This was discontinued in 1926. From 1938, members paid their caddies directly.

In 1929 the committee at Douglas was informed that it was becoming increasingly difficult to recruit boys to act as caddies. The committee decided in principle to recruit girl caddies, and the honorary secretary and his assistant were given the authority 'to look into question of providing suitable shed with closed door' for the girls.[4] The committee was eager to cater appropriately for the girls, and at its September meeting that year it was proposed that a builder be consulted regarding 'provision of sanitary accommodation for girl caddies and their housing in [separate] hut'.[5] In December 1929 the alteration of a storeroom for use by girl caddies was approved. It is not known if girl caddies were ever employed at that time in Douglas, as a committee minute from January 1931 suggests that objections from the local parish priest scuppered the plans: 'In connection with the action of Revd. Fr Murphy PP Douglas in preventing girl caddies from working for the club. It was decided that no action be taken until a reply was received from the Dean (Revd. Dr Sexton) on the subject'.[6] The general-committee minute books record no further information on the subject, and in the absence of any record of girls acting as caddies at Douglas at the time, it can be assumed that the committee bowed to the ecclesiastical pressure.

Caddie misbehaviour often figures in the minutes of general-committee meetings. At times, there were over sixty caddies at the club, and as they gathered each day at the caddie shed in the hope of employment, a certain amount of horse-play and jostling was to be expected. In March 1922 the committee decided that 'a paling be erected enclosing a space around the Caddie Shed so as to keep Caddies under better control'.[7] In those years, golf balls were relatively expensive, and the low-paid caddies were occasionally tempted to pocket a found ball for later sale. In September 1922 caddie C Sullivan was dismissed for not having returned a ball found by him at the sixteenth hole.[8] The professional apparently occasionally facilitated the caddies who wished to sell the found balls. In 1926 the then professional, J Sheridan, was called to account regarding the practice, but he 'denies sale to members of secondhand balls obtained from caddies'.[9] In 1945 two caddies were dismissed following the theft of two golf balls:

> The secretary reported on an incident which occurred recently when the golf balls of two members were stolen from the 18th fairway. The Garda subsequently questioned two of the Caddies, and as a result it is understood that the Garda are proceeding with a prosecution against the two Caddies for the robbery of the balls. The services of the two Caddies in question have been dispensed with.[10]

Caddies were also occasionally reported to the committee for trespassing on the lands adjoining the course in search of lost balls. Members were regularly warned not to purchase balls from caddies.

Caddies were at the lowest level of a golf club's hierarchy, and they were sometimes a convenient target for blame when something unseemly happened. In September 1929 a sum of money was taken from a workman's clothes that had been left in the engine room:

> Every effort had been made to trace the culprit from amongst the Caddies present on the occasion but without result. After some discussion as to the action to be taken with the Caddies it was proposed that … the Caddie Master should prepare a list of undesirable or unsatisfactory caddies and that as occasion offers the Hon Secy should dismiss them.[11]

It was always a rule of the club that a caddie could carry only one bag per round. On occasion, caddies attempted to carry two bags and thereby double their payment. In July 1940 it was reported to the committee that a number of caddies had refused to caddie for members when they were prevented from carrying two bags each. They subsequently tried to intimidate the younger caddies from carrying the clubs. Twelve named caddies had been ordered off the club grounds on that day for their misbehaviour. The committee decided to dismiss two of the caddies, suspend six for a month, and to permit four to resume work as they were married men.[12] In 1946 a similar incident was reported to the committee, and six caddies were suspended.[13] In a 1952 incident, a caddie refused to carry for a member when he discovered that the member's playing partner was going to carry his own bag. The committee took a dim view of this behaviour, and decided that 'such conduct on the part of a caddie could not be allowed to go unchecked'.[14] The disciplinary action is not recorded. At another time, a caddie was dismissed for 'inattention and impertinence', while at a committee meeting in 1970, 'the fact that a caddie partakes of liquor sitting on a couch in the hall' was raised.

In 1931 the caddies at Douglas went on strike, and the committee nominated four of its members to have discussions with them with a view to addressing their grievances. It was decided that the caddies would be given permanent numbers, and that a member would draw a number when engaging a caddie. It would seem that the strike arose due to members favouring some caddies with frequent employment while others were often passed over.[15] At least some of the caddies continued to harbour dissatisfaction, and at Christmas £5 was given to the caddie-master to be distributed amongst the permanent caddies 'with the exception of those concerned in the incident of the burning of the Caddie Shed on 10/12/31'![16]

The number of caddies working at Douglas varied greatly, and while the regular, full-time caddies presented themselves for work most days, the number of casuals fluctuated greatly. As the latter were mostly made up of schoolboys, weekends and school holidays would see more of them looking for work. The minutes of the general committee at Douglas record the distribution of Christmas gratuities to caddies for many of the years between 1936 and 1973, and often the numbers of regular and casual caddies receiving these gratuities are given. In 1936, 43 caddies in all were given a Christmas gratuity. In 1940 twenty-five regulars and thirty-five casuals were paid. Through the 1940s there were an average of fifteen regular caddies and twenty casuals at Douglas. For the 1950s the average number of regulars fell to eight, while there were twenty-two casuals. In 1964 only seven caddies in all were regularly working at Douglas, and this had fallen to two by 1972. Cummins and O'Callaghan were the names of the last two caddies who regularly worked at Douglas and who received Christmas gratuities. They are last mentioned in 1973.

After the Second World War, the use of caddies declined in the US, in Britain and in Ireland as players resorted in increasing numbers to the caddie cart. Caddie fees were also considered by many to be an avoidable expense. In 1953 the editor of *Irish Golf* magazine lamented the decline of the caddie:

> And now the caddies are a dying race! Economy has introduced the use of mechanical aids, although championship courses still retain a few representatives of the old school, and the ranks of a unique profession are being rapidly thinned. Perhaps some gifted poet will mark the end of an epoch with a fitting lament, for golf will be the poorer when the last caddie hands in his bag.[17]

Geoffrey Cousins, in his *Golf in Britain: A Social History from the Beginnings to the Present Day*, considers the advantages and disadvantages of the caddie cart:

> ...it cannot give advice, clean clubs, replace divots or give the line for putting. But it is never late on parade, requires neither lunch money nor tip, and can be depended upon not to cough or sniff 'on the stroke' or make cynical comments on one's style to other caddies.[18]

The practice of using a caddie has continued for many competitive fixtures, but the tradition of ordinary members employing caddies for leisure-time golf has all but disappeared.

Right: Victor Morecroft, caddie-master at Douglas from 1926–64.

4 *Fire! May 1921*

In the early hours of Thursday morning, 26 May 1921, the pavilion of Douglas Golf Club was completely destroyed in an arson attack carried out by a unit of the IRA. The *Cork Examiner* of the following day reported, under the headline 'Cork Burnings – Many Conflagrations', that 'The large pavilion at Douglas Golf Links was set on fire between two and three o'clock. It burned fiercely for some hours, and ... was totally ruined'. The *Irish Times* of 28 May carried the short official report of the burning issued by the authorities in Dublin Castle the previous day, giving an earlier time for the attack: 'A number of armed civilians set fire to, and completely destroyed, Douglas Golf Club, Cork at six O'clock on Thursday morning. The damage is estimated at £10,000'. Both the *Cork Examiner* and *Cork Constitution* of that day also carried the report. On 30 May the *Cork Examiner* published a photograph of the destroyed clubhouse. The striking features of the photograph are the two tall chimneys at either gable, standing over ten metres in height, and the group of twenty or so people gathered outside surveying the damage. The incident did not merit any further coverage in the press as the level of hostilities between the Crown forces and the IRA at the time was such that news of many other outrages was coming to hand on a daily basis.

Why was Douglas Golf Club targeted by the IRA for such an attack? Club folklore tells that the clubhouse was burned in error, that Cork Golf Club at Little Island was the intended target due to the popularity of that course amongst the British military stationed at Victoria (now Collins) Barracks in the city.

The War of Independence that began in 1919 became increasingly intense in the latter months of 1920 and in the first half of 1921. Cork was the most violent county during these revolutionary years, and the people of the city lived in an atmosphere of fear, intimidation and suspicion. At the height of the conflict, ambushes and shootings were a daily occurrence, while by night kidnappings and disappearances sustained an atmosphere of terror. Arson attacks on houses and business premises by both sides in the conflict escalated as the cycle of reprisal and counter-reprisal became increasingly violent. In the period between January and July 1921, 165 buildings were destroyed in Cork. Travel and communications were virtually paralysed as many road and rail bridges in the county were destroyed in the same period, while roads were frequently blocked or trenched, and telephone wires cut.

The immediate series of events that led to the burning of the Douglas clubhouse began with an IRA attack on an RIC (Royal Irish Constabulary) patrol in the Blackpool area of the city in which three policemen were killed. As a so-called 'official reprisal' for this, the British army destroyed four houses in the locality on 24 May. This in turn led to a counter-reprisal by the IRA, and between the evening of Wednesday 25 and the morning of Thursday 26 May, five arson attacks were carried out. The homes of four unionists – 'well known loyalists',[1] as the *Cork Examiner* termed them – were destroyed: those of Mrs Maude Jacob and Mr W Hirst Simpson at Castle View, Blackrock at about 10pm on Wednesday evening; that of Mr Ebenezer Pike at Carrigrohane at about midnight of the same night; that of Sir Alfred G Dobbin JP, in Montenotte at around 8am on Thursday morning. The fifth attack – some time between 2 and 6am that morning – destroyed the Douglas clubhouse. The caretaker, Joseph Power, was permitted by the attackers to remove his belongings and some other items from the clubhouse before the building was set on fire.

The attacks were disciplined, planned actions, and were carried out by the 2nd Battalion of the No. 1 IRA Brigade, which was commanded by Mick Murphy. The brigade publicly took responsibility for the action. While the rationale for attacking the four residences can be understood, the attack on the clubhouse, in contrast, seems puzzling. Mick Murphy, in his statement to the Bureau of Military History on his activities during the War of Independence, said that they burned the building because Douglas Golf Club was 'a den of imperialism'.[2] This may well have been the perception held by Murphy and his men, as golf-club membership was, in the main, the preserve of well-off, upper-middle-class, business or professional men who would have been quite conservative in nature. IRA volunteers in Cork city were mainly upper working class/lower middle class,[3] and in the atmosphere of the time could quite understandably have regarded the club as fair game, seeing its members as 'on the other side'. It is also possible that members of the British military had played golf as visitors to Douglas Golf Club. A tramline that passed relatively close to Victoria Barracks on the northside of the city would have conveniently brought players to Douglas, having changed trams on

CORK BURNINGS.

OFFICIAL REPORT.

Dublin, Friday.—The following was issued by Dublin Castle this morning:—

At 10 p.m. on the 25th, a number of civilians set fire to the residence of Mrs. Maude Jacobs, loyalist, of Castle View, Blackrock, Cork. After ejecting the inmates, the house was completely destroyed as also was an adjoining house belonging to Mr. Hurst Simpson. The damage is estimated at about £6,000.

At 6 a.m. yesterday a number of armed civilians set fire to Douglas Golf Club, Cork, completely destroying it. The damage is estimated at £10,000.

The residence of Sir Alfred Dobbin at Montenotte, Cork city, was set on fire at eight o'clock yesterday morning. The house was entered by a party of armed men, who ordered Sir Alfred and his family to leave. Petrol was then poured on to the floors of the various rooms, which were then set on fire. The damages is estimated at between £15,000 and £20,000.

CORK LAST NIGHT.

Some shots were fired in Cork last night between 8 and 10 o'clock, most of them in the north-western area of the city. There were, however, no admissions to the Infirmaries resulting from the firing.

BOMB AND BULLET VICTIMS.

Mr. Christopher Walsh, of the "Examiner" staff, and Mr Peter Murphy, of Messrs. Suttons, Ltd., are progressing favourably at the South Infirmary, where they are being treated for wounds received early in the week.

Report of the burning of the clubhouse, *Cork Examiner*, 28 May 1921.

The remains of the clubhouse after the arson attack of 26 May 1921 (*Cork Examiner*, 30 May 1921).

Patrick Street. A military connection with Douglas Golf Club is suggested by the mention of the 'Military Cup' at a committee meeting on 7 March 1922. It was decided at that meeting to rename the cup the '24 Cup'. The only source for such a trophy would have been the British military stationed in Cork.

It is extremely doubtful that the clubhouse was burned in error for that of Cork Golf Club. The IRA volunteers were from Cork and knew their city intimately. In an account of the burning recorded in the history of Douglas Golf Club in the club newsletter in 1977, it is claimed that 'an order was received by the Cork IRA from HQ in Dublin to "burn Cork Golf Club, Douglas, used by British Military from Cork Barracks"'. The writer of the piece cites no source for this quotation. The wording of the 'order', confusing the Cork and Douglas golf clubs, seems a little convenient as an explanation for the 'error theory'. It is unlikely to have happened in that way. At that time, the Cork No 1 Brigade acted in an independent fashion, and would have decided upon and organised its own actions. Sanction may have been sought or orders may possibly have been received regarding an action of greater significance, but the burnings of 25 and 26 May were a local response to a British action of the previous day.

Whatever the reason for the attack – whether deliberate or as a result of confusion – the members of Douglas Golf Club had lost their clubhouse and their golf equipment, which most members at the time stored in clubhouse lockers. Attacks on golf clubs were rare during the conflict, but the clubhouse at Skerries Golf Club was also burned down, and in another golf-related incident an Auxiliary major was shot dead on the golf course at Tralee in April 1921. In 1922, during the civil war, the clubhouse at Tullamore Golf Club was burned[4]

Aftermath

On Friday 27 May 1921, the day after the fire, the general committee of the club met at the Imperial Hotel on the South Mall. R McKechnie, club captain, was in the chair, and five other members of the committee attended: J G Musgrave, C Blake, T Kelleher, J N Healy and M English, the honorary secretary. 'The burning of the Pavilion and the advisability of resuming play on the links was discussed at length'.[5] No decision was taken on the matter, and the committee decided to await the outcome of the special general meeting of club members that was to follow.

The meeting of members was chaired by Fr Matt McSwiney, and was attended by sixty-eight people in all. Fr Matt McSwiney was co-opted as president for the remainder of the year due to the death in April of Fr R A O'Gorman, president for 1921. The eagerness of some to continue playing on the course in spite of the loss of the clubhouse led to a proposal that 'play on the links be continued under existing conditions'. This was withdrawn, however, and the meeting decided to leave the question of resuming play in the hands of the committee. The *Cork Constitution* of the following day, in its report of the meeting, noted that 'it was unanimously decided to temporarily suspend play on the links for a period not to exceed ten days, in order that the committee might be given sufficient time to make such arrangements for the resumption of play as they consider desirable'. It was also decided to appoint a sub-committee to organise a fund to compensate the resident caretaker/steward Joseph Power and the other 'inside staff' for their losses in the fire. It is noteworthy that the minutes record no condemnation of those responsible for the arson attack, nor expressions of anger or outrage, which would have been very understandable in the circumstances.

The general committee met again four days

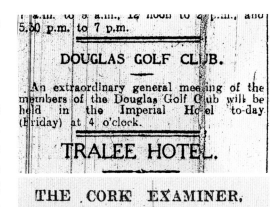

Top:
Cork Examiner, 27 May, 1921.

Middle:
Cork Examiner, 31 May 1921.

Bottom:
Cork Examiner, 1 June 1921.

later, on 31 May. The future of the club was in the balance, and it was unanimously agreed that the club would be wound up if sufficient funds were not raised from a 'proposed loan of £10 (Ten Pounds) per Gentleman Member in Cash' to start reconstruction.[6] A new club would be formed by those members willing to subscribe. The lady members were to hold a separate meeting to decide an amount they wished to subscribe.

The special general meeting that followed was attended by ninety members, gentlemen and ladies, and discussed the proposals for raising money: a loan of £10 per member and a bank loan to be covered by guarantees from members, every member to sign the guarantors' list. Other meetings followed in the subsequent weeks, and a loan guaranteed by club members was negotiated with the Munster & Leinster Bank. The proposed £10 loan by members seems to have changed somewhat, as entries in the account ledger for 1921–29 show that gentlemen members paid £5 and ladies £2 10s into a reconstruction fund, while only a small number paid £10. Up to 31 December 1921, 131 members had paid £587 13s into the fund.

While the majority of members seem to have been eager to save the club from closure and to contribute to the reconstruction of the clubhouse, a significant number were less keen. Through the second half of 1921, the minutes of the general-committee meetings record a constant effort to collect outstanding subscriptions. Letters were written to the defaulting members, and a collector was appointed to collect the outstanding monies. Eventually, the club solicitor was consulted as to how the matter might be resolved.[7] In November a circular letter was sent to those members who had not yet contributed to the reconstruction fund.[8]

The number of members in the club in 1921, paid-up or otherwise, is not known, but the account-ledger figures for 1922 show 284 people, gentlemen and ladies, as having paid subscriptions in that year, forty-one of whom paid an entrance fee and were presumably new members.[9] The arithmetic suggests a membership of at least 243 in 1921, and only about half of these seem to have contributed to the reconstruction fund, given that 131 are recorded as having paid in 1921.

The annual subscription – which stood at £5 for gentlemen and £2 10s for ladies in 1921 – was not raised and, indeed, continued at that level for the next twenty-five years, when it was eventually raised in 1946!

The general committee took other measures to save money. In July 1921 it was decided to reduce the wages of staff significantly: J Curran, the club professional, had his weekly wage halved to £1; Joseph Power, the caretaker/steward, had his wage cut from £3 to

£2 per week; William Magee, the senior groundsman, had his pay cut from £4 to £3 10s per week. In addition to the wage cuts, one of Magee's assistants, 'the boy Coughlan', was let go.[10] The weekly wage bill for groundsmen, Magee's assistants, fell from an amount that varied between £8 15s and £9 to under £7, suggesting that their number was reduced to three from four. The varying wage bill for ground staff suggests that their numbers varied from week to week, with the employment of casual staff as the need arose.

For the ten days or so that the course was closed for play following the fire, members of Douglas Golf Club were invited by the Monkstown, Muskerry and Cork golf clubs to use their courses free of charge.

To enable a resumption of play at Douglas with some measure of comfort, three huts were lent by member J G (Jimmy) Musgrave for use as temporary premises.[11] In September the committee decided to advertise for 'a 30x60x20 foot Sectional Hut',[12] which arrived at Douglas from Crosshaven the following month and with the others served the club as clubhouse, caddie shed and pro shop. The committee decided 'to purchase two large household buckets for the men's lavatory', and to acquire stoves for heating.[13] In December member D P McCarthy gave the club a gift of paint to decorate the huts, and a decision was made 'That ladies lavatory be built on to outside of existing hut'.[14] The accommodation was far from ideal and in stark contrast to the much-praised original clubhouse, but served the needs of members and staff for four years. The large 'sectional hut' was still used by the ground staff at Douglas into the 1970s.

Entries in the account ledger for 1921–29 suggest that members had to forego the pleasures of their own bar for only a short time. For 26 May 1921, nine shillings is shown under the heading 'Bar Receipts'. As this was the date of the fire, it is likely that it is an amount carried forward from previous income. A temporary bar of some kind was hastily installed in the temporary accommodation, as the weekly accounts from 9 June show healthy bar receipts. For the week ending 9 June, less than two weeks after the fire, the bar took in £9 19s 10d, over £14 in each of the two subsequent weeks, and amounts varying between £10 and over £20 per week for the rest of the year. For the week ending on New Year's Eve 1921, the bar took in the highest amount: £34 16s 11d. Clearly, the Douglas members were in high spirits at year's end, and as the bells in the city below rang in a new year, an uneasy peace was still holding following the Truce in July that ended two years of armed conflict. Having survived another major setback, the partying members must surely have felt a unifying and indomitable club spirit as they sang 'Auld Lang Syne' together.

1921 Captain's Chain

Douglas Golf Club lost its clubhouse and all it contained in the arson attack of 26 May 1921. This object, inscribed 'Douglas G.C. 1921 Captain's Chain', suggests that a group of club members decided to create a chain of office as a replacement for a more dignified one, probably lost in the fire. This 'Captain's Chain' was made from an empty State Express cigarette box, signed by a group of members and perforated to take a cord. One can imagine this group of early members wishing to find a suitable symbol of office to hang around the neck of 1921 club captain R McKechnie at a boisterous club get-together, the ceremony performed with mock pomp and much laughter! Many of the signatories were later officers of the club.

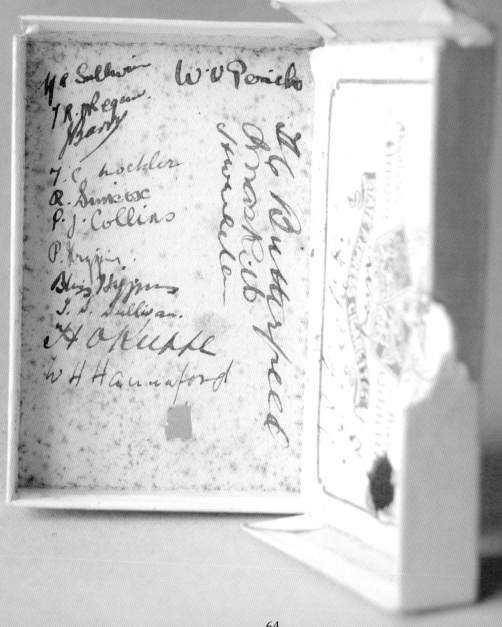

Redmond Simcox

by Liam Connolly

Redmond Simcox, born in 1904, was the youngest son of James and Kathleen Simcox. In 1925, at the age of twenty-one, Redmond assumed the captaincy of Douglas Golf Club.

Redmond grew up at Bloomfield House, Monfieldstown, near Rochestown. The Simcox family were bakers by trade, and Redmond's father was lord mayor of Cork in 1911 and again in 1912. In his teenage years, Redmond spent his leisure time learning the fundamentals of golf at Douglas, where his brother Richard was a founder member and a keen player. Richard Simcox featured in a number of the reports of the early competitions held at the club in 1910 and 1911. Such was the ability and aptitude of Redmond for the game of golf that by the age of twenty he had a handicap of scratch.

The early golfing tradition of appointing club captaincy to the best golfer in the club (as confirmed by winning the Scratch Medal) had long been discontinued by the 1920s, but one must wonder if it had any bearing on the appointment of Redmond as captain of Douglas in 1925. He was only twenty-one years of age, but his golfing ability was second to none in the club or, indeed, in Munster.

The year 1925 was a very busy one in Douglas. The building of the new club-house was nearing completion, and the course was being redesigned by the leading golf-course architect, Dr Alister Mackenzie. Funding for the cost of these works was commencing. The captain found the time to attend to all these matters whilst playing golf at the highest level, including playing in the Irish Close Championship at Portmarnock.

Following his year as club captain, Redmond concentrated on his golf, and reaped the rich reward of winning the South of Ireland Championship at Lahinch in 1926. In the final, he defeated the defending champion, M Crowley of Portmarnock, 7 and 5. The 'South' is the oldest of the provincial championships, and was inaugurated in 1895. Redmond and his brother Richard were regular visitors to Lahinch, and it is recorded that Redmond was very kind to his young admirers and, indeed, regularly arranged to have a basket of freshly baked bread brought from the family bakery in Cork to O'Dwyer's shop in Lahinch. Redmond repeated his victory in 1927 with a win by 2 and 1 over W G McConnell of Royal Portrush. The 1927 championship was the last 'South' to be played on the old course at Lahinch. The

Facing page: Redmond Simcox at the age of twenty-two, standing between Hubert O'Keeffe (left), and George Duncan (right).

Mackenzie course was in play for the 1928 championship. Redmond's only other appearance in the final was in 1936, when he was beaten 4 and 3 by T F Ryan of Tipperary. These victories in the 'South' established him as one of the leading players of his time. In 1936 Redmond also reached the final of the Cork Scratch Cup, but lost to the defending champion, J D McCormack, by 4 and 3. He won the trophy for the first time in 1928, and was victorious again in 1934, 1942, 1947 and 1949.

International golf matches were not as organised in the 1920s as they are now. The first Quadrangular International matches were held at Troon (Scotland) in 1932. In the period 1900 to 1931, only five representatives from Munster played on the international team, three of whom played before 1914. John Burke of Lahinch and Redmond Simcox of Douglas were the only two Munster representatives who played the international team between 1920 and 1931. International recognition did not come easily for southern players at that time. Redmond was named on the team to play Scotland at Newcastle, County Down, in 1927, and was a reserve on the team in 1928. He then experienced an unbroken spell on the Irish team, from 1930 to 1935, playing a total of thirty-two times in sixteen matches as a member of Douglas. Subsequently, he played for Ireland as a member of Cork Golf Club a further ten times in five matches in 1936 and 1938. The Douglas members of the 1930s were very proud of their international representative when they saw Redmond's name and club affiliation on the team sheets.

The Amateur Championship, first played in 1885, was considered to be one of the majors in the 1920s and 1930s. Its status was greatly enhanced by the achievement of the immortal Bobby Jones when he won the Grand Slam (Open, US Open, Amateur and US Amateur championships) in 1930. It was very rare in the 1930s to have an Irish entrant in the Amateur Championship. Redmond Simcox was one of the few Irishmen who entered at that time. The records of the Royal and Ancient Golf Club of St Andrews show that Redmond entered the championship in 1929 at Sandwich, Royal St George's, in 1930 at St Andrews, in 1931 at Westward Ho!, Royal North Devon, and in 1949 at Portmarnock. He was beaten in the first round in 1929, and in the second in 1931. His most notable performance was in the memorable championship in 1930 at St Andrews, won by Bobby Jones, when Redmond got to the fourth round, where he was beaten 3 and 2. Redmond achieved something of a record when he won his third-round match at that event 7 and 6 in just over an hour. He made a nostalgic appearance in the Amateur in 1949 when it was played in Ireland for the first time, at Portmarnock. In the first round, he was drawn against his Cork colleague and good friend, George Crosbie, whom he beat by 3 and 2. Regrettably, he lost 2 and 1 in the next round.

Redmond played golf to the highest level throughout his long career. He is remembered as a superb striker of his irons, using a big, wide-arched swing. Though he adopted a crouched putting style, he was regarded as a dependable putter. His many domestic successes include the Senior Cup in 1931 and 1939 and the Barton Shield in 1938 with Cork Golf Club, and losing finalist in the Irish Close Championship in 1938. He played in the Duncan and Havers exhibition match at Douglas in 1926, and was a member of the Douglas Barton Shield team that lost the national final in 1929. Redmond played as a member of Cork Golf Club in the Senior Cup of 1931 as it was the norm at that time for players to play for other clubs if their home club was not entering a team in the particular competition.

In January 1936 Redmond resigned his full membership of Douglas Golf Club and transferred to Cork Golf Club. He played his international matches in 1936 and 1938 – when he captained the team – as a member of Cork.

Redmond's involvement in the administrative side of golf started at a young age – when he was captain of Douglas in 1925 – and continued throughout his life. He was captain of Lahinch in 1929, following in the footsteps of his good friend and fellow Corkonian, William O'Dwyer. Redmond was captain of Cork Golf Club in 1932–33, captain of the senior international team in 1938, and received the ultimate recognition for his lifelong contribution to all aspects of the game of golf in Ireland when he was president of the GUI in the years 1950–52.

Redmond came from a family that was deeply involved in the formative years of Douglas Golf Club. His mother cut the tape at the opening of the new clubhouse in 1926. As lord mayor, his father James presented the Lord Mayor's Cup, more commonly known as the Simcox Cup, to the club in 1911, and Redmond presented Douglas with the Bloomfield Cup in 1929. Both trophies are keenly played for to this day.

Even though in the latter years of his life Redmond was very much associated with Cork Golf Club, it should be remembered that his formative and early years as a golfer were spent in Douglas Golf Club. Redmond Simcox died in 1969 at the age of sixty-five.

Top: Alf Padgham (left), and Redmond Simcox (right), in 1932.
Bottom: Redmond Simcox.

5 *The Phoenix Rises: 1920s*

During the 1920s Douglas Golf Club renewed itself, built a new club-house, reconstructed its course and began to make its mark on the competitive golf scene. The military and political conflict of 1919–21 had impacted very directly on the club, but the club seems to have

Douglas clubhouse, 1929.

been unaffected by the civil war that was fought from June 1922 to May 1923. On 8 August 1922, the Free State National Army landed a force of men in Passage West, and a two-day battle was fought in the Rochestown and Douglas areas as the republican 'Irregulars' resisted the National Army's advance on Cork city. Sixteen were killed, and many were wounded in the clashes. Access to Douglas Golf Club would have been very difficult and dangerous at this time, and there would have been military activity in the immediate vicinity of the course, if not on the course itself. The minutes of the general committee of the time make no mention of the action, nor is any reference made to the difficulties and dangers of the time. The only 'political' reference in these minutes occurs on 30 November 1923

– five months after the end of the civil war – when the following is recorded: 'Application from Republican Office, 56 Grand Parade, to suspend play until such time as all the prisoners were released'. This related to republican prisoners still being held by the Free State authorities. The committee decided to take no action.

A New Clubhouse

In addition to the monies loaned by members for the creation of a reconstruction fund following the fire of 1921, Douglas Golf Club also received compensation for its loss from the government of the new Free State. An extraordinary general meeting was held on 6 September 1923 to discuss the assessor's award of £5,426 for club losses: £2,500 was for the building, £1,831 for individual members' personal losses, and £1,095 for miscellaneous club fittings. This assessment was accepted, and the following November the general committee appointed the president, Fr Matt McSwiney, and the former honorary secretary, Mick English, 'to proceed to Dublin to interview Mr Brennan, Financial Secretary to the Treasury [i.e. secretary of the Department of Finance], relative to the compensation claim arising out of the burning of the Pavilion and personal effects of members in May 1921'.[1] The minister for posts and telegraphs in the new government was Corkman J J Walsh, and it is believed that his good offices were used by the club's representatives to get a sympathetic hearing.[2] The committee meeting of 11 December expressed satisfaction with the outcome of the meeting in Dublin.

As the committee worked to further its compensation claim, plans were being drawn up for the new clubhouse. In October 1922 Messrs O'Flynn and O'Connor, Architects, were asked to draw up sketch plans for the proposed building,[3] but it was February 1924 before the committee made a final decision as to its preferred design. The architects had submitted different proposals that the committee viewed, 'and after mature discussion one was decided on and he [honorary secretary] was instructed to advertise for tender for its completion at earliest possible moment'.[4] Four tenders were considered at a meeting on 17 July 1924, and the lowest, that of Denis Duggan & Sons for £3,117 6s 9d, was accepted. The other tenders came from Coveney Bros, S Murphy Bros and John Kearns & Son, and were up to £1,000 more expensive. By January 1925 the building was nearing completion, and committee members met there to view the work and to decide on minor alterations.[5]

The first tranche of compensation money was paid in February 1924 when £2,985 3s 6d was received to cover the losses of members' equipment and club furniture and fitings.[6] In December 1924 the committee was getting anxious about the delay in the payment of compensation for the loss of the clubhouse in 1921, as the work on the new clubhouse was by then well advanced. The honorary solicitor was asked to investigate.[7] He was successful, as a payment of £1,096 2s 10d was received in late January, and a further £394 15s 0d was paid in March.[8] Neither the minutes of the general committee nor the account ledger for 1921–29 record any further payments, although just under £950 was outstanding from the compensation award. This may have been paid at a later date and not recorded, but the £1,490 17s 10d received in compensation for the loss of the building in 1921 was over £1,600 short of the estimated cost for the new building.

An extraordinary general meeting was held in April 1925 to address the financial and other issues arising out of the building of the new clubhouse, which was to be officially opened five weeks later. The meeting decided to borrow £2,000 from the Munster & Leinster Bank, the loan being guaranteed by the members. It was also decided to repay the money lent by members in 1921 to fund the purchase of huts and their adaptation for use as temporary premises. Twenty-four of the attendance of thirty-eight had promised guarantees of £50 each by the close of the meeting. When the agreements were signed with the bank later that year, guarantees to the value of £2,575 had been given: twenty-nine guarantees of £50 and forty-six of £25. The guarantors were asked to state their occupation when signing the agreement, and over sixty complied, giving an interesting sample of the occupations of members of the time.[9] Fourteen were 'merchants', ten were either doctors or dentists, and seven were accountants. There were three each of commercial agents, directors, civil servants and managers, while there were two each of stockbrokers, pawnbrokers, builders and commercial travellers. Amongst the others were a cinema proprietor, a university teacher, a stationer and a gentleman (see appendix, pp. 92–3). The value of these guarantees was recognised by the club when the seventy-five guarantors were given preference (after club officers and the guarantors of 1916 and 1921) in the allocation of lockers in the new clubhouse. In addition, rule 6 of the revised rules of the club that came into effect in 1926 made the following provision: 'While the 1925 Guarantee to the Munster and Leinster Bank remains in force, at least two-thirds of the total number of the Officers and Committee of the club shall be elected from the Members who acted as Guarantors'. This provision still applied in the 1946 edition of the rules. Issues relating to the club water supply, the purchase of a tractor mower and the need for course-improvement works were also discussed at this meeting.

P J Collins was honoured by the club for his fund-raising efforts

G. MAY 25, 1925.

DOUGLAS GOLF CLUB.

New Pavilion—Opening Ceremony.

Four years ago the Douglas Golf Pavilion was burned down, and the outlook for the continuance of the club looked rather doubtful. All the furniture, fittings, and the members' clubs and effects were destroyed, practically nothing being salved, and the steward and his family were homeless. However, with the loyal help of a few members, one in particular, and the steward, tents, huts and corrugated iron sheds were got together and the nucleus of a temporary clubhouse was in being in a few days. The general body of the members maintained their allegiance to the club and the crucial period was safely passed. The huts for the past four years were the happy meeting place of large numbers of enthusiastic golfers and the membership steadily increased, so that at present the club has the largest membership roll, both men and women, outside the metropolis.

The re-building of the old clubhouse, which was completely destroyed, was taken in hands last autumn and after several unavoidable delays, including through a thunderstorm the demolition of the re-built walls before the roof had been placed upon them, the completed building was on Saturday taken over from the contractors.

The new pavilion is a handsome bungalow structure covering the entire area of the old clubhouse, with the addition of the space formerly occupied by a verandah. Situated on the Maryborough heights it commands a magnificent view of the city, the surrounding hills as far away as the Galtee and Knockmealdown Mountains being easily visible, whilst views of the river and Lough Mahon complete a panorama rare to find in any country. A pretty porch entrance leads into a spacious lounge room, which connects with a splendid large luncheon room capable of seating at table about 70 persons. These two rooms extending for over 60 feet along the front of the building, facing north-east, are lighted by large casement windows, and have an oak wainscotting surmounted by a very artistic wallpaper. A door leads back from the lounge into the smoke-room, whence another door leads into a very large and excellently fitted men's locker-room containing about 200 lockers. This room is heated by a hot-water system, and on a side upstairs lobby there is a very fine drying room. There is also a door leading direct from the locker-room into a luncheon-room and another door to the toilet room, which is fitted in a most up-to-date fashion with a plentiful hot and cold water supply. From this latter room a door leads out to the links. The ladies are provided with another large locker room, lighted by a magnificent bay window overlooking the third tee. There is an office and a committee room at the south side of the pavilion, and a very fine kitchen, which is fitted in every way to meet the demands of

Report on the opening of the new clubhouse, Cork Examiner, 25 May 1925.

in this period. He was made an honorary life member in 1926 in recognition of his work in raising £600 – almost twenty per cent of the cost of the new building – in the space of two years. He was later club president in 1930 and 1931.

Official Opening of Clubhouse

The general committee decided to invite Mrs Kathleen Simcox, the widow of James Simcox, to officiate at the official opening of the new clubhouse on Saturday 23 May 1925, as the club president, Mr H Longfield, would be absent. The Simcox family from nearby Bloomfield House had been associated with the club since its foundation, and James Simcox had presented the Lord Mayor's Cup (now called the Simcox Cup) to the club in 1911, while his sons Richard and Redmond were accomplished Douglas golfers. The Cork Examiner of 25 May gave a full account of the opening and the subsequent competitions, as well as a detailed description of the new building:

> The new pavilion is a handsome bungalow structure covering the entire area of the old clubhouse, with the addition of the space formerly occupied by a veranda. Situated on the Maryborough heights it commands a magnificent view of the city, the surrounding hills as far away as the Galtee and Knockmealdown Mountains being easily visible, while views of the river and Lough Mahon complete a panorama rare to find in any country. A pretty porch entrance leads into a spacious lounge room, which connects with a splendid large luncheon room capable of seating at table about 70 persons. These two rooms extending for over 60 feet along the front of the building, facing north-east, are lighted by large casement windows, and have an oak wainscotting surmounted by a very

artistic wallpaper. A door leads back from the lounge into the smoke-room, whence another door leads into a very large and excellently fitted men's locker-room containing about 200 lockers. This room is heated by a hot-water system, and on a side upstairs lobby there is a very fine drying room. There is also a door leading direct from the locker-room into a luncheon-room and another door to the toilet-room, which is fitted in a most up-to-date fashion with a plentiful hot and cold water supply. From this latter room a door leads out to the links. The ladies are provided with another large locker room, lighted by a magnificent bay window … There is an office and a committee room at the south side of the pavilion, and a very fine kitchen, which is fitted in every way to meet the demands of the members for hot and cold luncheons, teas, etc., completes the structure.

Having declared the pavilion open 'with a few happily chosen words', Mrs Simcox was presented with an inscribed gold key as a souvenir of the occasion. Following this, a series of competitions was held. The first was a mixed foursomes against bogey, which had an entry of sixty-four and was won by the pairing of Mrs James Power and Mick English. A ladies' 'approaching and putting' competition was held next, and was won by Mrs K Simmons. The golf concluded with a long-drive competition, which was won by Redmond Simcox, club captain and twenty-one-year-old son of Mrs Simcox. Of the twenty-seven entrants for this competition, Simcox alone broke 200 yards, winning with a drive of 217 yards. According to the newspaper account, 'a little informal dance in the luncheon room completed a very happy and enjoyable day'.

The gold key presented to Mrs J (Kathleen) Simcox on the occasion of the official opening of the clubhouse on 23 May 1925.

The *Irish Field* of 1 May 1926 was also full of praise for the new clubhouse, and for the members of the club who had overcome such obstacles to have yet another fine building at their disposal:

> the splendid pavilion which looks out on the fine course bears silent testimony to the love of the members for the game and their club … the members of the club rendered the committee every assistance, and even when, after the burning, they had to put up with any amount of inconvenience, they never murmured; in fact the more they suffered the more determined they became to get things to rights.

Although the new clubhouse was officially opened and highly praised, there were some ongoing problems. The main floorboards were damp and were causing damage to the linoleum covering. It was decided to remove the linoleum until 'the floor was thoroughly fit to receive it permanently'. The committee met again less than a week later, and the architect was asked to have the floorboards replaced. The gents' lavatories were also giving trouble, and there were leaks in the roof.[10] There was also some dispute about the architect's fees. The committee delayed payment as it endeavoured to establish if such fees had been included in the club's compensation claim.[11] On establishing that they had been, a deputation from the committee met with the architect and agreed payment with him, securing a reduction of £86.[12]

A Change of Course

Alister Mackenzie (1870–1934) is one of the best-known and highly regarded golf-course architects of the early decades of the twentieth century. He was born near Leeds in 1870, and worked first as a medical doctor before turning to golf-course design. He served as a surgeon with the British army during the Boer War, where he became interested in camouflage. During the First World War, he worked with military engineers and specialised in the camouflage of military earthworks. When he turned to golf-course design after the war, this knowledge of camouflage informed his work. He published his *Golf Architecture: Economy in Course Construction and Greenkeeping* in 1920, in which he sets out the principles that guided him in his design work. His designs rely heavily on the existing topography and features of a site, and are characterised by the sensitive adaptation of nature to produce challenging yet beautiful courses. He worked on a number of courses in Ireland in the 1920s, including Muskerry, Monkstown, Cork and Douglas, as well as at Lahinch and Limerick. He later worked in Australia and the US, where he died in 1934.

Dr. A. MACKENZIE

Golf Course Architect

MOOR ALLERTON LODGE LEEDS

Scale of Professional Charges and Conditions of Agreement

1—The general supervision which the Architect will give to the work is such periodical inspection by him or his deputy as may be necessary to ensure that the work is being carried out to his intentions, but constant superintendence of the work does not form part of the duties undertaken by him, and is not included for in the following scale of charges.

2—The Architect is empowered to make such deviations, alterations, additions, and omissions as he may reasonably consider desirable in the client's interests, in carrying out the work, provided that no material addition to the cost is caused thereby.

Scale of Charges

1—If the estimated cost exceeds £2,000, the percentage to be 6 per cent. plus all travelling and hotel expenses.

2—If the estimated cost does not exceed £2,000, the percentage to be 10 per cent. in the case of work costing £1,000 graduated to 6 per cent. in the case of work costing £2,000, plus travelling and hotel expenses.

3—For preliminary advice and report on the selection and suitability of a site for a Golf Course, or on the reconstruction of a Golf Course, 10 guineas and expenses a day.

4—In all cases where the material, labour, or carriage, in whole or in part, are provided by the client, the percentage of the estimated cost shall be calculated as if the work had been executed and carried out by a contractor.

NOTE—This scale of professional charges is based on the revised scale 1919 of the Royal Institute of British Architects.

The Architect's remuneration shall be payable by instalments from time to time, as the work proceeds.

His name is associated with some of the world's best-known courses – Augusta National (with Bobby Jones), Cypress Point, the West Course at Royal Melbourne Golf Club, and many more.

While the construction of the clubhouse was underway the committee also considered the state of the course at Douglas, which had been in play for fourteen years. Muskerry Golf Club had invited Dr Alister Mackenzie to draw up plans for an extension of its course from nine to eighteen holes. Mackenzie presented his plans to that club in August 1924, and the work on the course was completed in spring 1925. On 8 October 1924 the committee at Douglas decided 'that Dr A Mackenzie be asked to inspect the links and give report of his ideas and suggestions at a maximum of £10'.[13]

There is no record of Mackenzie visiting Douglas at that time, but a plan of the course was drawn by E Peard to be forwarded to Mackenzie.[14] Three weeks later, the committee had received a sketch of Mackenzie's proposed alterations, and the drawing was hung in the clubhouse for the attention of members.[15] The following May, when the work on the new clubhouse was in its final stages, a decision

Left:
Dr Alister Mackenzie's scale of charges, as sent to Douglas Golf Club.

Right:
Dr Alister Mackenzie (1870–1934), one of the world's best-known course architects in the early twentieth century, who redesigned the Douglas course.

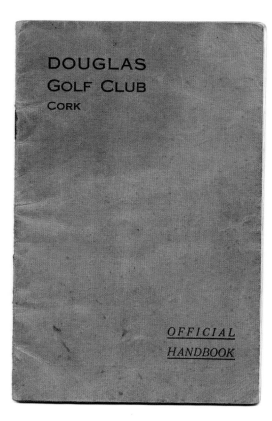

Above:
Douglas Golf Club
Official Handbook, 1929.

Right: from the top:
Fourth, thirteenth, fifteenth and
sixteenth holes as they looked in
the late 1920s.

was made to proceed with the work on the course as outlined by Mackenzie. The main construction work was carried out by the British Golf Course Construction Company of Headingly, Leeds, a company run by Mackenzie's brother. The work was estimated to cost £800.

In the spring and early summer of 1925, Cork Golf Club at Little Island had work done on its course by the British Golf Course Construction Company, and presumably the firm transferred to Douglas on completion of its work at Little Island. By December 1925 the estimate of £800 for the work had been almost reached, and the committee instructed the contractors to continue.[16] Douglas Golf Club's account ledger for 1921–29 records that three men were employed for a ten-week period between March and May 1926 in turfing the course. They were paid directly by the club, and their work completed the reconstruction and alterations. Following the work at Douglas, the British Golf Course Construction Company team moved to Monkstown, and carried out works there.

There is no record of the precise alterations Mackenzie made to the course, but his design served the club until the late 1990s. A guide to the course, with photographs, published in 1929 shows the course to be quite open and bare-looking, with very little tree cover. Fr Daniel P Fitzgerald – who became a member of Douglas in 1932 at the age of sixteen – remembers the course in its virtual treeless state:

> … in 1933, anyway, there were hardly any trees apart from the big tree at the corner of the twelfth, and over on the fourteenth there was a tree that could catch your tee shot. It was almost in the middle of the fairway. Apart from those two trees there wasn't a single trace of a tree. The tenth went down, the eleventh came up. There wasn't a single tree separating those. Going down the twelfth long ago, you could go onto the eighteenth fairway.[17]

The *Irish Field* of 1 May 1926, commented on the reconstructed course, and was impressed by Mackenzie's work:

> [Mackenzie] has so altered the confirmation of the ground about the greens as to give the whole course a very pleasing appearance … it bears at every turn the impress of his golfing genius, and the putting greens, which are larger than usual, are of that gently undulating type which form a feature of some of the best greens on the other side of the Channel, and resemble, as much as it is possible to make them, the seaside putting greens so beloved of the real golfer.

Following the reconstruction work on the course, its yardage was 6,079, with a bogey, or par, of 75. The card of the course was as follows:

No	Yards	Bogey
1	249	4
2	330	4
3	410	5
4	158	3
5	436	5
6	386	4
7	190	3
8	466	5
9	328	4
10	324	4
11	382	4
12	410	5
13	350	4
14	460	5
15	140	3
16	321	4
17	309	4
18	430	5

In 1930 the amateur record for the course was 71, held by Redmond Simcox, while the professional record, 69, was held by Arthur Havers. Havers had achieved this score during a series of exhibition matches he played at Douglas with George Duncan in September 1926.

The eighteenth green in 1929.

GOLF
The Palace Cup

On 27 May 1925, four days after the new clubhouse was officially opened, the Palace Cup was first played for at Douglas. The minutes of the general committee for 10 February of that year record that the honorary secretaries of Douglas and Cork golf clubs met with R M Magrath – manager of the Palace Theatre in Cork and a member of Douglas – to discuss the arrangements for the first playing of the Palace Cup. The trophy was presented by the directors of the theatre 'to the golfing community of Cork', and was to be played for annually or biannually. The competition was to be stroke-play over thirty-six holes, with a handicap limit of 12, and was to be played on an eighteen-hole course, the venue to change annually. The directors of the theatre also agreed to give a replica each year as long as those directors remained in position.

The first winner of the Palace Cup was M Ryan of Muskerry Golf Club, a 7-handicapper who played the thirty-six holes in 162, giving him a net score of 148. The runner-up was Mick English of Douglas, who finished 1 stroke behind. The June 1925 edition of *Irish Golf* described the misfortune that befell English and which probably denied him the win:

> … at the second hole in the first round he had played two perfect shots, and he could scarcely have missed a 4, but an ex-caddy picked the ball up and was going away with it, when the shouts of some spectators made him drop it in a bunker. English and his partner had not seen this, and when he came up he decided to play the ball where it was, and it cost him 6.[18]

Details of the Palace Cup.

The presentation of the cup took place at the Palace Theatre. The winner was not able to attend, and William Hickey, captain of Muskerry, accepted the cup on his behalf. A week later

> all the prominent golfers who took part in the competition, were to be seen in action on the excellent film taken specially by a Gaumont Graphic man from London. It was an excellent picture, and the proprietors and manager were congratulated on their enterprise in having secured a very interesting record of the first contest for the Cup.[19]

Other Golf Trophies

A number of other trophies were added to the cabinet at Douglas during the 1920s. Dr W Magner, a founding member of the club, donated the Magner Cup in 1922. A M Roche, who had a jeweller's shop on Patrick's Street, donated the Roche Cup in 1923, and its first winner was J Wilson. The same year, Raymond Morrogh presented a cup for competition for members playing off 9 or under. The Tramore Cup was presented to the club in 1923 by John Heffernan, and it was first played for in March 1924, the first competition having been postponed due to a heavy snowfall; the first winner was D Daly. The St Patrick's Day Cup was presented in 1925 and the club Championship Cup in 1927. In 1928 M J Henchy presented the Rathmore Cup to Douglas, and it was first won by Fred Lambkin, while the ladies of the club were presented with the Derby Cup by the committee in that year also. In 1929 Redmond Simcox, club captain in 1925, presented the Bloomfield Cup.

Duncan and Havers at Douglas

In 1926 Portmarnock Golf Club invited George Duncan of Wentworth and Abe Mitchell of St Alban's to play a series of exhibition matches at the Portmarnock course over five days in September and October of that year. Douglas Golf Club and Malone in Belfast also issued invitations to the pair, and the result was a mini-tour beginning at Douglas for two days, followed by five days at Portmarnock, and concluding at Malone Golf Club. Immediately prior to the tour, Mitchell pulled out, and his place was taken by Arthur Havers of Coombe Hill Golf Club.

George Duncan was enjoying a successful career as a professional, and had won the Open in 1920 as well as having ten top-ten finishes in that competition. He won the Belgian Open in 1912, and finished in the top ten in the US Open in 1921 and 1922. He went on to play for Britain in the first Ryder Cup, in 1927, and played again in 1929 and

Details of trophies presented to the club in the 1920s.

Clockwise from the top: Roche Cup, 1923, Rathmore Cup, 1928, Bloomfield Cup, 1929, Derby Cup, 1928, Tramore Cup, 1924.

Above:
Group of Douglas
members at the Duncan
and Havers exhibition
matches played on 25–26
September 1926.

Below:
Advertisement relating
to the event, *Cork
Examiner*, 18 September
1926.

1931. Arthur Havers was also at the top of his game at the time: in the Open he finished in the first ten five times, and won the title in 1923. Like Duncan, he played on three British Ryder Cup teams: 1927, 1931 and 1933. It was quite a coup for Douglas to have such accomplished and well-known professional golfers coming to the club, and the event attracted much newspaper comment and general public interest. The *Cork Examiner* of 23 September 1926 wrote as follows:

> The interest which has been aroused by the series of exhibition matches to be played by George Duncan and Arthur Havers over the Douglas Golf Course on next Saturday and Sunday has far exceeded the anticipations of those concerned in organising the event. Players of the International fame of these two professionals have not been seen in Ireland for a long period of years, and the opportunity afforded this weekend at Douglas of

witnessing golf of championship standard is one that should not be missed by the general public, apart altogether from the golfing community …

In view of the heavy expenditure which the engagement incurs on the Douglas Club, a field charge of 2/6 for visitors will be made each day. Members will, of course, receive free badges. The Automobile Association men will have charge of the parking of motor cars, for which there will be space for close on two hundred. The catering for both days is being carried out by the Tivoli Restaurant Co., and ample accommodation is being provided to meet the luncheon and tea requirements of all visitors, in addition to the members of the club.

The exhibition matches took place on Saturday 25 and Sunday 26 September, and over 500 spectators turned out each day as Douglas showed off its new clubhouse and recently reconstructed course. The *Cork Examiner* of the following Monday gave a very detailed account of the two-day event, as well as publishing a number of photographs. That newspaper's correspondent felt that the exhibitions by the visiting professionals were a great opportunity for recent converts to the game:

... the vast majority of those who are members of the

Above:
Duncan and Havers exhibition matches, September 1926.
From the left: James G Musgrave, Charles Blake, Arthur Havers, Mick English, Hubert O'Keeffe (president), Redmond Simcox, George Duncan and V M Morrogh (captain).

several clubs in the neighbourhood of the city ... may be said to be the rank and file, who have joined the 'Royal and Ancient Army' in hundreds in recent years, and whose enthusiasm for the pastime is vastly in excess of their knowledge of how the game should be played. For them, and the others who have attained a good standard of proficiency, the exhibition matches ... were of absorbing interest.

Despite the large attendance each day, no problems were reported. 'The arrangements for the carrying through of the competitions were on an elaborate scale and were perfect in every detail, with the result that not a hitch occurred'.

The features of Havers' game that were noted in the newspaper were his long driving and 'accurate pitch approach shots'. It was Duncan's putting, apparently, that most impressed the spectators over the two days:

Duncan's putting was what tickled their fancy particularly. His rapid survey of the line some yards behind the ball, his quick march up to it, and then his unhesitating hit which sent it to the hole. One spectator, after seeing this a few times, remarked – 'Why putting is just a joke with him.'[20]

In the first match of the day, on Saturday, the two visitors played each other over the eighteen holes, stroke-play. Havers won with a 73 against Duncan's 76, and won 'a special money prize', presented by the club president, Hubert O'Keeffe. In the afternoon, Duncan was paired with top Douglas golfer Redmond Simcox against Havers and another Douglas man, Mick English, in a fourball foursome. This was won by Duncan and Simcox, 1 up. On Sunday morning, Duncan and Havers played another stroke-play match. Havers won again, and went around in 69, a professional record for the course. The club captain, V M Morrogh, sponsored the prize for this match. In the afternoon, two other Douglas worthies, J G Musgrave and Charles Blake, joined the professionals in a fourball match. Duncan was by now finding his form, and he played the first nine in 31, 6 under bogey, or par. Although his second nine were not as good, he and Musgrave beat Havers and Blake.

The weekend was considered an unqualified success, and the preparation and work of the club officers 'was a striking example of what good organisation and cordial co-operation can achieve in an undertaking of the kind'. Car ownership was by now on the increase, and the challenge of dealing with the numbers of vehicles attracted by the event was ably met by the club: 'So numerous were the motor cars that special arrangements had to be made for their parking and these worked smoothly, and the Civic Guards and officials of the Munster Motor Association directed the traffic into and from the grounds'. As the *Cork Examiner* remarked, 'the men of the Douglas club, when they do anything, believe in doing it well'.[21]

The visit of Duncan and Havers to Ireland was to have a lasting impact on the golf scene in this country. The pair travelled on to Portmarnock for their engagements there, and at a dinner hosted by the Portmarnock club in their honour, George Duncan suggested that an Open Championship be held at Portmarnock. The suggestion was acted upon, as Duncan felt such an event 'would have the support of 20 or 30 of the "Big Men" of the game in England and Scotland'.[22] The first Open Championship of Ireland was played in August 1927, and was won by George Duncan.

The *Cork Examiner* Professional Tournament

A week after the Duncan and Havers visit, Douglas Golf Club hosted the second *Cork Examiner* Professional Tournament. In 1925 the proprietors of the newspaper presented £50 each to Cork, Muskerry and Douglas golf clubs as sponsorship for tournaments to be confined to Irish professionals. The first of these had been played at Cork Golf Club in 1925 and had been won by L Wallace of Ormeau. The Douglas tournament was played over three days, 4–6 October, and had thirty-four entrants competing for a first prize of £20. The runner-up prize was £10.

The qualifying round over thirty-six holes on the first day saw eight go forward to the next round. Douglas professional, J Sheridan, failed to qualify, but Jim Bailey – who was to replace Sheridan the following year as Douglas professional – made it through. Bailey lost out in the next round match-play stage. The final on the third day was between L Wallace (unattached) and W Nolan of Portmarnock, Nolan winning on the thirteenth hole of the second eighteen, 6 and 5.

The officers and members of Douglas were by now experienced in organising big events, and the newspapers again lavished praise on them for the excellence of their work: 'The arrangements for the tournament were faultlessly carried out by Mr M English, the Hon Secretary of the club, and the other officials and members, who gave

A photomontage from the *Cork Examiner*, 5 October 1926, of some of the professionals playing at the *Cork Examiner* Professional Tournament at Douglas in October 1926.

valuable assistance'. The visiting professionals 'were guests of the club and were entertained to luncheon and tea each day, as well as being provided with free caddies, while the Victoria Hotel motor bus and members' cars were at their disposal for going to and from the course'. In his acceptance speech, W Nolan, the tournament winner, also praised the club members: 'The arrangements were admirable in every particular, and the generosity and hospitality of the members was quite embarrassing. They [the professionals] all felt deeply grateful for the splendid time they had been given'.[23]

Barton Shield

In 1929 Douglas reached the final of the Barton Shield, played at Portmarnock Golf Club. It was not to be the club's finest hour, as Redmond Simcox and S H McCarthy were beaten by four holes by J D McCormack and C Robertson, while J G Musgrave and M J Henchy lost to M Crowley and H E Bell by eleven holes. This gave Portmarnock victory by fifteen holes. Victory in the Junior Cup the following year would go some way to restoring Douglas pride!

GOLFERS
Redmond Simcox

Redmond Simcox.

Pre-eminent among Douglas golfers in the 1920s was Redmond Simcox. He was born in 1904 and grew up at Bloomfield House, a large red-brick residence on the southern shore of the Tramore River estuary. He was already a member of Douglas in 1921 when the surviving records of the club begin, and such was his talent that by May 1924 his handicap was reduced to scratch. He was captain of the club in 1925, and represented his club, province and country many times in his amateur career. In 1926 Simcox became the first Douglas golfer to win the prestigious South of Ireland Championship at Lahinch. In that year, J G Musgrave also played but was beaten in the fourth round by Dr M Barrett of Muskerry, but Simcox was to exact a little revenge for his club colleague by beating Barrett in the semi-finals. In the final, Simcox played M Crowley of Portmarnock, the title holder from 1925, and beat him 5 and 4. The *Irish Field* of 21 August 1926 commented that Simcox 'made a few mistakes here and there with simple mashie shots, but he was better all round than his opponent ... He putted beautifully'. The account also noted:

> None at Lahinch grudged Simcox his victory ... All through the tournament he played convincing golf and his success over Michael Crowley, the holder, was as deserved as it was unexpected in some quarters. The winner is one of the best golfers which the South has

produced for many a year, and he gave Cork one of the few big things which the county has achieved in Irish Golf … Simcox is a fighter, and a much better player than his friends thought him.

The *Cork Examiner* report on Simcox's win was relatively short, and concentrated mostly on Crowley's costly errors in the final: on the second hole his caddie dropped a club on his ball, incurring a penalty for Crowley who became upset and played his next shot recklessly. Following that, Crowley 'cracked up', as the report put it, and 'to have beaten Simcox he would have had to be playing well above his normal form'.[24]

Redmond Simcox retained the South of Ireland title in 1927. S H McCarthy and J G Musgrave also played in the championship, but the former was beaten in the third round, while the latter lost in the fourth round. Simcox alone of the three Douglas men went to the semi-finals, where he beat O Brown of Tuam to reach the final. In the final, played over thirty-six holes on Friday 12 August, Simcox met William McConnell of Kingstown (now Dún Laoghaire; his club is given as Royal Portrush in the GUI records). The *Cork Examiner* of 13 August gave a detailed account of the match, and remarked that 'the plain fact of the matter is that the better golfer won, and that about puts it in a nutshell!' The quality of golf was not good, apparently, but Simcox led from the first through to the thirty-fifth hole, where he clinched victory by 2 and 1.

In 1936 Simcox resigned his membership of Douglas and switched to Cork Golf Club, though he continued to be a pavilion member at Douglas, his first club.

S H McCarthy

Like Redmond Simcox, Scott H McCarthy – known as 'Spot' – was already an accomplished golfer when club records begin in 1921. He was a member of the Douglas team that won the Cork Senior League in 1920, and in February 1923 he became the first Douglas golfer to have his handicap reduced to scratch. He was a natural left-handed player, but such was McCarthy's ambidextrous skill that he also had a club handicap for playing right-handed in confined competitions! He played a number of times in the South of Ireland Championship but never won. He was also a member of Monkstown Golf Club and Cork Golf Club, and was on the Monkstown team that won the Barton Shield in 1933. He later played on the Cork Golf Club teams that won the Barton Shield in 1937 and 1938.

An incident recorded in the minutes of the general committee at Douglas in 1928 shows that 'Spot' McCarthy was not always an impeccably behaved club member. A special meeting of the general committee was held on 23 April that year to deal with 'the incident of Mr S H McCarthy driving his motor car over the 1st, 10th and 11th greens on the evening of 18th April'. A proposal to expel him from the club was defeated by ten votes to three, and a proposal that he be suspended for six months was defeated by seven votes to five. Eventually, he was suspended for six weeks, seriously admonished and warned as to his future conduct; this suggestion was carried by eight votes to four.

J G Musgrave

J G (James Garfield) Musgrave was a key member of Douglas Golf Club in the 1920s and into the 1930s, both as a player and administrator. He was one of the seven trustees of the new Douglas Golf Club formed in 1916, and was a member of the general committee at the time of the burning of the clubhouse in 1921. He was very active in ensuring the survival of the club at that time, and was club captain in 1928 and 1929, and was later a club trustee. As a player, Musgrave first comes to notice as a member of the Douglas team that won the Cork Senior League in 1920. He played in a number of South of Ireland Championship, reaching the fourth round in 1926 and 1927. He was a member of the Douglas team that won the Junior Cup in 1930, and played for Monkstown when that club won the Barton Shield in 1933. From 1933 to 1937 J G Musgrave was the chairman of the Munster Branch of the Golfing Union of Ireland, and was a member of the international selection committee appointed by the GUI in those years. He was also a keen rugby player in his youth, and was a member of Cork Constitution rugby club. He was president of the Munster Branch of the Irish Rugby Football Union (IRFU) from 1913 to 1919, and was president of the IRFU in 1930–31. Musgrave Park in Cork was named in his honour.

The Douglas team that won the Cork Senior League 1920.

Standing, L–R:
W V Pericho, S H (Spot) McCarthy, J B Coghlan, R M Magrath, D Kelleher.

Seated, L–R: J O'Brien, J G Musgrave, C Blake, M English.

Front, F Lambkin.

Membership and Finance

As peace eventually became established after 1923, golf again went through a period of growth. Between 1920 and 1924 nineteen golf clubs were established in Ireland, and as the decade advanced this momentum grew: thirty-one new clubs were founded between 1925 and 1929.[25] While some established clubs were finding it difficult to retain members in these years, Douglas Golf Club seems to have fared quite well. At the neighbouring club at Monkstown, for example – then a nine-hole course – membership during the 1920s fell to between eighty and 100, down from a high of about 300 ten years before.[26] In 1921 Douglas had something over 243 members, while through the following seven years membership averaged 302 in total, men and ladies.[27] In 1925, for example, there were 194 men and 117 ladies in the club, the ratio in the following year was 191:135, and in 1927 was 181:123. Resignations and deaths were balanced by the admission of new members. In 1922 forty-three new members joined Douglas, paying an entrance fee of £2 2s each, in 1923 forty-three joined, in 1924 fourteen, and in 1925 thirty-three. The entrance fee for men increased to £5 5s from July 1925, though 'old members who wished to rejoin could do so without entrance fee'.[28] An entrance fee of £2 2s for ladies was introduced from August 1925.[29] Rule 14 of the club gave the committee some discretion in relation to entrance fees: 'The Committee shall have the power, when, and as they think fit, to impose an Entrance Fee, and fix the amount of same.'

The subscription rates remained unchanged until 1946, and stood at £5 for men and £2 10s for ladies. In addition, most members paid an annual locker rent of six shillings for men and five shillings for ladies. The majority of members kept their clubs in lockers at the clubhouse, as transporting them was quite difficult at a time when car ownership was not yet widespread. Many members travelled by tram to Douglas village, and walked the last half-mile up Maryborough Hill.

In the late 1920s the financial position of the club was giving some cause for concern. Membership numbers fell a little in 1927 and 1928, and the income from subscriptions also fell. In 1926 this income was £1,211 11s, and it fell to £1,092 19s 6d in 1928, a fall of ten per cent. In the same period, the income from the bar – the other principal source of revenue – fell by just over fifteen per cent.[30] The middle years of the decade had been expensive for Douglas given the building of the new clubhouse and the course reconstruction.

APPENDIX

1925 list of guarantors for £2,000 loan from Munster & Leinster Bank

H Scott	£25	Work manager, Ford
John Crofts	£25	Merchant, N Main Street
T J O'Callaghan	£25	Cashier, Lady's Well Brewery
D Forde Lagge	£25	Stockbroker, South Mall
C S Hosford	£25	Merchant, North Main Street
C W Fielding	£25	Pharmacist, Rock Lawn, Douglas Road
T O'Gorman	£50	Merchant, Sunday's Well
P Doolan	£25	Civil servant, 2 Morningside
E H Willis	£25	Commercial Agent, 10 Patrick's Street
J F McCarthy	£25	Commercial Agent, 10 Aldergrove
D Sullivan	£25	Civil Servant
James N Healy	£25	Accountant, Grattan Hill
R McKechnie	£50	Merchant, Pembroke Street
F Lambkin	£25	Accountant, 7 Frankfield Terrace
J J O'Leary	£25	Merchant, Frenche's Quay
Wm E Williams	£50	Merchant, Ashton Place
Hubert O'Keefe	£50	Dentist, Woodsgift
P A O'Regan	£25	Dentist, Grand Parade
E D H McCarthy	£50	Director, Cook Street
John Heffernan	£50	Pawnbroker, Shandon Street
John Riordan	£50	Merchant Tailor
[illegible] Twomey	£50	Pawnbroker, Douglas Street
John Hoare	£50	Commercial Agent, Connaught Avenue
Thomas Kelleher	£25	Builder, Mount Verdon Terrace
Thomas R O'Regan	£50	Merchant, Summerhill
Stephen Whelton	£25	Cinema Proprietor, 3 Grosvenor Place
G Hunt	£25	Manager, Tylers
Michael Dorgan	£25	Mosely Villa, Ballintemple
Joseph [illegible]	£25	Medical Doctor, Patrick's Hill
J Power	£50	Merchant, Winthrop Street
H F Longfield	£50	Grange Erin
J Moloney	£25	Bank Clerk, Sunday's Well
W J O'Callaghan	£50	10 Winthrop Street
M Henchy	£25	Merchant, Rathmore House
Denis Lucey	£25	Medical Doctor, South Mall
Daniel P McCarthy	£25	Merchant, Castle Street
J S Kirkpatrick	£25	

Alfred McDonagh	£25	Stationer, 124 Patrick's Street
H Golden	£50	Accountant, 28 Maylor Street
M English	£50	Engineer, 20 Winthrop Street
J A Dunlea	£25	Accountant, 7 Saint Patrick's Terrace
W V Pericho	£50	Dentist, South Mall
W D White	£25	Merchant, McCurtain Street
W T O'Sullivan	£50	Merchant, New York House
Jeremiah Murphy	£50	Builder, North Mall
Frank Bradley	£25	Merchant, North Main Street
A M Roche	£25	Jeweller, Patrick's Street
D Madden	£25	University Teacher, Wellington Road
A St J Atkins	£25	Secondary Teacher
James G Musgrave	£50	Merchant
T S Reynolds	£25	Doctor, Douglas
Redmond Simcox	£50	Merchant, Douglas
J Maskill	£25	Civil Servant, 7 Park Villa
John Booth	£25	Medical Doctor, Sidney Place
Bernard Kilbride	£25	Manager, Charlemont Terrace
Eugene Gayre	£25	Assistant Secretary, Harbour Board
James G Crosbie	£50	Ballybrack
P J Collins	£50	Director, Suttons, Charlemont Terrace
Stephen Morrogh	£50	Surgeon Dentist
James Henchy	£50	Merchant, Sunnyside, Saint Lukes
Charles Blake	£50	Stockbroker, 12 Marlboro Street
Matthew Moloney	£25	Accountant, Douglas
E J Fitzpatrick	£25	Commercial Traveller, 20 Patrick's Hill
Patrick Morris	£25	Ballinlough Road
Christopher O'Herlihy	£25	Accountant, Friar Street
Wm F O'Brien	£25	Traveller, Lady's Well Brewery
Aidan de Fleury	£25	Accountant, R & H Hall Ltd
John Mailiff	£25	Shopkeeper, 5 Pembroke Street
J [illegible]	£50	Medical Doctor, South Mall
J Twomey	£25	Director, M D Daly & Co., College Road
J Stanley Sullivan	£50	Merchant, Eglantine, Douglas Road
Daniel R Baker	£25	Merchant, 6 Herbert Park
Vincent Morrogh	£50	Gentleman, Montenotte
?	£25	Medical Practitioner
?	£25	Mount Grange

Fr Daniel Fitzgerald

In the late 1930s and early 1940s Daniel Fitzgerald became Douglas Golf Club's most promising young star. He played off a handicap of +1, and would surely have won many honours for himself, for his club and country but for the impact of the Second World War and his departure to China as a missionary priest in 1946. Fr Dan was ninety-three years old on 28 June 2009, and is the club's longest-serving member.

Fr Dan was born in 1916, and grew up at 10 Old Blackrock Road in Cork. His father John was a member of Douglas Golf Club, and used the title Sir John Fitzgerald. This title had been inherited from his father, Sir Edward Fitzgerald, who, as lord mayor of Cork, had been knighted in 1903 by King Edward in recognition of his work in promoting the Great Exhibition in the city in 1902 and 1903. Fr Dan began playing golf at Douglas with his father, and was elected a member in October 1932 when he was sixteen years old. He had played hurling and was a natural left-handed player, but as very few left-handed clubs were available at the time, he had to play his golf right-handed. In September 1933 Fr Dan left Cork for Dalgan Park, where he trained to be a missionary priest with the Columban Fathers, being ordained in 1939. From 1933 he was able to play golf only during the summer holidays but still managed to improve very quickly, winning the Palace Cup in the summer of 1934 playing off a handicap of 7.

Above, left to right: C F Murphy (president), Fr Dan Fitzgerald and P J Collins (captain), taken at Killarney Golf Club on the occasion of the Munster final of the Senior Cup, 1942.

Fr Dan was ordained a Columban Father in 1939, and was due to travel to China as a missionary priest but was prevented from doing so by the outbreak of war. For the duration of the war, he worked for the Cork diocese, and as his duties were not too onerous he was able to continue playing golf. 'I used to go out to Douglas from the Blackrock Road on my bicycle. There were not many playing and the course was quiet. I'd stay there all day hitting golf balls,' he recalls. He won Harry Atkins' Captain's Prize in 1941, and following that his handicap was cut to +1. In 1942 Douglas played Cork Golf Club at Muskerry in the Munster section of the Senior Cup, though the competition was not played at a national level for the duration of the war. In his match Fr Dan beat Jimmy Bruen on the last green. Douglas played Lahinch in the Munster finals at Killarney, and here Fr Dan played and beat John Burke, another great amateur golfer.

William (Bill) Magee was greenkeeper at Douglas for many years up to his death in 1936, and often acted as official starter for competitions at the club. Fr Dan remembers waiting to tee off for his second eighteen holes in the competition for the Palace Cup in 1934 and feeling quite nervous as a large group of spectators had gathered at the first tee to watch the players play off. 'They're not much help,' he recalls remarking to Magee. 'You'll be no damn good until you can miss it in front of them,' Magee replied!

Fr Dan recalls being very impressed with John McKenna when he came to Douglas as the club professional in 1937. Up until that time, he says,

a professional was regarded as just a small cut above a caddie …

Above: Detail from the Palace Cup, which Fr Dan won in 1934 at Douglas.

you didn't expect to find as a professional any one who had gone beyond the primary school. And I met this man over in the pro shop in Douglas and I remember saying to myself, 'Gosh, sure he could be a teacher, he could be a lawyer, he could be anything.' A very quiet, retiring man but obviously there was something about him. Always struck me that he was a very good fellow.

John McKenna also had a high opinion of Fr Dan. In a newspaper interview in 1984, he recalled: 'Fr Dan Fitzgerald was probably the best player I saw here in my time. He was plus one and could play to it.'[1]

He remembers many Douglas golfers from those times – Dan McCarthy, Harry Golden, Dr 'Packer' Kiely, Mick Henchy, Charles Murphy and others. Fr Dan enjoyed a great friendship with Jimmy Bruen, and played against him and with him on many occasions in the late 1930s and early 1940s. In 1946 Fr Dan sailed for China to eventually begin his missionary work, and on a stopover in Hong Kong received word that his friend Jimmy Bruen had won the British Amateur Championship, the first Irishman to do so. At the Douglas AGM on 26 February 1947, it was decided to make both Fr Dan and Bruen honorary life members of the club. Two months later, Fr Dan wrote from China to thank the club for conferring that honour on him:

> Many thanks for your letter which reached me safely last month. Though it's a long way from Douglas to these parts, I haven't lost interest in the spot where so many happy days were spent, and the decision of the members at the General Meeting to make me an Honorary Life Member of the club is something which I appreciate very much. It was very kind and thoughtful of you all, and I would like to express my sincere thanks for yet another kindness received by me from the Douglas Golfers. With best wishes to you and all the old friends, not forgetting the staff.[2]

In 1949 the communists took power in China, and Fr Dan and the other Columban Fathers were kept under virtual house arrest and suffered many privations before being expelled in 1952. Fr Dan's memories of Cork and especially of Douglas Golf Club sustained him through the lonely and difficult years in China.

> I didn't think I'd see much of Cork again. It was like, in a way, leaving everything you were accustomed to. But somehow the Lord gave me the help. The communist times weren't great but somehow you felt that there was something bigger than yourself helping you … I remember in the bad days it was a bit of a help to look back to the days in Douglas where everybody was so friendly.

He returned to Cork in 1952, and played again at Douglas – but with a handicap of 8 – before he was posted to Australia in 1954, where he worked until 1961.

On his return, Fr Dan was based in Dublin, and played a little golf there. His visits to Cork and to Douglas became less frequent as his father had died and many of those he had played with in the 1930s and 1940s had also passed away.

He recalls being impressed with Douglas golfers like Éamonn McSweeney, John Morris and Bill Kelleher on his occasional visits to Douglas in the 1950s and 1960s. He maintained his friendship with Jimmy Bruen up to Jimmy's death in 1972, and played an occasional game with John McKenna. Fr Dan later served in Scotland before returning to Ireland. He now (2009) ministers in the parish of Nenagh in County Tipperary.

Fr Daniel Fitzgerald was a very talented golfer, and while the Second World War and his departure to China prevented him achieving his full golfing potential, his role as a priest also had an impact. Many golfing clergymen were reticent about publicising a devotion to their chosen pastime, and Fr Dan also felt that reticence:

> At that time, you see, golf was not regarded as a terribly democratic game, and for a priest to be extra good at it, well …! I'd say jokingly to people, when I go to meet St Peter I'm not going to mention the subject unless he brings it up, because he'd want to know what else I did besides play golf!

Reflecting on his golfing life, Fr Dan fondly remembers many fourballs played with friends at Douglas; he recalls cycling out to the course at a time when few people had cars, when the course was very open and lacking tree cover, and when sheep grazed the fairways and sometimes the greens, to the constant annoyance of Bill Magee, the greenkeeper. He remembers his golfing friends and the camaraderie of Douglas Golf Club, and he adds: 'John McKenna stands out always as being a great friend, a great golfer. There was something special about John.'

On 21 June 2009, midsummer's day of centenary year, Fr Dan visited Douglas Golf Club again, seventy-seven years after he had first become a member. Modest as ever, he did not announce his visit, and would have quietly left again but that he was recognised by some members. President Seán McHenry then introduced him to the members present, and briefly outlined his golfing career. As he afterwards toured the course in the comfort of a golf cart, his keen eye surveyed the changes, and he remembered his golfing companions of old, many of whom had been founder members of the club.

Fr Dan is modest about his achievements. When pressed about his talent, he mischievously replies: 'I was more ornamental than useful'!

Fr Dan Fitzgerald at Douglas, 21 June 2009.

6 Testing Years: 1930s & 1940s

The energy, resilience and vigour that the members of Douglas Golf Club showed in the 1920s dissipated somewhat during the following decade. The club had a relatively new clubhouse, a reconstructed course, and members were enjoying the fruits of their hard work and investment. It is understandable that the high levels of energy and commitment demanded of them following the fire of 1921 and the subsequent rebuilding works could not be maintained. External factors also impacted on the club as the economic downturn of the 1930s lowered living standards and affected business. There were increasing demands from club employees for wage increases, and it was difficult at times to maintain membership numbers. A number of members who had been significant in the early growth and survival of the club died during these years. Mick English, captain in 1920 and long-time honorary secretary, died in 1932, and J G Musgrave, who was key to the club's survival in 1921 and served as captain in 1928 and 1929, died in 1937. Despite the difficulties, the club carried on, secured an extension on the lease on the course and modernised aspects of its administration.

In 1931 the club suffered something of an administrative hiccup. The annual general meeting of that year was delayed by over two months due to the laxity of the honorary secretary, F Cussen, in performing his duties. As a result of this, the post of honorary secretary was abolished by decision of the AGM in April 1931, as were the posts of assistant honorary secretary and honorary treasurer. The paid position of full-time secretary (later, secretary-manager) was then created. The first appointee to the new post was an old Douglas stalwart, Mick English, who was paid £100 per annum. Following the death of English in 1932, Maurice Reidy was appointed, and he served until 1950.

William (Bill) Magee died in 1936, having been a member of the ground staff at Douglas since before the First World War, and greenkeeper since the early 1920s. His green-keeping skills and good humour had endeared him to many members. The November edition of *Irish Golf* published a short obituary of Magee:

Facing page: Group of Douglas members at the clubhouse, 1944.

For over 25 years he has officiated at that club and during that time proved himself one of the most conscientious and valued employees, never sparing himself where his work was concerned. The greens, of which so much is thought of, are entirely due to Magee's unceasing care. He was a general favourite with all the members who will indeed miss his unfailing good humour and cheery disposition.

Magee was succeeded by Bob Ryan (also referred to as J Ryan in the club records) who had been a member of the ground staff since 1920. He served the club as greenkeeper for the next thirty-seven years and died in 1973.

The departure of some of the club's best golfers in the 1930s contributed to a lack of success on the national stage in the later 1930s and 1940s: Redmond Simcox, Douglas' most accomplished player, relinquished his Douglas membership in favour of Cork Golf Club, and contributed to that club's success in the Barton Shield in 1937 and 1938, and in the Senior Cup in 1939. S H McCarthy also played

Below:
Douglas players and supporters at Killarney for the Munster final of the Junior Cup, 1930.

on those winning Barton Shield teams. Douglas did take a national title in 1930, with the Junior Cup victory at Lahinch, and reached the national finals of that competition on four subsequent occasions in this period: 1931, 1934, 1939 and 1948.

Junior Cup Victory, 1930

Douglas Golf Club's only major win on the competitive golf scene in this period was the Junior Cup victory in 1930. In May of that year, Douglas comfortably beat Muskerry in the semi-finals of the Munster section, which was a matchplay competition, with six of the seven Douglas players winning their matches. J G Musgrave, J Jerome, H Whelan, M H Prentice, M J Henchy and T R O'Regan won, while C Blake lost.

In the Munster final, played at Killarney in early June, Douglas met Limerick Golf Club. The competition was eighteen-hole stroke-play, with the best five scores to count. The weather was extremely warm and proved uncomfortable for the players. The *Cork Examiner* remarked that 'the heat was excessive and the players departed from

IRISH JUNIOR CUP.

MUNSTER SECTION.

Semi-Final:—

Douglas	v.	Muskerry.	
	Pts		Pts
C. Blake 0		D Bresnan 2 up ...	1
J G Musgrave 5 & 4	1	R Whyte	0
J Jerome 4 & 3 ...	1	K John	0
H Whelan 5 & 4 ...	1	J Morrissey	0
M H Prentice 2 up	1	F Phillips	0
M J Henchy 4 & 3	1	P Kiely	0
T R O'Regan 7 & 5	1	W F O'Connor	0
Total 6		Total , ...	1

The Munster Final of this competition will be played at Killarney on Thursday, 5th prox., when Douglas G.C. will meet Limerick G.C. in an 18 holes stroke, the best five scores to decide the winning team to represent Munster at Lahinch in the Inter-Provincial on June 26th.

Below: Junior Cup victory at Lahinch, 1930.
Standing L–R:
H Whelan, F Lambkin,
W T O'Sullivan,
M J Henchy, C Blake,
V Morrogh, M H Prentice.
Seated, L–R: R J Murphy,
T R O'Regan, J G Musgrave,
D P McCarthy.

the strict etiquette of golfing attire, discarding pullovers and jackets'.[1] Having trailed initially, Douglas pulled ahead of Limerick and won by 8 strokes.

The national finals of the Junior Cup were held at Lahinch on 27 and 28 June. In the semi-finals, Douglas beat Lisburn 4–3, J G Musgrave, V M Morrogh, H Whelan and T R O'Regan winning their matches. They went on to play the holders, Killiney Golf Club, in the final. The Douglas players played exceptionally well, and had the most comprehensive of victories, winning all of their seven matches. The Douglas team was J G Musgrave, J Jerome, V M Morrogh, M J Henchy, H Whelan, D P McCarthy and T R O'Regan.

Other Golfing Highlights

In the 1930 Barton Shield, Douglas lost to Monkstown in the Munster semi-final at Cork Golf Club. The Douglas pairing of Redmond Simcox and S H McCarthy beat Monkstown's W Dwyer and G Crosbie by 6, but the other Douglas pair, C Blake and M J Henchy, were beaten by 7 by Rex Murphy and P J Hussey. While success at provincial and national levels seemed somewhat elusive in subsequent years, Douglas did occasionally make its presence felt.

Douglas Golf Club repeated its 1930 Junior Cup Munster success in 1931, and travelled to Rosse's Point for the national finals. Unfortunately, the team was unable to repeat the feat of the previous year, and was beaten in the semi-finals by Dublin University, 5–2. The Douglas team was J G Musgrave, J Murphy, M Henchy, M English, H Whelan, D P McCarthy and T R O'Regan. The two Douglas winners were M Henchy, 1 up, and H Whelan, 3 and 1.

In June 1934 Douglas again got to the national finals of the Junior Cup, at Rosslare, and had a bye through to the final against Knock, but were beaten 4–1. The Douglas team was J G Musgrave, W H Strong, D P McCarthy, M Henchy and P Crowley. D P McCarthy was

Rule book, 1946.

the only member of the team to win a match, 2 up.

In 1939 Douglas won the Munster final of the Junior Cup by beating Limerick at Lahinch, 3–2. The Douglas players were T O'Donovan, G P Crosbie, G Power, P Murphy and S Skuse. The national finals were played that year at Rosse's Point, and in the semi-finals Douglas beat Bangor 3½–1½, but lost the final to County Sligo 3–2. H O'Sullivan and M Gleeson won their matches, but the other Douglas players, T O'Donovan, J Henry and S Skuse, lost theirs. The correspondent of *Irish Golf* expressed some sympathy for the Douglas players: 'this club deserves great applause for their great effort against the home team. It was indeed hard luck having gone so far, to be just pipped at the post. However, there's always the next time.'[2]

In the 1948 Junior Cup campaign Douglas beat Lahinch in the

Munster final at Ballybunion 3–2. Daniel P McCarthy, Jim Myles and Con Harrington won their matches, but Sam Thompson and Michael Gleeson lost theirs. The finals were played at Royal Portrush, but Douglas lost to Rathmore, the eventual winners, in the semi-finals.

In 1949 the Douglas ladies won the Munster section of the Senior Cup at Limerick, and played in the national finals at Baltray, County Louth, in June. They would have to wait another three years to take their first national title, however, as County Louth won the event that year for the fourth time in a row.

During the mid-1930s, Daniel P Fitzgerald, one of Douglas Golf Club's most accomplished golfers (see feature, pp. 94–7), began to make his mark on the competitive golf scene. At this time, he was a seminarian studying for the priesthood in County Galway, and only played golf during his holiday periods. In 1934 he won the Palace Cup, at the time 'one of the most coveted golfing trophies in the South',[3] playing off a handicap of 7. By 1936 his handicap was down to 4, and he played under a pseudonym, a practice very much favoured by clergymen who felt that many in their flock would not look too kindly on their priest spending time on a golf course. In golf reports in the press in the years following 1936, he appears as 'Daniel P', 'Daniel Pat' or 'P Daniels'. He was ordained in 1939 and was based in Cork from then until the end of the Second World War, during which time his golf flourished. By 1941 he was playing off scratch, and after winning the President's Prize that year with a gross score of 63 – equalling the course record – his handicap was reduced to +1.

The high point of Fr Dan Fitzgerald's golfing career at Douglas was in 1942 with the Senior Cup team that reached the Munster final in Killarney. Douglas had beaten Cork Golf Club at Muskerry in the early stages of the competition, and Fr Dan had caused a stir by defeating Jimmy Bruen on the eighteenth green in their match. In the final against Lahinch, he again had an historic win when he beat the famous John Burke of Lahinch – again, on the eighteenth green – in the final. Douglas unfortunately lost the final to Lahinch. Fr Dan's ability was now widely recognised, and *Irish Golf*, mixing its metaphor a little, called him 'a Daniel among the tigers with a vengeance'![4] That magazine also wrote: 'Undoubtedly the biggest surprise in Southern golfing circles was the recent defeat of Jimmy Bruen by "Daniel Pat" in a Senior Cup match. "Daniel Pat" conceals the identity of a young clergyman and he is a player of no mean repute'. The account went on to note that the highlight of the finals was 'Daniel Pat's' defeat of John Burke.[5] The Douglas Senior team was 'Daniel Pat', J Henry, M Gleeson, G P O'Brien and P J McInerney.

Fr Dan Fitzgerald, 1942.

...date the memory of the late ... DAVID WHITE R.I.P. 1933

DOUGLAS GOLF CLUB
· LADIES BRANCH ·
THE COLLINS CUP
· PRESENTED BY ·
P.J. COLLINS Esq.
1933.

1933.	Mrs. J.A.HA
1934.	Miss K.D.MA
1935.	Mrs. C.P.NEC
1936.	Miss K.E.OCAL
1937.	Miss E.M.HOLL
1938.	Miss M.HOWA
1939.	Miss M.HOWA
1940.	Mrs. P. COVENE
1941.	Mrs. GR OBME
1942.	Mrs. W.JOCK OVA
1943.	Mrs. SD RAHERT
1944.	Mrs. G.P.OBNEN
1945.	Mrs. M.KECARTH

Douglas G. Club
THE STAFFORD CUP
1933
PRESENTED BY R.G.STAFFORD

Fr Dan continued to play golf at Douglas until he went to England in 1945, and from there to China in 1946. He continued to do well in various club competitions, and was a member of the Douglas team that won the Senior League in the summer of 1942.

Trophies

The most beautiful and valuable piece of silverware in the Douglas collection is the White Memorial Trophy. It was presented to the club in 1933 by the father of Walter David White, who died that year having contracted pneumonia after being caught in a blizzard while driving to Dublin to attend a rugby international. On the back of the cup, a very detailed image of the clubhouse at Douglas as it looked in 1933 is chased, and the design includes a motor car and an image of a young man, presumably the deceased.

Two other trophies were also presented that year: the Stafford Cup, presented by R G Stafford and first won by M J Henchy, and the Collins Cup, presented to the ladies of Douglas by P J Collins, president in 1930 and 1931. The first winner of the Collins Cup was Mrs J A Halpin.

A New Professional

James Bailey had been the professional at Douglas since 1927, and he was especially noted for his club-making skills. In 1937 the committee was expressing some dissatisfaction with Bailey's work, and decided that he would have to resign if he could not manage to maintain a stock of clubs in his shop, presumably of his own manufacture.[6] The situation did not apparently improve, and it was decided to dispense with his services in October, though he continued to be employed on a week-to-week basis until a new professional took up duty.[7] John McKenna's appointment as Douglas professional in December 1937 was an astute move on the part of the committee (see feature, pp. 122–5). McKenna was of one of Ireland's most promising young professional golfers at the time, and later proved to be one of the best golf coaches in the country. It was felt by many that Douglas was not achieving its potential on the competitive golf scene, and it was hoped that John McKenna's arrival would have a positive impact. *Irish Golf*, in its issue of February 1938, noted:

> The appointment of J McKenna as professional to this club has met with the entire approval of the members. There is plenty of hidden talent amongst them and it is now hoped that McKenna will not be too long in discovering some. As it is, the general standard is far below what it should be.

Facing page: clockwise from top:

Details from the White Memorial Trophy, presented to the club in 1933 in memory of Walter David White. Note the view of the clubhouse from the eighteenth green and the motor car, chased on the reverse of the trophy.

Detail of the Stafford Cup, presented in 1933.

The Collins Cup, presented in 1933 to the Ladies' Branch.

GOLF PROFESSIONAL
wanted for Douglas Golf Club (CORK)
Apply by letter to Secretary, stating terms expected.

As a competitive professional, McKenna certainly made his mark in the late 1930s and throughout the 1940s: in the latter decade, for example, he had a top-ten finish in each of the ten annual Irish Professional Championships, winning the title in 1945 and 1948; in 1947 he won the Dunlop £500 tournament at Portmarnock. With Harry Bradshaw and Fred Daly, McKenna made up the trio that dominated Irish professional golf at the time. The great successes the Douglas ladies enjoyed in the Senior Cup from 1952 and at interprovincial and international level is acknowledged to have been due in no small measure to the coaching of McKenna. While Douglas enjoyed no victories on the national stage in the 1940s, John McKenna's achievements did attract much positive press coverage for the club.

Membership Issues

In this period, the optimum membership for the club was considered to be 250 men and 120 ladies. These numbers were not always realised, and there was variation from year to year. The average annual intake of new members in the years 1935–49 was thirty-six, but it was difficult at times to fill the vacancies that occurred, especially in the early years of the 1930s. Vacancies arose due to resignations, deaths and the striking-off of members for non-payment of subscriptions. An editorial in the January 1934 edition of *Irish Golf* commented on the problem of resignations from golf clubs, and exhorted golfers contemplating resignation to think twice:

> Do not let any of us resign our club membership because of a mistaken idea of economy. Golf, and all it means to our health and interest in life, can never be expensive. The man who gives up golf degenerates in health and spirits, becoming a mere automaton between his home and his office.

In February 1930 it was decided to abolish the entrance fee for new members 'as total roll of members falling in recent years'.[8] An

106

effort was made to recruit new members, and five years later the membership situation had improved to the extent that entrance fees and a waiting list were reintroduced. The fee for men was £2 2s 0d, and for ladies £1 1s 0d. The corresponding annual subscriptions were £5 and £2 10s 0d. Clergy were to be exempt from the entrance fee and waiting list.[9]

Through the late 1930s and into the 1940s, the demand from ladies, in particular, for membership of Douglas Golf Club far exceeded the availability of vacancies, and the committee frequently struggled in its efforts to deal with the situation in a manner that was fair to applicants and in the best interests of the club. In November 1937 it was decided to restrict the number of lady members to a maximum of 120, and to give preference to the wives of members when any vacancies arose. There was at this time continuing pressure on the club to admit more lady members, and in an attempt to accommodate those pressing for membership, a new category of five-day lady membership was created. Numbers in this category were to be limited at the discretion of the committee, and play was restricted to weekdays only for an annual subscription of £2 2s 0d.[10] The demand from ladies for membership continued, and in 1939 their membership numbers were raised by ten to 130. Even during the early years of the Second World War, when rationing, shortages and many other privations were impacting heavily on people's lives, more ladies sought membership of Douglas than could be accommodated. Preference was still given to members' wives, and this was extended to their daughters in 1941.[11] The number of lady members was eventually raised, in 1943, by a further ten, to 140.[12] In 1945 it was decided to regularise the situation regarding the admittance of ladies, as the committee was often dealing with this on an ad hoc basis. From March of that year, the wives, sisters and daughters of gentlemen members were to have preference over all other applicants 'in the ratio of two vacancies to be reserved for the former, as against one vacancy for the latter', and they were to be elected in order of date of application.[13] In November 1946 it was decided to clear the waiting list for ladies, and twenty-seven were elected for membership for 1947.[14] As the decade came to an end, the pressure eased, and in 1949 there were no ladies on the membership waiting list.[15]

The imposition of an entrance fee and the amount of that fee varied depending on the demand for membership: early in 1930 the fee was abolished as the club endeavoured to attract new members, while a fee of £2 2s 0d was imposed from 1935, when membership numbers had reached an acceptable level. By March 1938 the committee found itself for the first time in its history having to severely restrict the election of new gentlemen, or ordinary, members. It was found necessary to establish a waiting list for those seeking member-ship, and priority was to be given to men of single-figure handicaps in an attempt to improve the club's competitive advantage following the departure of some high-achieving members. The entrance fee was raised to £3 3s 0d, no further country members were to be admitted for some time, and the limit of 250 on the number of ordinary members was strictly enforced.[16] The pressure from aspiring members eased as the Second World War progressed, and in 1943 the entrance fee was waived for the duration of the war. It was imposed again in July 1945, only to be withdrawn four months later.[17] Through the later 1940s, Douglas Golf Club attracted more applicants than could be accommodated, and in 1946 it was decided to raise the number of ordinary members to 260 in an effort to partly satisfy this demand.

Income and Expenditure

The specifics of the finances of Douglas Golf Club for the years up to 1921 are not available due to the destruction of all club records in the burning of the clubhouse in May 1921. An account ledger for the period 1921–29 survives, as do the ledgers for the years from 1941. However, there is a gap in the record from 1930 to 1940, and no account ledgers for that decade survive. In comparing club income and expenditure in the early 1940s with that recorded for the 1920s, it is clear that very little changed over that twenty-year period: wages remained relatively static –as did many other costs – and the varia-tions in income were not overly significant. In circumstances such as these, and in the almost complete absence of inflation, detailed financial planning, budget projections and the myriad other provi-sions that clubs and other organisations currently make were still very much in the future.

From 1941 to 1945 the total annual wage bill for the course, or 'outdoor', staff was around £640. This group was made up of a greenkeeper and three assistants, though additional casual workers were taken on occasionally. The clubhouse, or 'inside', staff consisted of the steward, or caretaker, and an attendant up to 1929, and a manageress and assistant thereafter. Their total annual wage bill was just under £200. These annual wage costs, totalling in the region of £840, changed very little over the twenty-five years or so from the early 1920s to the mid-1940s. In 1922, for example, the club professional was paid £2 per week, supplemented by income from lessons. When John McKenna was appointed professional fifteen years later, in December 1937, his basic weekly wage was still £2, and though he was paid occasional bonuses during the war years (1939–45), his wage was not increased from £2 until 1945. During the 1920s the club greenkeeper, William Magee, earned £4 per week, but this was subsequently reduced, and he was earning fifteen shillings less when he died in 1936. His replacement was Bob Ryan, and his weekly wage did not break the £4 mark until the late 1940s. In 1925 a caddie-master, Victor Morecroft, was employed at £2 per week, and his wage stayed at that level until 1937, when it was raised by five shillings per week. It remained at £2 5s 0d for a further ten years until it was raised to £3 7s 6d in 1947. However, like a number of other club employees, he was paid occasional bonuses during the years of the Second World War in lieu of wage rises.

During the later 1930s, there was pressure from the employees of the club for wage increases resulting, one presumes, from the increasingly difficult economic conditions of the country at the time. Prices for agricultural products had collapsed, and a tariff war with Britain – Ireland's principal trading partner – resulted in increased unemployment and a depressed economy. The committee resisted demands for wage increases by simply refusing them or by repeatedly deferring consideration of them. Small increases were sometimes grudgingly granted, however, and John Spillane of the outdoor staff, for example, was given an increase of 2s 6d in 1937 to bring his weekly wage to £1 17s 6d, while the greenkeeper, Bob Ryan, had his weekly pay of £2 5s 0d raised by five shillings in the same year. The committee was capable of compassion, however, and an incident in 1936 gives an indication of what conditions were like for many people in a period of sustained hardship. E Murphy, a member of the outdoor staff, was granted £10 by the committee following the death of two of his children to cover their burial expenses 'and to provide nourishment for the other members of his family who are ill with scarlet fever'.[18]

It was 1943 before the issue of wage increases was fully addressed. In October of that year, it was decided to pay annual bonuses to staff in lieu of pay rises. Mrs Murray, the manageress in the clubhouse, was given £16, Bob Ryan, the greenkeeper, received £15, and six other employees received sums between £5 and £13.[19] This bonus, which was paid annually up to 1947 for some employees, was a significant amount, and represented up to fifteen per cent of annual pay. The bonus was paid in monthly instalments. After the end of the war in 1945, pressure was renewed on the committee to grant wage rises to staff, in spite of the continuing payment of bonuses, and, in the case of some employees, increased bonuses. In March 1947 significant wage rises of fifty per cent were granted, but the payment of bonuses was discontinued. In the following years, regular wage increases were given as Douglas Golf Club – along with every other employer, business and organisation in the country – entered an era of continuing inflation. Up to the mid-1940s, it cost in the region of £3,000 annually to run the affairs of the club, but as that decade ended, rising costs in the wider world impacted on the club, and this, coupled with increased wage demands by staff and the increasing costs of maintaining a golf course and facilities, led to increased subscription rates.

Douglas Golf Club, in common with all other golf clubs, relied on a number of sources for its income. The bar and members' subscriptions made up the lion's share of this, followed by green and competition fees, locker rents and entrance fees. In the late 1920s the annual bar income averaged £1,894, but between 1941 and 1945 this annual income fell to £1,562, reflecting the more difficult conditions of the war years. Following the war, conditions improved but so did costs, and the income of the club bar shows this with an annual average income of £2,556 for the five-year period from 1946. In the 1920s, annual income from members' subscriptions averaged £1,137, while in the period 1941–45 this averaged £1,376 though subscription rates had remained unchanged over those decades. This average increase can be explained by larger membership numbers in the 1940s. Subscriptions were increased in 1946, the first increase in over twenty-five years, and subscription income consequently grew. At the club AGM in February of that year, it was decided to raise the ordinary subscription to £6 6s 0d (including locker rent) and pro rata for other grades of membership.[20] This led to a thirty-per-cent rise in subscription income, from £1,414 in 1945 to £1,860 in 1946. The annual subscription was raised again two years later, to £7 7s 0d, even though the committee had hoped to have the rate for 1948 set higher at £8 8s 0d.[21] The annual average income from members' subscriptions for the five years 1946–50 was £2,080, a fifty-per-cent increase on that for the previous five years.

While a virtual stagnation of wage and other costs in the period from 1921 to the end of the Second World War left the subscription rate of Douglas Golf Club unchanged for twenty-five years, the changed conditions in post-war Ireland, with the slow beginnings of persistent inflation, led to the first subscription-rate rise in 1946. From then, the members' subscriptions were seen as the ideal and obvious source of increased club income – more especially as membership became more coveted and valued.

The Impact of War

Ireland was not a combatant in the Second World War, but the hostilities *did* impact on this country through rationing, shortages, restrictions on travel and a host of other measures introduced by the government under special emergency powers. Indeed, the war years were known in Ireland, officially and colloquially, as the 'Emergency'.

Uncertainty, coupled with a necessary caution and conservatism, led to developments in many facets of Irish life being put on hold 'for the duration', and although golf continued to be played, the game was not immune from the restrictive affects of the war. The editor of *Irish Golf*, perhaps only a little tongue-in cheek, saw golf as an antidote to the horror of war:

> It is more than likely that the coming year will try us hard, be we neutral, or belligerents. It is imperative, therefore, to provide an antidote to the poison of war and all its propaganda. We strongly advise all non-golfers who desire to retain their sanity to at once take up golf. By doing so they will create problems for themselves that will make even the horrors of war seem but passing phases.[22]

The Golfing Union of Ireland cancelled the Irish Amateur Open and Close Championships, the Barton Shield, the Senior and Junior Cup competitions for the duration of the war. The Open Championship of Ireland was also cancelled for those years, and no amateur international competitions were played between 1939 and 1946. While the South of Ireland and the other major provincial championships were played during these years, the difficulties confronting those wishing to travel long distances to such events resulted in a reduced entry and a lesser standard of competition than might otherwise have been the case. This devalued somewhat the status of those events. Competition tended to become more local, and golfers relied more on their own clubs for a competitive outlet. Inter-club competition did not cease, and in the Cork region, for example, the Senior and Junior Leagues continued to be played. Between 1941 and 1945, however, the Munster Branch of the GUI did run competitions along the lines of the Junior and Senior Cup for Munster clubs, and Douglas enjoyed some success. In 1941 Douglas won the Cork section of the Junior Cup, beating Fermoy in the final, and went on to meet Lahinch at Killarney in the Munster final, where they were beaten three matches to two. In 1942 Douglas again reached the Munster final of the Junior Cup, but were beaten by Limerick. Douglas were also beaten in the Munster final of the Senior Cup, but managed to cause a stir on the path to the finals with Fr Dan Fitzgerald beating both Jimmy Bruen and John Burke, two of Ireland's greatest amateur golfers.

Members who relied on their cars for transport to their clubs had difficulty in acquiring fuel, and had to resort to public transport or some other means of travel. Monkstown Golf Club suffered a big decline in activity and members during the war years, and the club operated at a loss as many of its members lived some distance from the course and could not travel as easily or as frequently as they had in the past. Membership at Douglas did not fall, though members did suffer in the same way from fuel shortages and rationing. The tram to Douglas had ceased operating in 1932, and was replaced by a bus service from the city centre that continued to function during the war, though with a reduced frequency. The bus was used by many members, as were bicycles, and by 1944 the committee at Douglas had become concerned about the club's responsibility for members' bicycles: the minutes for 11 April of that year record that the secretary was asked 'to enquire if the club has any responsibility for the bicycles of members parked in the platform provided by the club for that purpose'. Seán McHenry, club president for centenary year, remembers playing golf at Douglas as a juvenile in the war years, and recalls the frequent telling of the 'great bicycle wager' story:

> During the war, members, apart from those with 'special' petrol allowances, came to the club in many ways: by bus to the Fingerpost and then walking up the hill, by horse-drawn carriage, and by bicycle.
>
> Dr 'Nudge' Callanan was one of the cyclists. One evening in the bar, a wager was made that he could not mount his bicycle at the Fingerpost, cycle up Maryborough Hill and not dismount until he arrived at the old wooden shed that served as pro shop and tool shed (in the middle of what is now the main carpark at the clubhouse). The challenge was set for a Saturday, and meanwhile the caddies had spread word of the event far outside the club, and 'bookies' were taking wagers in the club and in Douglas village.
>
> By the time 'Nudge' Callanan mounted his bicycle at the Fingerpost on the appointed Saturday the hill was lined with members and spectators – with the greatest number at the steepest part of the hill and lining the entrance itself. A relaxed 'Nudge' waved to spectators and friends as he easily negotiated the early part of the journey, but matters became more serious as he came near to the club. By the time he was level with the club entrance, his progress was painfully slow as he weaved from side to side of the hill trying to keep sufficient momentum to stay on the bicycle, and he still had to ascend the steepest challenge of all, the route from the entrance to the shed. Those who had wagered on success had written off their investment, while the others were already celebrating theirs.
>
> The cheering died away as 'Nudge' did not turn in the club entrance but laboured slowly onwards, continuing

up Maryborough Hill while waving to the spectators to clear a way for him. He then disappeared slowly out of sight!

Moments later came the loud ringing of a bicycle bell and down the hill at furious speed came a laughing 'Nudge'. He shot through the entrance and his momentum made the last but steepest part of the climb an easy task until he finally dismounted at the shed.

And that is when the real controversy began. There were furious arguments between those on both sides of the wagers. I recall being told that some members did not speak to one another for a long time after, and that some wagers were never paid. In what were the drab and weary days of the war, that was an interlude that lived long in the telling!

Other Douglas members travelled to the club in some style, and again Seán McHenry recalls a group that included Mickey Roche, Frank Bennett and Tom Crofts arriving at the club in a horse-drawn coach!

During the First World War, golf clubs were obliged to set aside at least ten per cent of their land for tillage in an effort to maintain food supplies. Compulsory tillage orders were also made by the Irish government during the Second World War, even though Ireland was neutral, but the GUI negotiated an exemption for golf clubs in the Twenty-six Counties. Clubs in Northern Ireland had to comply with a similar order from the United Kingdom government.

In the early years of the war, there was a fear that Ireland would become directly involved in the conflict despite its declared neutrality. Britain was at a strategic disadvantage during the Battle of the Atlantic due to its return of control of the so-called Treaty ports at Lough Swilly, Berehaven and Cork Harbour to Ireland in 1938. German U-boats inflicted heavy losses on Allied shipping, and some believed that Britain would attempt to get back the ports, by force if necessary. It was also feared that Germany would invade Ireland following a defeat of Britain or as part of an effort to invade Britain. As part of the counter-invasion measures, golf courses were instructed to put obstacles on their fairways to prevent the landing of hostile aircraft. At Douglas, a sub-committee was formed in 1940 'to advise on the staking of the course to prevent landings of aircraft'.[23] Older Douglas members remember the stakes and barbed wire on the course, and also the deployment of a unit of the Local Security Force, which maintained a watch for aircraft from the vantage point of a ditch adjacent to the eighth fairway. Measures such as these lessened as the war progressed and the perceived threat of invasion receded.

The war effort in Britain and the difficulties of Irish manufacturers in accessing and importing raw materials quickly led to shortages of many manufactured goods. Golf was affected by a severe shortage of golf balls that became particularly pronounced as the war progressed; consequently, golfers became increasingly unable to replace lost or damaged balls. In January 1942 the committee at Douglas was forced to restrict the sale of balls. From 13 January, only members were permitted to purchase balls at the club, and only at the rate of one ball every two months! In addition, John McKenna, the professional, was instructed 'to keep a record of the issues [of balls] to each member with dates of same'.[24] In early 1942 the GUI set up a committee to examine the problem and to look also at the growing black market for golf balls. This committee had discussions with the Irish Dunlop Company – the principal supplier and manufacturer of golf balls in Ireland – with a view to ensuring supplies to Irish golfers. Following these discussions, Dunlop produced remoulded golf balls, and as there were inconsistencies as to weight and size, the council of the GUI decided 'that the limitations as to the weight and size of a golf ball be waived for golf in Ireland during the war and/or for the present golf ball emergency'.[25] Dunlop had to impose a quota on the number of balls supplied to clubs, and in May 1942 the secretary at Douglas was instructed to write to Dunlop to establish which year's sales were to form the basis of the quota allocation, and to find out from the professional the details of ball sales over the previous three years.[26] The following month, an answer had still not been received from Dunlop, and as the scarcity of supply had become such an inconvenience, the secretary was asked to contact the firm again.[27]

Golf balls had become rare and valuable, and golfers had consequently become increasingly careful. As William Menton noted in his history of the GUI: 'The five minute rule became somewhat stretched in friendly fourballs as the recovery of a ball from a wayward shot assumed paramount importance.'[28] At the AGM of Douglas Golf Club in February 1942, it was decided that a caddie would be stationed at the first and fifth holes to track and recover balls struck out of bounds.[29] The value of balls sometimes put temptation in the way of those seeking to make some easy money: in April 1945 the committee at Douglas considered an incident where the golf balls of two members were stolen from the eighteenth fairway during a game. The Gardaí were called to investigate, and two caddies were prosecuted for the theft of the balls.[30]

Building Works, etc.

Although the economic difficulties of the 1930s and the impact of war in the 1940s made life difficult for many, Douglas Golf Club managed to keep membership numbers at their maximum, and to generate an income sufficient to maintain the course and facilities to a continuing high standard. In 1935, for example, it was decided to improve the entrance from Maryborough Hill and to surface the driveway properly from the entrance to the clubhouse. The sum of £119 was spent on work at the entrance, but the cost of asphalting the driveway was considered excessive.[31] In 1938 an extension costing £789 was built and the clubhouse roof was re-covered in asbestos tiles.[32] In the 1940s there were problems with dry rot in the bar and dampness on the north side of the clubhouse. Remedial work was undertaken to address this, and the roof was again repaired. P Coveney was a prominent member of the club in those years, and his expertise in building-related matters was frequently sought by the club. In these years, the stewardess and greenkeeper were provided with living accommodation. In 1945 it was decided that the living quarters of the greenkeeper and the professional's and caddies' sheds needed upgrading. These buildings had been acquired in the early 1920s as temporary emergency accommodation, but had become permanent fixtures over the subsequent twenty-five years. Due to wartime restrictions, there was difficulty in sourcing timber for repairs to the greenkeeper's quarters.[33]

Matters were left stand for nearly two years until July 1947, when architect E P O'Flynn was asked to prepare plans for an extension to the clubhouse, including living quarters for the stewardess Miss Egan. At a special general meeting in December, the committee was empowered to borrow the money for the building work as at least £8,000 would be needed, so the annual subscription was increased by £1 1s 0d to £7 7s 0d for ordinary members as a contribution towards the building fund.[34] Some of this work was completed by late 1948, and the lounge and dining room were improved. However, it seems that the planned large two-storey extension with accommodation for the stewardess was not proceeded with in full, as in May 1949 the architect was asked to prepare plans for a three-bedroom bungalow for her.[35] Tenders for the building were invited, and that of Messrs O'Shea at £3,010 was accepted. A bank loan was to be sought to cover the cost of building. Matters were delayed somewhat as the financial position of the club was examined by a sub-committee. Following its deliberations, the prices of all drinks in the bar were raised, and a series of dances, dinners and whist drives was proposed as a means of raising money. In December 1949 it was decided not to proceed with the bungalow as planned, and a more modest set of plans were drawn up. The cost of the revised building was estimated to be £1,450, and John Barrett was engaged to undertake the building work. By October the building work was finished, and £73 8s 11d was paid to Roches Stores for linoleum, curtains and other fittings for the new bungalow.[36] Early the following year, two of the old huts were demolished, and the third – which served as living quarters for the greenkeeper – was renovated.

A New Lease on the Course

The lease held by Douglas Golf Club from Patrick McAuliffe on its lands had been executed on 30 December 1916 at an annual rent of £120, and was to run for a period of thirty-one years. In 1933 a special meeting of the general committee decided that it was time to review this lease with a view to getting an extension on it. There was also the question as to the club's right to a plot of ground on the north-western boundary of the course, which had been fenced off by Michael McAuliffe, the son of Patrick, to whom the lands owned by Patrick had been transferred in 1923.[37] The club president, James Henchy, was asked to approach McAuliffe with a request for an extension of fifty years on the lease at an annual rent of £146 until the expiry of the then current lease in 1947, and at a rent of £172 for the remainder of the period.[38] This offer seems to have been unsuccessful, as in January 1934 an improved offer of £170 per year for fifty years – including the use of the plot on the north-western

Details from the renegotiated 1934 lease.

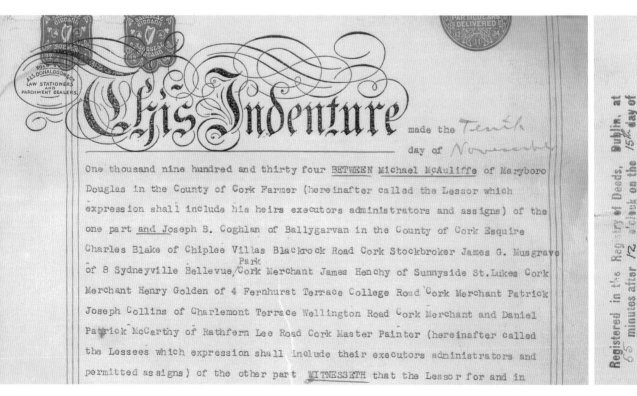

boundary – was made to McAuliffe.[39] By May McAuliffe still had not replied to the offers, and the committee decided to offer to purchase the land outright in an effort to bring matters to a conclusion.[40] This offer seems to have brought the issue to a head as a new lease for a fifty-year term at £170 per annum was agreed the following month, and the details were forwarded to J C & A Blake, Solicitors, of 27 Marlboro Street so that the final documents could be drawn up. The acreage of the course is given as ninety-eight acres and one rood, and does not include the land located across the Carrigaline road to the south-west included in the leases up to this date. It was also written into this lease that the lessor had the right to graze up to 270 sheep and lambs on the course, and 'that all the manure on the course shall be collected by the Lessees [i.e. the club] or their servants and any not needed by the Lessees for use on the course shall be the property of the Lessor and … shall be placed … to the right of the fifth green'. The new lease is dated 10 November 1934, and is signed by the seven trustees of Douglas Golf Club: Joseph B Coghlan, James G Musgrave, Charles Blake, Henry Golden, Daniel P McCarthy, James Henchy and Patrick J Collins. The first three of these had also been signatories to the 1916 lease.

Following the death of Michael McAuliffe in 1949, his daughter intimated that she was interested in selling the McAuliffe house and lands, including the land of the course leased to the club. The asking price of £8,000 was considered too high, and following a valuation

1934 lease: signatures of the seven club trustees, Joseph B Coghlan, James G Musgrave, Charles Blake, H Golden, Daniel P McCarthy, James Henchy and P J Collins.

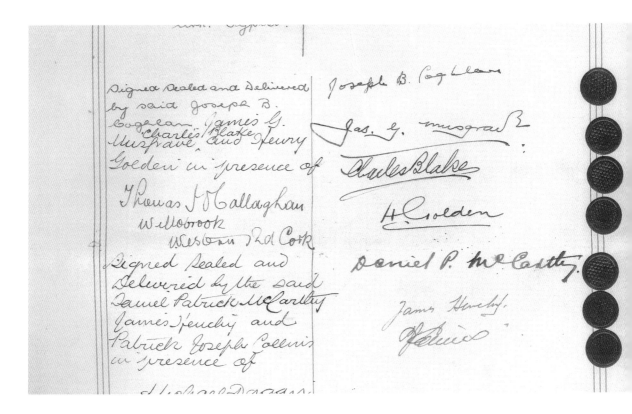

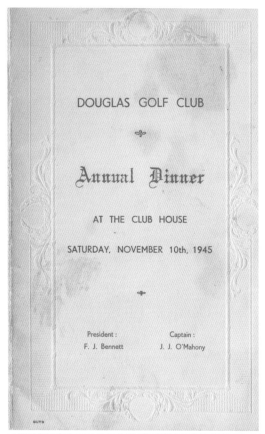

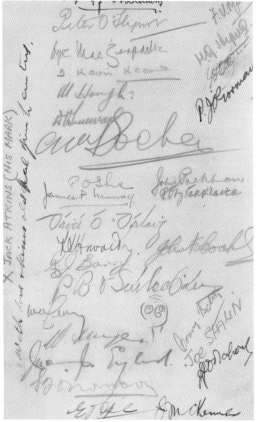

by Marsh & Sons, an offer of £4,000 was made by the club to Miss McAuliffe.[41] In May Miss McAuliffe said she would accept £6,000 for the house and lands, and a special general meeting of the club was held to discuss the matter. This meeting decided to offer a maximum of £3,000 for the land of the golf course and an additional four acres, or a maximum of £5,000 for the full lot, including the house.[42] This offer was not apparently accepted, and by the AGM in February 1950 no further progress had been made on the matter. A year later, in April 1951, the issue arose again, and a sub-committee was formed to examine the advantages or otherwise of getting an extension of the lease or, alternatively, the outright purchase of the course.[43] The minutes of the committee meetings where the matter was discussed suggest that there was no real urgency or desire to progress the outright purchase of the course, and neither the potential vendor nor the club pursued the matter very vigorously. The annual rent of £170 was reasonable and affordable, and 1984, when the lease would expire, was still a long way off.

Douglas Golf Club survived the economic difficulties of the 1930s and the impact of the Second World War and its aftermath. Membership was maintained almost at its maximum throughout the period, and the club finances were kept in relatively good order. The lease on the course had been renegotiated and was secure until 1984 at a very manageable rent. John McKenna, one of Ireland's best professionals and coaches, was now based at the club, and a new generation of golfers, Zelie Fallon, Éamonn McSweeney, Tadg Higgins and others, were about to bring the successes to Douglas that were so long awaited.

Left:
Menu from the annual dinner of 1945, with the signatures of many members on the reverse.

Professionals at Douglas

As golf spread and became popular in Britain and Ireland in the 1890s, the professional became essential to the life of a club. Members relied on the professional to take care of the upkeep and maintenance of the course, to supply and repair clubs, to remould gutta-percha balls, and to teach the skills of the game. The first professionals were mostly Scottish, and the first professional in Ireland, appointed at Royal Belfast in 1889, was Alexander Day from Musselburgh in Scotland. Some came to be professionals through their skill at club manufacture and repair, while others did so by virtue of their superior skill at the game of golf, and in the late nineteenth and early twentieth centuries the exceptions were those who could leave their work and travel to play in tournaments and exhibition matches. In those early years, the status of the professional was quite low in the hierarchy of golf – essentially, just a little higher than that of a caddie. In many clubs, the professional was allowed enter the clubhouse only by the back door, and socialising with members was frowned upon, if it happened at all. Professionals were usually not allowed use the members' locker rooms at professional championship events. As Geoffrey Cousins has written: 'They worked hard and long to earn their money, but the job was congenial in many ways, providing a healthy active life and associations, however distant, with people of superior birth and social standing. Professionals were in general respected, if not accepted as equals by the members'.[1] The status of the professional changed later, especially in the 1930s, with the emergence of golfers like Henry Cotton and Walter Hagen, and a successful touring professional was able to earn significant sums in prize money and sponsorship. Hagen neatly summed up the change with his famous quip: 'I don't want to be a millionaire, I just want to live like one!' Their image changed as the media and the public saw these sportsmen as role models and icons. The supremacy of the amateur ethos was eroded over time, and by the 1970s a successful amateur was expected to turn professional rather than being criticised for doing so.

John McNamara, 1909–14

John McNamara was the first professional at Douglas Golf Club. He was born in Lahinch, and prior to coming to Douglas in 1909 he was employed at Muskerry, Rushbrooke and Tramore Golf Clubs. In 1914 he played in the Irish Professional Golfers' Association tournament, representing Douglas. He left Douglas in 1914 and joined the British army. There is no record of him returning to work at any golf club in Ireland or Britain after the First World War.

S M McDonald, 1918

Guy's Cork Almanac and Directory 1918 lists S M McDonald as the Douglas professional for that year. This is the only mention of McDonald in connection with Douglas in the available records. *The British Professional Golfers 1887–1930: A Register* lists S McDonald as being the professional at Omagh from 1914 to 1919, and at Limerick from 1923 to 1925.[2]

John Curran, 1919–22

Before coming to Douglas, John Curran is recorded as having served at Youghal from 1914 to 1917. At Douglas, he was initially paid £2 per week, but this was reduced to £1 following the burning of the clubhouse in 1921. He was given notice by the club in April 1922 and his employment ceased on 27 July that year. After leaving Douglas he worked at Crosshaven, of which course there is little information, and Kinsale, before taking up duty at Bandon on a permanent basis in 1930. He died in 1964.

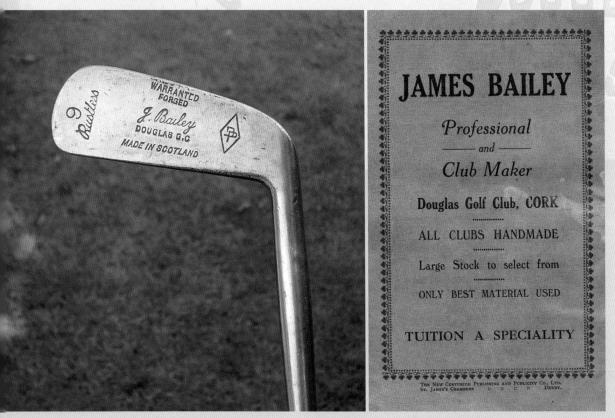

Left: A James Bailey iron. *Right:* Advertisement from 1929 official handbook.

James Sheridan, 1922–27

James Sheridan began work at Douglas on 1 August 1922, having worked at Milltown immediately prior to that. In 1924 he was allowed keep the profit from the sale of golf balls at the club in return for a ten-shilling reduction in his weekly wage. In 1925 he was censured by the club for failing to keep lesson appointments and for not having the pro shop open at the appointed times. The following year, he was in trouble again for selling second-hand golf balls obtained from caddies. The club asked him to retire early in 1927.

James Bailey, 1927–37

James Bailey was highly regarded as a teacher and club maker. Before coming to Douglas, he had worked at Dundalk, Greenore, Great Orm in Wales, Hermitage, Kingstown, Portmarnock and Milltown, where he had been assistant to Tom Shannon. At Douglas, he was paid £2 per week and was allowed charge 2s 6d per hour for lessons. He also made some income from the sale and repair of clubs, but was not permitted to sell second-hand golf balls. The clubs he made were considered to be of a very high quality, and a number of Douglas members still have their prized Bailey clubs. In July 1937 the club wanted Bailey to resign as he was not able to keep his pro shop stocked with clubs, presumably of his own manufacture, and he was employed on a week-to-week basis until John McKenna was appointed at the end of 1937.

John McKenna, 1937–76

See feature over (pp. 122–5).

Gary Nicholson, 1977–

Gary S Nicholson was born in Tramore, County Waterford and first played golf on the course there at the age of seven. After leaving school, he spent some years training to be an accountant, but tired of office work and left Ireland for Canada. His golf had been steadily improving, and when he emigrated he was playing off a handicap of 4. In Canada, he turned to golf as a career, and became a professional in 1967. That year, he graduated from the Canadian PGA Business School. He worked first as an assistant at the Marine Drive Golf Club in Vancouver, and later worked at two other clubs in the city before being appointed professional at the Lions Golf Club Centre, also in Vancouver, in 1975. Gary returned to Ireland in 1976, and took up duty at Douglas on 1 January 1977. He has served the needs of the members for over thirty-two years, and has had the satisfaction of seeing players like John McHenry, John Morris junior, and Eavan Higgins benefit from his coaching and achieve at the highest level of the amateur game.

Gary Nicholson.

John McKenna

John McKenna was Douglas Golf Club's professional from 1938 until his retirement at the end of 1976. He was born in Dublin in 1905, and was a member of an illustrious Irish golfing family. His father James was the first resident professional at Lahinch Golf Club in 1893, and he was later attached to Portmarnock, Carrickmines and Rossmore golf clubs before going to Armagh in 1924, where he remained until his retirement in 1950. He played in the first Irish Professional Golf Tournament held at Royal Portrush in 1895, and was a founding member of the Irish Professional Golfers' Association in 1911. John McKenna's uncles John and Patrick were also professionals.

John McKenna played hurling and football in his youth before he became seriously involved in golf after the family moved to Armagh in 1924. He won Armagh county-championship medals in football in 1931 and 1932, and became an assistant to his father at Armagh Golf Club before taking up his first appointment as professional at Bundoran in 1936. He had first come to prominence as a golfer in 1932 when he was beaten in the final of the Ulster Championship. He played in the Irish Open in 1935, and the correspondent of *Irish Golf* commented: 'young J J McKenna of Armagh played excellently and will yet be one of our best players. He is going the right way to be so at present'.[1] In 1937 he came second in the Irish Professional Championship and established himself at the top of the game in Ireland. In late 1937 Douglas advertised for a professional to replace James Bailey, and John McKenna expressed an interest. He came to Douglas on 21 November 1937 to be interviewed and to play some rounds of golf with 'specific members'. All went well, and he was offered the position in December, which he accepted.[2] John McKenna was paid £2 per week and worked from 10am until dark. He charged 2s 6d per hour for lessons, 3s 6d for a round of golf or a fourball.

John McKenna was a club professional par excellence: he was a very talented teacher, and devoted most of his energies to coaching, seeing his principal duty as bettering the game of the members of his club. He played only two or three tournaments each year, but despite this apparent lack of regular competition, he beat the best on a number of occasions, and always impressed with his skill and temperament. For twenty years – from the mid-1930s to the mid-1950s – Irish professional golf was dominated by three players: Fred Daly, Harry Bradshaw and John McKenna. While Daly and Bradshaw travelled abroad and competed in Britain and elsewhere, McKenna disliked travelling, and confined himself to the very limited Irish circuit. Fred Daly, who won the Open in 1947 and had top-four finishes on four subsequent occasions, said of McKenna:

He was very much in the same grade as myself and the Brad [Harry Bradshaw] but unlike us he did not drive himself. We were over in Britain all the time but he went there only twice and that was the difference because we won our bit of glory over there.[3]

McKenna's reluctance to travel was commented on in the golfing press. He won the Irish Dunlop £500 tournament in 1947, and *Irish Golf* commented:

Everyone at Portmarnock was asking how it was that John Mckenna was not over in England taking part in the big professional events there. Well might the question be asked, as the Douglas man's golf is good enough for any company. In Cork he has little of that needle golf essential to players in big events, yet he went through the Dunlop Tournament playing as few loose shots as any. We all hope he will try his luck over the water, for outside his play he seems possessed of a watertight temperament, taking everything that comes imperturbably.[4]

Harry Bradshaw, ten times Irish professional champion and second in the 1949 Open after a tie, also felt that McKenna missed out by not travelling: 'There was very, very little between the three of us in those days, just that Fred and myself played the British circuit and John did not'.[5] McKenna did travel to Britain in 1945 after the end of the Second World War to play in the Daily Mail-sponsored 1,500 Guineas Tournament at St Andrews. He came joint thirteenth but shot a 74 in his second round in dreadful weather conditions, a score that impressed all commentators. Bradshaw also played in that tournament, and remembered the return ferry crossing to Ireland: 'John was very seasick. He told me then that he would never go over across the water again. And I don't think he did either.'[6] McKenna spoke about his unwilling-

ness to travel in a newspaper interview in 1984: 'I hardly ever went across-channel. The money there was a pittance, £50 for the winner and the like. I preferred to stay at home and give lessons, there was more money in it.'[7]

Between 1939 and 1949 John McKenna had a top-ten finish each year in the Irish Professional Championship, winning the title in 1945 and 1948. In 1945 the event was played at Newlands, and McKenna's friends and rivals, Daly and Bradshaw, finished second and third respectively. Following McKenna's victory, *Irish Golf* commented: 'I frankly confess I had no idea McKenna is so good as he is. To my mind he has one of the best grooved swings in the country – and best of all appears to have a temperament always kept in a refrigerator.'[8] In 1947 John McKenna won the Dunlop £500 Tournament at Portmarnock. On the way to victory, he beat Harry Bradshaw in the quarter finals by one hole, and reigning Open champion Fred Daly in the semi-finals by 5 and 4. This achievement is all the more noteworthy as the victories over his two rivals came on the one day. In the thirty-six-hole final, he beat Jack McLoughlin by 7 and 6. The *Irish Golf* correspondent again lamented McKenna's reluctance to travel: 'It struck me forcibly that it was a pity so fine a player did not cross the Irish Sea oftener, as if he did, he would be there or thereabouts in any events he played in.'[9] The following year, 1948, McKenna again won the Irish Professional Championship, and in 1951 he played in the Open when it was held at Royal Portrush, the only time it was played in Ireland, finishing with an aggregate of 302.

It is as a teacher and coach that John McKenna is best remembered. The Douglas ladies who played on the successful Senior Cup teams of the 1960s and 1970s acknowledge the impact of McKenna's teaching. Ann Heskin recalls the successes of those years: 'There wasn't a team in the country to touch us. Why? John McKenna. We had talent and it was fostered by John McKenna. As a teacher he took such an interest in us. Marvellous at the finesse of the game, the finer points. He was a complete perfectionist.'[10] 'Mack', as he was affectionately known, coached five women internationals from Douglas: Zelie Fallon, Girlie Hegarty, Anne O'Brien, Ann Heskin and Oonagh Fitzpatrick (Heskin). In a profile of McKenna in the programme for the 1971 Dunlop Irish Professional Golf Tournament, Dermot Russell writes of McKenna's fame as a coach: 'The modest McKenna has a big name as a teacher now … Try asking the top grade players, the ones who slip quietly to Douglas for a quick lesson when things go wrong.'

John McKenna spent almost forty years at Douglas as a well-loved and greatly respected professional popular with the members. 'The real proof of his standing with the members of his home club is to be seen every Sunday morning when, wet or fine, a gay group gathers at his shop to exchange the latest golfing gossip and to spend some moments in congenial gossip.'[11] Tall and thin, he was 'a slim stylist with golf in his blood, greatness in his nature'.[12] Elsewhere, he is described as 'A patient teacher and a club maker of some renown, altogether another total golfing package from the McKenna family tree.'[13] John McKenna retired at the end of 1976, and he died in 1995.

7 *The Middle Years: 1950s*

Douglas Golf Club survived, and indeed thrived at times, during the difficult years of the 1930s and 1940s. The club had maintained its membership numbers, and was in a financially secure position. It was felt by many, however, that the club was not achieving its potential in competitive golf: the last major success was the Junior Cup of 1930, and no individual player had made an impact since the departure of Fr Daniel Fitzgerald in 1945. In the May 1948 edition of *Irish Golf*, this lack of success was noted, and put down to a dearth of ambition:

> We hope Cork golfers are not taking after those of Dublin, for the latter are largely satisfied to get down to handicaps of four and the like – and then crying 'Enough!' They just lack sweet ambition ... Douglas club has a course that should produce fine players, but the Douglas members do not seem to suffer from the 'limelight bug'.[1]

This changed in the 1950s with the Douglas ladies winning their first Senior Cup in 1952, and the men winning a second Junior Cup in 1955. Zelie Fallon and Girlie Hegarty became the first Douglas ladies to be chosen to play at international level, and the success of Douglas men like Éamonn McSweeney and Tadg Higgins showed that the 'limelight bug' was still somewhat infectious!

Up to the 1950s golf was still very much a game for the middle and professional classes. Many established golf clubs were now fifty years old or approaching that milestone, and traditions had become established. Clubs had helped develop social and business networks, and the children of the first generation of members very often maintained those traditions, while new members, usually chosen from amongst the acquaintances of existing members, easily fitted into the existing club milieu. In that way, a club ethos and set of values was sustained. A club such as Douglas – where membership was valued, sought after and not lightly given up – could easily become very insular and draw its members from an increasingly narrow range of people. The challenge was, and is, to recruit members from outside the existing members' range of social, business and familial contacts, especially when good golfing talent is sought and needed.

Facing page, clockwise from top left: Dermot Barry, Terry McSweeney, John Coakley, Jerome O'Driscoll and Conal Boyle. Photographs taken at Douglas, 1954.

Éamonn McSweeney, 1955.

The post-war world of the 1950s was different in many ways to that of the previous decades. The strict lines of social division were beginning to loosen a little, and advancement on merit rather than through social connection became more common. As early as 1943, the editor of *Irish Golf* felt that the Second World War was going to be a turning point for society and for golf, especially in efforts to democratise the game. In the March edition of the magazine, he suggested that the post-war world would be very different and socially more equitable: 'in a much-changed world the idea should be to make golf more than ever a game for all. Up to now golf has largely been the pastime of those comfortably off. Difficult though it may be, we should endeavour to make the game open to all classes.'[2]

This 'democratisation' happened to an extent at Douglas, and some new members were elected from outside the usual pool of potential members. These were people with proven golfing talent or with a potential to become good golfers who previously would not have considered becoming members of the club, or who would not have met the criteria for election. Éamonn McSweeney was one such person. He had worked as a part-time caddie at Douglas from about 1937, when he was fifteen years old, and had occasionally played a round there. His golfing talent was recognised, and he was invited to become a member of the club in 1952. The annual subscription at the time was £8 8s 0d, and Éamonn remembers having to borrow some of that money. At first, he felt that he did not really belong in the club, his background being very different to that of the majority of members, and he sometimes had a sense that he was not regarded as a social equal. Éamonn had become a member to play and to excel at golf, and that he did, his handicap falling to 1 in a very short period of time, and within three years of joining Douglas, he was number one on the Junior Cup team that won the national title. His golfing success gave him the confidence to overcome his initial reluctance, while his obvious talent established his credentials in the eyes of the members.[3]

Douglas Ladies' First Senior Cup, 1952

The Senior Cup for ladies was first contested in 1926, and apart from a win for Cork Golf Club in 1927, no club from Munster won the trophy in the succeeding twenty-five years (the Senior Cup was suspended 1940–45). The competition was dominated by clubs such as County Louth, Milltown and Royal Portrush until Douglas dramatically broke through with a stunning victory in 1952. That win heralded a golden era for the ladies of Douglas Golf Club, with a further eleven Senior Cup victories in the following decades, as well

1952 Senior Cup
winning team.
Standing, L–R:
Mrs M O'Byrne,
Miss M Murphy,
Miss E O'Callaghan.
Seated, L–R:
Mrs Z Fallon,
Mrs P McKenna,
Mrs M Riordan.

as frequent representation at international level. That first Senior Cup win also propelled Zelie Fallon to national prominence.

Mrs Peg McKenna, wife of the club professional John McKenna, captained the team of Mrs Zelie Fallon, Miss Marjorie Murphy, Miss E O'Callaghan, Mrs M O'Byrne and Mrs Myra Riordan. They beat Cork, Muskerry and Limerick on the way to taking the Munster title, and travelled to Newcastle for the finals 'fortified with limitless courage and the fervent good wishes of all Munster folk'.[4] In the semi-finals, Douglas met Royal Portrush, a club with three Senior Cup titles and which had on its team Mrs Z Bolton, a British international and Curtis Cup player. All the Douglas players notched at least one winning point against Portrush, Mrs Zelie Fallon beating Mrs Bolton.

In the final, Douglas played Milltown, which had won the title the previous two years, and had six titles in all. Douglas won 3–2, Mrs Zelie Fallon beating Miss Hanna 6 and 5, Miss Marjorie Murphy beating Mrs Butler 5 and 3, and Miss E O'Callaghan beating Mrs Tunney 3 and 2. Mrs M O'Byrne and Mrs P McKenna of Douglas lost their matches. The victory was of huge significance for Douglas Golf Club as a whole, not just for the ladies. The twenty-five-year stranglehold of Ulster and Leinster clubs on the Senior Cup was broken, and the winning of a national title was a confidence boost for all Douglas players. The team captain was deservedly praised, the *Irish Golf* correspondent writing that it was 'almost impossible to assess the debt the winning side owes to the leadership and inspiration of Mrs McKenna'. The club now had reason to celebrate, and 'general rejoicings were the order of the day and of several gay nights to boot, when the new champions returned home from their successful northern expedition'.[5] It was also acknowledged that the emergence of the Douglas ladies onto the national golf stage was greatly helped by the coaching and mentoring of John McKenna.

Amongst the ladies who benefitted from McKenna's coaching was Zelie Fallon (see pp. 141–3), who won her first full international cap for Ireland in 1952, having been chosen as a substitute in 1951. Her first international outing in the Home Internationals was at Troon, and she held her international place every year until 1968. She won a further cap in 1970, and was Ireland captain in 1972. Zelie Fallon won the Munster Senior Championship in 1955, 1956, 1957, 1959 and 1964.

Girlie Hegarty (see pp. 144–5) was another Douglas player who came to prominence at this time. She was runner-up in the Irish Close in 1953 and 1956, she won her first international cap in 1955, retained it in 1956, and was Ireland captain in 1964.

Tadg Higgins

Tadg Higgins was another who broke the mould of the usual Douglas member. He joined in 1954 at the age of twenty-eight, having achieved success as a pitch-and-putt player. Pitch-and-putt had grown in popularity, especially in the Cork region, in the late 1940s and early 1950s, and good players were often invited to join golf clubs where their talent at the short game could be developed for the longer course. Within eighteen months of joining Douglas, Higgins' talents were being noticed in the golfing press:

> [Tadg Higgins] is going from open meeting to open meeting and winning all before him. His handicap descended from fifteen to five in less time than it takes to narrate, and the experts predict that this talented 'novice' has yet to reach his golfing peak. The Douglas club have a great find in Tadg Higgins, one of the most deadly putters in the business.[6]

In January of the following year, the same magazine noted that

Tadg Higgins with the Cork Scratch Cup, 1959.

Higgins 'continues to defy bogey with some astonishing performances'.[7] He maintained his standards, winning the prestigious Cork
Scratch Cup in 1959, when he beat one of Ireland's foremost internationals, George Crosbie, in the final by 4 and 3. His immaculate
putting gave him the advantage over Crosbie, the report in the *Cork
Examiner* noting that 'he used this club [putter] only 26 times as
against 38 by Crosbie'. The newspaper also quoted Christy O'Connor
as remarking that Higgins' putting was 'the best I have seen in competitive golf'.

Tadg Higgins won the An Tóstal scratch competition at Douglas
in 1960, and played on the Douglas Senior Cup team that was beaten
in the national semi-final in 1962. He was unbeaten in all his matches
in that campaign. He also played for Munster on a number of occasions. Tadg Higgins died at a relatively young age in 1976.

Junior Cup Victory, 1955

The achievements of players like Éamonn McSweeney and Tadg
Higgins were still a little in the future when Dominic Coffey penned

an article in *Irish Golf* in July 1954 that was quite critical of the underachievement of Douglas Golf Club players:

> The critics have asserted, and not without due cause, that the approach of the Douglas club to knock-out events is too slap-happy – if I may borrow an expression of our American cousins. A long string of defeats in the Irish Cups and local leagues, broken only by some progress in the Barton Shield of a year or two ago, points the moral only too clearly. The talent is definitely available, but the players, somehow, fail to do themselves justice when the die of combat is cast. The killer instinct, necessary to all sports from heavyweight boxing down to Wimbledon tennis, is not part and parcel of the Douglas make-up. A desire to win at all costs can lead to abuses and bad sportsmanship, but it is carrying things to the other extreme to class this factor as a plague to be avoided at all costs. The other teams take trouble to cultivate the quality, which can be the difference … Having waxed outspoken on this matter, it is only fair to congratulate the Douglas representatives on their true sportsmanship. They have never failed to field a team in all scheduled events, and have [won] the Cork Junior League for 2 seasons in succession.

Within a year, Coffey had to eat his words when in June 1955 Douglas Golf Club won the Junior Cup for the second time in the club's history. By now, Éamonn McSweeney was at the height of his golfing prowess, and he led the Douglas team to beat 'a rampant Lahinch side' in the Munster final on the Lahinch course. Having been all square after four matches, 'McSweeney proved himself a worthy leader by snatching a win'.[8] Douglas then beat Castlerea in the national semi-final, four matches to one: R Daly, J Condon, N McNamara and É McSweeney winning their matches, P J Connolly losing his. In the final, Douglas met a much fancied Hermitage side, and again É Mc Sweeney showed his leadership qualities. The *Cork Examiner* of 22 June wrote:

> There was sparkling golf in the top match of the Junior Cup when the big Hermitage man, H Murphy, found that it required birdie figures to take holes from the Douglas man, É McSweeney, in a match that went to the 19th with a Cork win. At the tie hole the Dublin man could not find the green where the Corkman was sitting pretty for a birdie four and the match. In the second match Richard Daly (Douglas) had a good win

Junior Cup victory of 1955.
Standing, L–R:
P J Connolly,
É McSweeney,
J J Condon,
N McNamara,
M J Gleeson.
Seated, L–R:
R Daly,
A W Stokes (captain),
J C Coulter (president),
C S P MacEnrí.

against the useful N P Cregan, whom he beat three and two.

J Condon won his match 5 and 4, while N McNamara won 2 and 1. P J Connolly, unfortunately, lost his final match, 5 and 4.

Irish Golf was lavish in its praise of Douglas, while saving a little sting for the tail! The winning team had

> cantered through by wide margins at the expense of Castlerea and Hermitage to win the Irish Junior Cup. Thus after a lapse of twenty-five years, Douglas have won this grand old cup, and the result should count for more than a few medals to a well-balanced side. Éamonn McSweeney and his colleagues proved that team spirit and the will to win could triumph over more fancied opponents … [The win] has brought a ray of light into the hitherto dark shadows of golf at Douglas. Richard Daly at number two supplied classic golf … while P J Connolly and J J Condon were in the fighting forceful mould. Niall McNamara, at number five, was the find of the season … We trust that this win will be the renaissance of stroke-play in the Douglas club, which has the reputation of neglecting solo play in favour of the less testing fourball.[9]

The full Douglas panel was É McSweeney, R Daly, P J Connolly, J J Condon, N McNamara, M J Gleeson and C S P MacEnrí.

Apart from hitting the headlines for winning national trophies a couple of times in the 1950s, Douglas Golf Club also continued

Detail of the Distillery Challenge Trophy – better known as the Distillers' Cup – presented to the club in 1954 as the An Tóstal Scratch Cup.

to cater for its ordinary members – those who never achieve greatness but who, by their continued membership and participation in club competitions and activities, sustained the club. In May 1950 the club held its first Open Week, which very quickly established itself as an annual feature on the local golf calendar. In the early 1950s the Irish tourist industry, with the backing of government, initiated the An Tóstal festival. Cities, towns, sporting organisations and other bodies were encouraged to organise annual cultural and sporting events in the early summer that would attract visitors and encourage tourism in Ireland at a time of economic difficulty. As part of the new Open Week, an annual An Tóstal golf competition was organised by Douglas Golf Club from 1954, with the An Tóstal Scratch Cup, presented by the Cork Distilleries Co. Ltd, as the centrepiece of the golfing activity (this trophy is now called the Distillers' Cup, and is played for annually on New Year's Day). After the An Tóstal initiative ceased in the early 1960s, this competition came to be called the Douglas Scratch Cup.[10] In 1956 the An Tóstal Scratch Cup was won by Mick Power of Muskerry, who shot a record 69 in his second round of the thirty-six-hole competition. Mick Power was born in the Douglas clubhouse many years before when his father, Joseph Power, was the resident steward there.

An Tóstal exhibition match at Cork Golf Club, April 1953. *L–R:* John McKenna, Henry Cotton (1953 Ryder Cup captain), Jimmy Bruen, Bill O'Sullivan.

An An Tóstal competition was organised in April 1953 by Cork Golf Club. Henry Cotton, the famous professional and 1953 Ryder Cup captain, came to Cork and played an exhibition match with Dr Bill O'Sullivan of Killarney against Jimmy Bruen and John McKenna, the Douglas professional. Over 3,000 spectators turned out for the match, and though McKenna and Bruen did not win, McKenna's 70 'rekindled the desire of local golfers to see this retiring former champion again enter the open competition lists'.[11]

In April 1954 Douglas organised an exhibition golf competition as part of its An Tóstal contribution. Harry Bradshaw and Fred Daly, Ireland's two foremost professionals, accepted invitations to play at the Douglas event, and they were joined by leading amateurs Joe Carr and Jimmy Bruen in a series of matches played on 23–24 April. The other three golf clubs in the Cork area agreed to assist in the stewarding of the events and to share any profit or loss. Douglas, however, would retain all bar profits![12] Harry Bradshaw made a great effort to set a new course record at Douglas during the event. He needed to get a birdie on each of his final three holes to achieve this, but failed on the eighteenth when he missed his putt for birdie. The event incurred a financial loss, and when only two of the other three Cork clubs paid their agreed share of that loss, the Douglas committee made up the shortfall.[13]

An Tóstal exhibition match at Douglas, April 1954.
L–R: Harry Bradshaw, Jimmy Bruen, Joe Carr, Fred Daly

While Tadg Higgins, Éamonn McSweeney and others were the highest Douglas achievers in this decade, a number of others made their mark also, though to a more modest degree: John and Norman Butler, Bill O'Callaghan, Stan Reynolds, Sam Thompson, Seán McHenry, J J Heffernan, David O'Connell, Christy Synnott and Phil Roberts are amongst those whose names are most often mentioned in the golfing reports of the time.

Caddies and Caddie Carts

The post-war years saw a steady decline in the use of caddies by golfers not only in Douglas but throughout the golfing world (see feature, pp. 53–7). The caddie cart gradually replaced the caddie as a means of conveying one's clubs. The caddie shed, for long a feature of all golf clubs, was generally converted for use as a storage area for the new caddie carts. In the 1930s there had been upwards of sixty caddies at Douglas, both part and full-time, overseen by the caddie-master, Victor Morecroft. By 1954 this number had fallen to twenty-five, and the growing use of caddie carts led to the conversion of part of the caddie shed for caddie-car storage in the spring of that year. Within two months, this new storage area was found to be inadequate, and a further portion of the caddie shed as well as part of the coal-storage area were converted to house even more caddie carts.

Management Issues

The catering at Douglas Golf Club had been in the charge of manageress Miss B M Egan since 1944. This position replaced that of steward with the departure of Joseph Power in 1929. The manageress resided at the club with free accommodation, fuel and light, and had quite onerous duties. She was responsible for the catering in the dining room as well as having responsibility for the bar, including the keeping of accounts and stock books and the management of

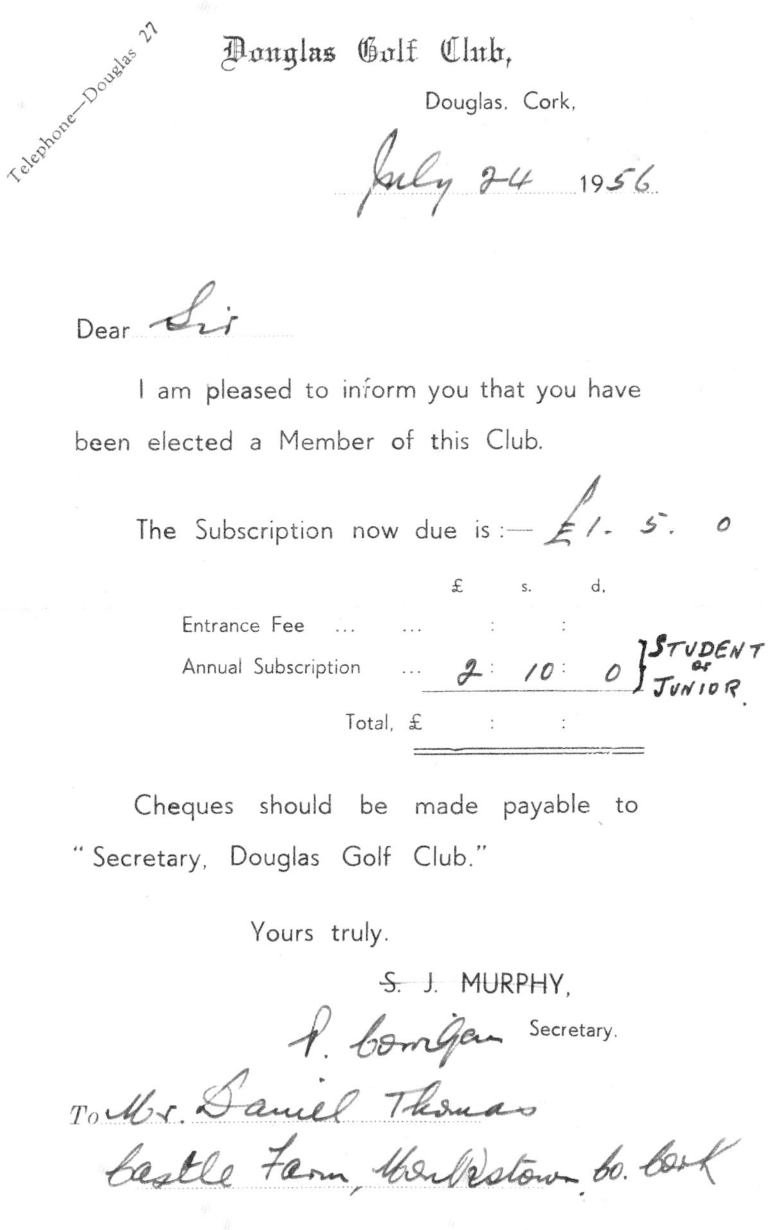

Telephone—Douglas 27

𝔇𝔬𝔲𝔤𝔩𝔞𝔰 𝔊𝔬𝔩𝔣 𝔆𝔩𝔲𝔟,

Douglas. Cork,

July 24 1956.

Dear *Sir*

I am pleased to inform you that you have been elected a Member of this Club.

The Subscription now due is :— *£1. 5. 0*

	£	s.	d.
Entrance Fee	:	:	
Annual Subscription ...	*2* : *10* : *0*		*STUDENT or JUNIOR*
Total, £	:	:	

Cheques should be made payable to " Secretary, Douglas Golf Club."

Yours truly,

S. J. MURPHY,

P. Corrigan Secretary.

To Mr. Daniel Thomas
Castle Farm, Monkstown, Co. Cork

Dan Thomas, captain in 1990 and president in 1999, becomes a member of Douglas in 1956 at a total cost of £3 15s 0d.

Douglas members at the clubhouse 1950, with President Jim Fallon (centre left) presenting a trophy to Joe O'Donovan (captain, 1960 and 1961).

any assistants employed for bar, kitchen or dining-room work. She also oversaw the cleaning of the clubhouse and the lighting of fires. Miss Egan resigned in 1950, and for the next seven years the committee struggled to satisfactorily manage the catering and bar service, having difficulty finding a person with the requisite skill and experience in whom they could have full confidence. Miss Egan was replaced by Mrs Henry Cody, who lasted barely three weeks in the position until she was in turn replaced by Mrs Lily Campbell in August 1950. Mrs Campbell stayed five months, and her replacement, Mrs Hackett, resigned in January 1952. Mrs Margaret Klincewizc was then appointed manageress, and she held the position until the end of 1956. The committee appointed Mrs Mary Kenny, a member of the waitressing staff at the club, as manageress in January 1957, and the arrangement appears to have been very satisfactory for the duration of Mrs Kenny's employment. There had been difficulties with the management of the bar accounts at different times prior to the appointment of Mrs Kenny, and on one occasion the Gardaí were called to investigate cash shortages. One former manageress took legal action against the club in 1953, the matter eventually being settled three years later. In December 1952 the committee decided to

appoint a bar committee of three members with a view to improving the management of the bar, and ensuring proper cash and stock controls.

In 1951 the annual subscription for ordinary members was £8 8s 0d, and pro rata for other categories. By 1957 these rates had risen by fifty per cent as wage and other costs rose more rapidly. The outdoor staff were granted wage increases in 1950, 1951 and 1952, and in December 1953 an extraordinary general meeting was held to discuss the increasingly difficult financial position of the club. The bank overdraft had exceeded £1,000, and over £200 had still to be paid in outstanding bills. The meeting felt that cutting expenditure would impact on the condition of the course, and 'extra money must be spent if the buildings were not to fall into a worse state of dilapidation than they are at the moment'. The men's locker-room roof was leaking and the floor needed a new covering, the bar and dining room were in need of redecoration, and the outer walls of the clubhouse were also in need of painting. It was decided by a vote of forty-one to twenty-nine to increase the annual subscription to £10 from January 1954 to address the financial shortfall.[14] Another wage increase was given to the ground staff in March 1954, amounting to an annual

L–R: Jim O'Hea, Geoff Thompson, Jack Murphy, Douglas Loane. Photograph taken at Douglas, 1954.

Left, L–R:
Charlie Murphy,
Harry Atkins.
Right, L–R: Mick
Henchy, Jerry Murphy,
Dan McCarthy.
Photograph taken at
Douglas, 1954.

cost of £91. The growing problem of members defaulting on their subscriptions coupled with increasing costs led in January 1955 to the committee seeking an increased overdraft facility of £1,800 – the equivalent of 180 full annual subscriptions.[15] Wage rises continued to be sought and granted in 1955, 1956 and 1958, and bar and catering prices were regularly reviewed and increased as necessary. The club's financial position was closely examined again in October 1956, and a proposal that members be asked to make a voluntary contribution towards covering a loss for the year of £650 was defeated in favour of a rise in the subscription for ordinary members by twenty per cent to £12.[16]

The question of a telephone for the secretary's office illustrates the club's attitude to spending at the time. In 1957 the club still had only one telephone, housed in a telephone box. In that year, the committee discussed having an extension made from this to the secretary's office as he frequently had to leave his office to answer telephone calls. It was decided that the proposed extension would be for incoming calls only. The committee eventually decided not to make the proposed extension as the cost of 15s 6d per quarter was considered too high.[17]

By the AGM of 1960, club finances had taken a turn for the better, and it was reported to the meeting that in 1959 bar profits had risen by twenty per cent, subscription income by fourteen per cent and green fees by fifteen per cent.

Zelie Fallon

Zelie Fallon was one of the most outstanding golfers to have come out of Douglas, and won honours at provincial, national and international level. She was born Zelie Godfrey in 1926, and grew up in Mallow, County Cork. She was a champion tennis player in her teens, winning the Irish under-fifteen championship, and she later won the Munster senior singles championship and played at interprovincial level. Zelie turned to golf in 1947 after she married Jim Fallon, later president of Douglas (in 1950), and as a profile of her in *Irish Golf* in 1959 noted, 'Almost from the start, her "feel" for a game, her skill in timing and her natural athletic ability were invaluable assets, and she showed wisdom in placing herself in the hands of the Douglas professional, John McKenna.' So rapid was her improvement and so stylish was her golf that in 1951 – barely four years after first taking up the sport – Zelie was chosen as a substitute on the Irish team for the Home Internationals.

Above: Zelie Fallon with the Irish Amateur Close trophy 1964.

She won her first full cap the following year when she played for Ireland at Troon, and had a very promising debut, beating her English opponent by 5 and 4. Zelie held her international team place every year until 1965, regained it in 1968, 1969 and 1970, and was non-playing captain of the Irish team in 1972. In 1964 Zelie was non-playing captain of the British and Irish three-member team that competed for the Espirito Santo Trophy, the Women's World Amateur Team Championship, at St Germain in France.

As well as winning her first international cap in 1952, Zelie Fallon was also a member of the first Douglas team to win the Senior Cup, and played a significant part in the victory, beating her Milltown opponent in the final by 6 and 5, having beaten British international and Curtis Cup player Mrs Z Bolton of Royal Portrush in the semi-finals. Zelie was a member of the Douglas Senior Cup team every year from then until 1975, winning the national title another five times in that period.

Zelie Fallon won the Irish Amateur Close title only once, in 1964, and would undoubtedly have won it once or twice more but for the dominance of Philomena Garvey, who won the event fourteen times between 1946 and 1963. In 1958 Zelie played in her first Amateur Close final, but came up against the legendary Miss Garvey, and lost at the thirtieth hole of the thirty-six-hole match. In 1959 Zelie played Miss Garvey in the first round, as there was no seeding in the draw, and made an early exit. The year 1964 was to be Zelie's, however, when the event was played at Royal Portrush. She had a 'walk over' in the first round, and won her next four rounds before meeting Pat O'Sullivan of Tramore in the final. That was the last year the final was played over thirty-six holes, and Zelie won the title on the thirty-seventh hole. She was the first Douglas player to win a national title, and the club marked the occasion with a dinner and presentations. Zelie played in only two more Irish Amateur Close Championship, losing in the quarter finals in 1965 and in the semi-finals in 1968.

Zelie Fallon was chosen for the Curtis Cup panel for the 1960 meeting with the US to be played at Lindrick, but she unfortunately did not make the team itself, an omission that disappointed not only herself but her club-mates and the golfing press. Zelie was playing her best golf at this time. In 1959 she had won the Munster Championship for the fourth time, and was playing for Ireland for the eighth successive year. In the 1959 Home International series, played at Hoylake, Zelie was paired with Philomena Garvey in the foursomes, and they beat the top pairings from England, Scotland and Wales. In the singles, Zelie beat her English and Welsh opponents, and halved her match against Belle McCorkindale of Scotland. In November 1959 a piece in *Irish Golf* praised Zelie's performance at Hoylake, and suggested that she would make the Curtis Cup team:

> There are solid reasons to expect that she will actually take part in the contest ... The difference between Mrs Fallon's past record and this sudden leap to fame was one largely of temperament. For years she had hit her shots consistently and well until the pressure came on in an important match, and then she became nervy and tentative on the short shots. This time her chipping and putting were immaculate and

confident, and having realised that she can beat any of the top-liners, she could achieve her ambitions of winning national championships and gaining a regular Curtis Cup place.

In Munster, Zelie won the Ladies' Senior Championship in 1955, 1956, 1957, 1959 and 1961. She was playing captain of the Munster team in the inaugural Interprovincial Series in 1964, and she was a member of the team from then until 1974, with the exception of 1967. She was non-playing captain in 1975.

From the mid-1970s Zelie Gaynor, as she became known following her second marriage in 1967, withdrew from more-serious competitive golf and enjoyed a more leisurely, though never casual, approach to the game. Zelie was part of the Douglas Golf Club family for fifty-seven years, and had found great support there following the death of her first husband, Jim Fallon, in 1953 after only six years of marriage. Zelie married Paddy Gaynor in 1967, and later had to endure the difficulty of being widowed for a second time. Douglas was always her alternative home and family, and in April 1994 she presented the club with a collection of the medals and brooches she had won during her illustrious career. These are now displayed in the clubhouse dining room. When Zelie died in 2004, she bequeathed her 1964 Irish Amateur Close trophy to the ladies of Douglas, and the minutes of the 2005 Ladies' Club AGM record: 'Zelie's wish was that we, the Ladies of Douglas, would play for this in an annual competition.'

Many will remember Zelie Fallon as she was described in a magazine profile when she was at the peak of her golfing career: 'Tall and dark, graceful in every movement, she is an ornament to any golf course on which she plays, and she typifies the smartly turned-out, elegant modern champion.' As one of her long-time Senior Cup team-mates said: 'She was a lady if ever there was one'.

Senior Cup winners 1961. *L–R:* Girlie Hegarty, Peg McKenna, Zelie Fallon, Eileen O'Callaghan, Anne O'Brien.

Girlie Hegarty

Mary Monica Cotter was born in Cork in 1910, and although called Monica as a child, her brother called his sister 'Girlie', and it is by that name she was affectionately known by her family, friends and all in the golfing world. Girlie grew up in Cork, on Connaught Avenue, and went to St Aloysius' school where she played camogie. In 1925, at the age of fifteen, she was a member of the school team that won the final of the Junior Schools' Camogie Cup. Nine years later, Girlie won an All-Ireland senior camogie medal with Cork. She was also an accomplished hockey player, and played with Midleton. In 1938 Girlie joined Muskerry Golf Club, but had played golf for some years prior to that: her daughter Ann has a trophy her mother won at an open competition in Ballybunion in 1937. Girlie and her friends often cycled from the city to Muskerry to play. She married Jerry Hegarty in 1942, and joined Douglas Golf Club through the good offices of the then honorary secretary Julianne McCarthy. Mrs J F Hegarty is how Girlie is named in most official golf records.

Girlie was coached by Douglas professional John McKenna, and improved her game while also rearing four children, the third of whom, Ann, has won three Senior Cups with Douglas as well as captaining the team on two occasions. Girlie's great golfing talent was recognised in 1955 when she won her first cap for Ireland in the Home Internationals, and she was chosen again the following year, joining the other Douglas international, Zelie Fallon. In 1964 Girlie captained the Irish team for the Home Internationals at Troon. In the 1960s, the Douglas ladies were amongst the most successful golfers in the country, winning four Senior Cups and quite a number of international caps. Girlie won Senior Cup honours with Douglas in 1960, 1961, 1967, 1968 and 1973. She was on the Munster Interprovincial side in 1970, and captained the team in 1971. Girlie, like Zelie Fallon, was unfortunate in that the Irish Amateur Close Championship was dominated by the virtually unbeatable Philomena Garvey through the 1950s. Girlie got to the final in 1953 but was beaten by Miss Garvey, and in 1956, when Miss Garvey did not play, Girlie won through to the final only to lose to Pat O'Sullivan of Tramore.

Girlie Hegarty also contributed greatly to the administrative side of golf. She was a committee member at Douglas for many years, and was lady captain in 1957. Girlie served on the Southern District executive and the central council of the ILGU, and on the LGU executive council. The culmination of her administrative career was her three years as president of the ILGU, from 1974 to 1976. In 1982 she was elected honorary life vice-president of the ILGU in recognition of her contribution

Girlie Hegarty, 1967.

to women's golf in Ireland. When her playing career ended, Girlie was an Irish national selector.

Girlie always worked to promote golf amongst younger players. In 1983 she donated a trophy to the club for an annual scratch competition for women golfers under twenty-two years of age. It was first played for in 1984, and the first winner of the Girlie Hegarty Trophy was Ada O'Sullivan of Monkstown. Girlie sadly died just three months later, on 23 November.

Girlie is remembered as a great golfer and one who expected the best from the teams she was involved with. She was a good off-the-cuff speaker and could use her wit and humour to great effect. Another Douglas member of long standing says: 'Girlie was tough, but if you were down no one could be kinder.'

8 *The Swinging Sixties*

The 1960s was a decade of great change in Ireland. Economically and socially, the country moved closer to the mainstream of Europe and America, and the older certainties were slowly eroded. Young people now found their voice through music, fashion and political activism, and they gained an increased confidence through better access to education. Developments in communications, the growth of television, increasing foreign travel, the spread of liberal ideas and growing affluence all combined to create a more democratic and modern society that lost much of the conservatism of earlier years. The game of golf evolved also, and in Ireland its playing base broadened and the membership profile of golf clubs changed as the newly affluent – many of whose parents would have never aspired to become members of a golf club – now took up the game and embraced club life. A correspondent of *Irish Golf* noted the great upsurge of interest in golf in the 1960s, and cited television coverage, the improved earning power of the young, and the perception that golf was no longer 'an old man's game' as reasons for this. Many 'graduates' from pitch-and-putt clubs were also moving on to the longer game, and wider car ownership enabled enthusiasts to travel further afield for golf as clubs close to centres of population reached capacity.[1]

William Menton in his history of the Golfing Union of Ireland also discusses this period of expansion of the game in Ireland, and identifies three principal reasons for the growth.[2] In 1959 the Dunlop Masters, effectively a tournament of champions, was held in Ireland for the first time at Portmarnock, and Irish golf enthusiasts had the opportunity to see in action Ireland's leading professionals, Christy O'Connor and Harry Bradshaw, as well as players from abroad. The event captured the public imagination, and 27,000 attended over the four days of the tournament. Christy O'Connor won the title by 4 shots, with Joe Carr in second place. Secondly, the Canada Cup tournament, now called the World Cup, was held at Portmarnock in 1960, and thirty countries were represented. Again, the leading professionals from abroad played, and even larger crowds turned out to watch what was the biggest golf event ever held in Ireland. The third event cited by Menton that helped popularise golf was the opening

Facing page, L–R: Seán McHenry, Jack Sheehan (president), Jack Lynch (Taoiseach) at Douglas, 1967.

147

of Ireland's first television station, Telefís Éireann, at the end of 1961. By 1963 forty per cent of households had a television set, and while general sports coverage occasionally included golf, the transmission of a series from April 1963 called *Shell's Wonderful World of Golf* proved hugely popular with viewers, golfers and non-golfers alike.

Douglas Golf Club passed its fiftieth birthday in 1959, and was in rude health as it began its second half century. The club started the decade by acquiring outright ownership of its course at Maryborough, and finances continued to be in a good state in spite of this purchase. At the annual general meeting in February 1961, 'the best balance sheet ever produced at this Club' was presented, and two years later the AGM was told that 'Douglas was never doing better' financially. The club developed a driving range, improved the clubhouse facilities, and built a new pro shop and caddie shed. The course was also improved, and Douglas hosted the Dunlop Irish Professional Golf Tournament in 1963. Bill Kelleher was the club's most successful male golfer in the early 1960s, playing seventeen times for Ireland as well as playing for Munster on thirty occasions and winning a number of prestigious tournaments. The ladies of Douglas won the Senior Cup in 1960, 1961, 1967 and 1968, and brought honour to their club and country when Zelie Fallon, Ann Heskin, Oonagh Heskin (later Fitzpatrick) and Anne O'Brien played for Ireland at different times during the decade, while Girlie Hegarty captained the Irish team in the Home Internationals of 1964.

Course Purchase, 1960

Under the terms of the club's 1934 lease, the landowner, J P Saunders (who had married Miss McAuliffe), had the right to graze up to 270 sheep on the course. While such an arrangement had its advantages in earlier years, as the sheep kept the rough in trim, by 1960 the standards demanded by players of their course and advances in the quality of course maintenance rendered the situation extremely unsatisfactory. At the 1960 AGM (the first time it was held at the clubhouse), reference was made to the damage being done to the area around the first green by the lessor feeding his sheep there. One speaker is recorded as having remarked: 'It would be a great job if we could buy the land,' to which another replied: 'It would indeed be a great blessing if we were rid of the sheep.'[3]

An approach was made to Saunders some time later by the president, B G Burkley, and captain, Joe O'Donovan. By August 1960 a special meeting of the committee was told that negotiations were underway and that the lessor had initially asked for £10,000 for the land. The club had by then spoken to its bank about taking out a loan for the purchase.[4] The following month, the committee had a lengthy discussion about the tactics to be used in the negotiation, and it was decided that Joe O'Donovan would act on behalf of the committee and the club.[5] The club offered £8,000, but Saunders would only drop the asking price to £9,500. Joe O'Donovan was asked to make a further approach, and to ask Saunders 'to give in writing his rock-bottom figure'. Meanwhile, a sub-committee of four was formed to deal with the financial implications of the purchase.[6]

This sub-committee met with the club trustees a week later, on 21 October, and Joe O'Donovan gave a detailed report on his negotiations, informing the meeting that the vendor was holding firm on his demand for £9,500. He also presented a plan to fund the purchase whereby 100 members would advance a loan of £20 each, and £1 would be added to the annual subscription to cover the cost of servicing the additional bank loan. The captain's 'vast amount of work' on the matter was acknowledged, but the president seemed not to be convinced of the wisdom of the purchase at that price, and pointed out that the club would have the use of the course for a further twenty-four years under the terms of the existing lease. 'Should we allow ourselves,' he asked, 'to be stampeded for people who might not even use the course then?' One of the trustees spoke in agreement with that point of view, while another remarked: 'The same people will always be called on … the same spirit does not prevail here as in other clubs. Perhaps in another five or ten years enthusiasm might be keener.' An intervention by the club's honorary solicitor, Mr B Galvin, seems to have swung matters in the captain's favour when he pointed out that the price of the land was not too high 'having regard to what an asset it would be to own and to what it would likely be worth in years to come.'[7]

Ten days later, the captain reported to a special committee meeting that he already had £1,200 promised by way of advances, and that he was confident of raising at least a further £500. The committee felt that an EGM would reject the proposed purchase as the asking price was too high, and the captain was asked to convey this to Saunders in the hope that he would drop his asking price.[8]

An EGM, attended by ninety-five members, was held at the clubhouse on 25 November to consider the resolution that the club would purchase the course and premises for £9,250, the vendor having agreed with the captain to drop his asking price by a further £250. The members were also being asked to approve a £1 increase in the annual subscription to fund the loan repayments. The president proposed the resolution and was seconded by the captain, who presented details of the negotiations to the meeting. He set out four principal reasons for the purchase, the primary one being the sheep problem. He told the meeting: 'Douglas is the only one of the four

Cork Clubs with sheep on it. If we could get rid of the sheep our course would improve. Our golf would be more enjoyable.' He also pointed out that the club was getting good value for money, and that the £1 extra on the subscription and the loan of £2,000 from members were a small burden. Lastly, he said that the purchase would secure the future of the club:

> The owner tells us that he will not agree to the renewal of the lease when the present one expires and council's opinion is that as the law stands we have no right of renewal. We may never again get the opportunity to make the future of our club secure, we should buy now.[9]

Some speakers from the floor spoke against the purchase, pointing out that the lease had another twenty-four years to run, while others felt that the price, at just over £100 per acre, was too high. One speaker, with a sense of how land values were to increase, said: 'We should not hesitate in buying as the price might be £40,000 in 24 years!' A motion to offer to purchase the whole of the Saunders property was defeated. This motion was proposed as some felt that land adjoining the first, fifth and eighteenth holes, not included in the proposed purchase, could be developed later to the detriment of the club. The original motion was then put to a vote, and it was carried overwhelmingly, with only five votes against.

Following the EGM, matters were left in the hands of the club solicitor, Barry Galvin, as agreement had to be reached with the vendor regarding rights of way over the course before final contracts were drawn up. In August 1961 the committee approved the issuing of the cheque for the final payment to complete the purchase of the course.[10] Dominic Coffey, writing in *Irish Golf*, praised the club for buying out its course, and singled out Joe O'Donovan, 'the diplomatic skipper', for particular mention. He continued: 'It is quite an achievement, in an age when land for building can fetch fabulous prices, for the members of this prospering club to buy out their own ground, and thus ensure that golf will continue to flourish for many generations on the gentle slopes of Maryborough Hill.'[11]

Proposals to acquire more of the land adjoining the course began to be put forward in the late 1960s, but as the purchases were not completed until the early 1970s, the matter is dealt with in chapter 9.

Course Improvements, 1962–63

J P Ryan was president of Douglas Golf Club for 1962 and 1963, and drove a lot of the change that saw the club consolidate and prosper through the 1960s. He proposed the setting up of the finance and membership committees, pushed the necessity for long-term planning, suggested and oversaw the development of a driving range, and was president when the Dunlop Irish Professional Golf Tournament was held at Douglas in September 1963. In the year prior to that tournament, a number of improvements were made to the course, which had remained virtually unaltered since the Mackenzie redesign nearly forty years before. In July 1962 discussions were held with Muskerry and Cork golf clubs regarding the employment of a course architect on a shared basis, but neither club was interested. Douglas then contacted the firm of C K Cotton on its own behalf, and following a communication setting out its terms, a committee meeting in October discussed the actions to be taken. The president pushed strongly for proceeding with a redesign, stating that the club needed a clear five-year plan as things were being done in a haphazard fashion up to then. Despite some resistance from committee members, J P Ryan prevailed, and it was decided to engage the Cotton firm to come and report on the course.[12] Commander Harris visited Douglas in late 1962 or early 1963, and suggested a programme of improvements for the course, many of which were carried out before the staging of the Dunlop tournament in September.[13] Eddie Hackett, who later became a very well-known golf architect in his own right, was a member of the Cotton team at the time.

A report in *Irish Golf* in August 1963 details some of the changes undertaken to remodel the course 'in accordance with current championship trends':

> All the old type of grass bunkers have been eliminated, and plantations of trees have been introduced at strategic points to heighten the natural quality of many of the holes. The approaches to many of the greens have been tightened by excellent sand-traps, and modern sand-hazards crop up also to penalise the wayward drive at the 2nd, 5th and 17th holes. The new look appearance of the Douglas course is completed by the introduction of tiger-tees at the 2nd, 5th, 13th, 16th and 17th holes, but this move is countered to some extent with a new forward tee at the 18th. The latter hole thus becomes a par four instead of the usual five ... strict bogey for the round totals 72.[14]

In 1965 the greens committee suggested to the general committee that the formation of a separate handicapping committee would ease its burden of work and lead to an improvement in overall efficiency.[15] The matter was raised again ten months later, and the greens committee again recommended separate handicap and course committees.[16] The wheels of change can sometimes turn slowly, and following a rule change it was 1968 before the recommendation was implemented. From the AGM of February that year, separate greens and handicap committees were elected.[17]

The Dunlop Irish Professional Golf Tournament, 1963

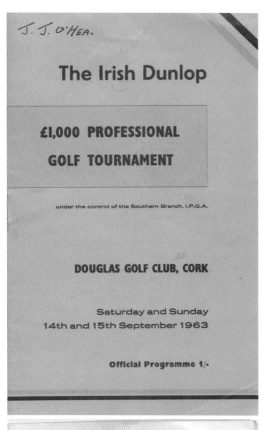

The prestigious Dunlop Irish Professional Golf Tournament was held at Douglas on 14 and 15 September 1963, the first time the event was organised outside Dublin, and was seen as a vote of confidence in the club and its course. It was a happy coincidence, no doubt, that Douglas president, J P Ryan, was managing director of the Dunlop manufacturing facility in Cork. Large crowds attended, especially on the second day, and the presence of Christy O'Connor, then Irish professional champion, was an added attraction. Forty-four professionals played two rounds on the Saturday, and the top twenty-four played two further rounds the following day, Sunday 15 September.

Nick Lynch of Sutton, a young professional aged twenty-five, led after the first day's thirty-six holes, having had a course record 68 in the morning and a 70 in the afternoon. The favourite, Christy O'Connor, was 5 strokes behind. On Sunday morning, Lynch and O'Connor were paired, and gave the huge gallery of over 2,000 value for their money when Lynch equalled his 68 of the previous day and O'Connor went one better with a new course record of 67. O'Connor was still 4 behind going out for the final eighteen holes, but it was felt that his greater experience would tell in the afternoon. The *Cork Examiner*'s golf correspondent wrote that the afternoon's round 'proved to be one of the most dramatic which this writer has seen through a summer of golf'.[18] By the turn, O'Connor had gained 2 strokes on his opponent, but poor putting by O'Connor allowed Lynch re-establish his 4-stroke lead by the sixteenth. O'Connor gained 2 strokes over the final two holes, but Lynch maintained his composure and won by a margin of 2, and pocketed the biggest prize of his career thus far, £175.

At the prize-giving speeches, Watty O'Sullivan of the Irish Professional Golfers' Association paid tribute to the excellent organisation of the

Starting Time a.m.	p.m.	Caddie No.	Name and Club	ROUNDS 1st	2nd	Total
9.30	1.40	1	J. McGuirk (Kilkenny)	75	78	153
		2	F. Condon (Monkstown)	76	78	154
		3	J. Williamson (Massereene)	80	83	163
9.38	1.48	4	R. J. Browne (A) (Foxrock)	73	72	145
		5	J. Kinsella (A) (Castle)	72	73	145
		6	W. Robertson (Belvoir Pk.)	81	78	159
9.46	1.56	7	J. Kelly (Tullamore)	76	72	148
		8	G. Brown (Rosslare)	82	76	158
		9	A. E. Bacon (A) (Castlerock)	74	80	154
9.54	2.04	10	C. K. Neill (Bray)	76	77	153
		11	C. Kane (Unattached)	74	74	148
		12	P. O'Boyle (A) (Elm Park)	81	83	164
10.02	2.12	13	E. Jones (Bangor)	76	71	147
		14	J. Henderson (Clandeboye)	75	72	147
		15	J. Carroll (Grange)	75	76	151
10.10	2.20	16	C. Connolly (Corbalis)	81	71	152
		17	H. Dobbs (Shandon)	82	74	156
		18	V. Steward (Ballycastle)	87	80	167
10.18	2.28	19	A. Murphy (A) (Royal Dublin)	77	76	153
		20	E. Bradshaw (Delgany)	no return		
		21	D. Williams (A) (Sutton)	79	80	159
10.26	2.36	22	D. O'Brien (Killiney)	73	76	149
		23	K. O'Connor (Elm Park)	80	85	165
		24	J. McKenna (Douglas)	74	74	148
10.34	2.44	25	J. McGonigle (Sligo)	76	76	152
		26	D. A. Stevenson (Royal Portrush)	76	77	153
		27	P. O'Connor (Royal Dublin)	77	71	148
10.42	2.52	28	C. Greene (Milltown)	73	73	146
		29	J. Craddock (Foxrock)	74	77	151
		30	J. Bradshaw (Edmondstown)	72	74	146

Match No.	Starting Time a.m.	p.m.	Caddie No.	Name and Club	ROUNDS 1st	2nd	Total
11	10.50	3.00	31	S. O'Connor (A) (Royal Dublin)	78	74	152
			32	H. Bradshaw (Portmarnock)	70	75	145
			33	D. Patterson (Warrenpoint)	no Score		
12	10.58	3.08	34	T. Curtin (A) (Unattached)	77	80	157
			35	D. Higgins (A) (Cork)	73	74	147
			36	F. McGlain (A) (Bundoran)	78	79	157
13	11.06	3.16	37	C. O'Connor (Royal Dublin)	71	72	143
			38	W. Sullivan (Rathfarnham)	73	75	148
			39	R. Kelly (Castlerock)	74	74	148
14	11.14	3.24	40	J. Martin (Unattached)	73	73	146
			41	N. Lynch (Sutton)	68	70	138
			42	P. Skerritt (St. Annes)	71	76	147
15	11.22	3.32	43	M. Murphy (A) (Royal Dublin)			
			44	T. Rooney (Mullingar)			

(A) denotes Assistant.

Hole No.	Yards	Bogey	Hole No.	Yards	Bogey
1	271	4	10	336	4
2	375	4	11	380	4
3	448	5	12	403	4
4	148	3	13	375	4
5	430	5	14	418	4
6	381	4	15	146	3
7	187	3	16	390	4
8	486	5	17	337	4
9	322	4	18	423	4
	3048	37		3208	35
				3048	37
				6256	72

REQUESTS TO SPECTATORS

1. Comply with instructions from Stewards.

2. Avoid any movement, disturbance, or noise while a player is making a Stroke.

3. Do not walk across the Greens or through the Bunkers or New Plantations.

4. Do not use Movie Cameras where their noise would distract the players.

tournament, and praised the club president, J P Ryan, and captain, J T McSweeney, for their work. The attendance was the largest ever for the event, and *Irish Golf* remarked: 'In view of the unusually big gate, the organisation of which was in the capable hands of Seán McHenry, it would seem that the Douglas venue provides not only a test of golfing ability but fine facilities for viewing.'[19] The *Cork Examiner* agreed:

> The tournament was magnificently run and the club … rated considerable praise from players and spectators alike. It was an exceptionally successful event and put Douglas in the top rank. The fact that so few players broke 70 speaks for its sternness as a test of golf.[20]

First and second-round scores as recorded in the programme by J J O'Hea.

1962 Douglas internationals Zelie Fallon and Bill Kelleher with club president, Jim Ryan (left), and club captain, James Kelleher (right).

Golf

In the 1960s Douglas Golf Club was rarely out of the golfing news. Bill Kelleher came to prominence shortly after joining the club in 1959, and within two years was playing off scratch (see feature on Bill Kelleher, pp. 167–71). He played on the Munster team from 1962 to 1966, and played for Ireland seventeen times between 1962 and 1964. Bill Kelleher made international headlines when he won the final match of the Home International series at Porthcawl on his international debut in September 1962 to give Ireland a tie for victory. As well as winning a number of scratch cups, he also made headlines when he won the South of Ireland Championship in 1964 after an epic final against John Nestor. He joined another former pitch-and-putt champion and Douglas scratch-man, Tadg Higgins, on the Senior Cup team that got to the national semi-finals in 1962.

In the early stages of the competition, Douglas comfortably beat Cork on their home course, and then beat the Munster favourites, Killarney, by an emphatic four matches to one. The Douglas team was Tadg Higgins, Bill Kelleher, Hugh Coveney, Norman Butler and Con Collins. According to the report in the *Cork Examiner*, Hugh Coveney was 'the hero of the night' when, 1 down after sixteen holes, he shot two birdies to win by 1. 'Splendidly-built, young Billy Kelleher showed again his all-round exceptional ability' as he won 6 and 5. 'Stylish Norman Butler … produced a blitz finish' for his win, while 'a diminutive Con Collins won a ding-dong battle' against his opponent, and finished 1 up. Tadg Higgins was the only Douglas player to lose his match.[21] Douglas were now through to the Munster final against Limerick, which was played at Ballybunion. Douglas beat Limerick

3 and 2 in a dramatic final that was decided on the twenty-first green when an on-form Tadg Higgins defeated Munster interprovincial Pat Walsh. The Senior Cup national finals were played at Royal Portrush on 24 July, and Douglas played Shandon Park in the semi-finals. Shandon Park had won the Senior Cup in 1960 and 1961, and were the form team again in 1962. Douglas were roundly beaten 4½ to ½, Tadg Higgins being the only Douglas player not to lose. In his match against John Duncan, he was 3 down but staged a magnificent fighting finish of 4, 4 and 4 to level. They were still square after the nineteenth when called in.[22] Shandon Park went on to beat Galway and win the Senior Cup for the third year in a row.

Éamonn McSweeney, John Morris and Christy Synnott were other Douglas players who distinguished themselves in scratch cups and open competitions in those years. *Irish Golf* reported Douglas Golf Club's championship in late 1963, which featured 'a grand struggle' between Bill Kelleher and 'a newcomer to the golfing scene', John Morris, playing off 2. Kelleher won with a new amateur course record of 67, equalling Christy O'Connor's record set in September.[23] In September 1964 the Douglas team of Christy Synnott, Jim O'Hea, Tadg Higgins, John Morris and Éamonn McSweeney won the Kinsale Scratch Cup, and in April the following year Bill Kelleher and Tadg Higgins narrowly beat Joe Carr and Noel Fogarty to win the Killarney Scratch Cup.

1962 Senior Cup Munster Champions. *Standing, L–R:* T Higgins, N P Butler, H P Coveney, E C Synnott, C Collins. *Seated, L–R:* J P Ryan (president), W A Kelleher, J J Kelleher (captain).

1969 Douglas internationals. *Back, L–R:* Anne O'Brien, Girlie Hegarty, Ann Heskin, with John McKenna. *Front:* Oonagh Heskin (left), Zelie Fallon (right), with lady captain, Mary Mackesy.

Douglas Ladies Show the Way!

While the men of Douglas deservedly made headlines during the 1960s, it was the ladies who firmly put the club on the golfing map with four Senior Cup victories, an Irish Women's Close champion and a number of Munster Senior Championship wins. Douglas ladies were also on every interprovincial and international team during the decade.

In 1960 the Senior Cup finals were played at Cork Golf Club. On their way to the finals, Douglas beat Lahinch and Cork, and in the semi-finals defeated the holders Royal Portrush. In the final, Douglas beat County Louth (Baltray), holders of six Senior Cup titles. The Douglas captain was Maura Coffey, and the other team members were Zelie Fallon, Girlie Hegarty, Anne O'Brien, Eileen O'Callaghan, Madeleine Murphy, and Peg McKenna, who only played in the match against Lahinch.

In 1961 Zelie Fallon was at the top of her game, and won a fifth Munster Senior Championship playing on her home course at Douglas. She later led the Douglas ladies to a third Senior Cup victory at Newcastle, beating Lahinch, Ballybunion and Cork to win in Munster, and then beating Galway and Tullamore before defeating old rivals Royal Portrush in the final. Zelie Fallon was captain, and the other team members were Girlie Hegarty, Anne O'Brien, Eileen O'Callaghan and Peg McKenna.

In 1962 the Douglas ladies again won the Munster final of the

1960 Senior Cup champions.
Standing, L–R: Eileen O'Callaghan, Madeleine Murphy,
Anne O'Brien,
Peg McKenna.
Seated, L–R: Zelie Fallon, Maura Coffey,
Girlie Hegarty.

Senior Cup but were not able to repeat the national victory of the previous year. Ann and Oonagh Heskin joined Douglas in 1963 at the invitation of Girlie Hegarty, and they very soon became members of the Senior Cup team, and in 1964 won the Munster area final of the Senior Cup, which was to be the first in a series of twenty consecutive provincial titles. Douglas dominated Munster ladies' golf until that remarkable run was broken in 1984. Their fourth Senior Cup was won in Castlerock in 1967. Oonagh Heskin was captain and the other members of the team were Anne O'Brien, Ann Heskin, Zelie Fallon, Girlie Hegarty, Eileen McDaid and Peg McKenna. They beat Donabate 4½ to ½ in the semi-finals, and overcame Royal County Down 3 to 2 in the final.

The Douglas domination of the Senior Cup in the 1960s continued the following year, 1968, and having comprehensively beaten Castletroy 5 to 0 in the Munster area final at Thurles, the team went on to the national finals at Lahinch. There, they beat Royal Portrush 3 to 2 in the semi-finals, and defeated Milltown 4 to 1 in the final. Anne O'Brien captained the side, and the team members were Oonagh Heskin, Ann Heskin, Zelie Gaynor (formerly Fallon), Girlie Hegarty and Peg McKenna.

In 1964 Zelie Fallon became the first Douglas player to win the Irish Women's Close Championship at Royal Portrush, beating Pat O'Sullivan of Tramore in the final at the thirty-seventh hole. This event had been dominated for years by Philomena Garvey, who

1967 Senior Cup champions.
Standing, L–R:
Eileen McDaid,
Anne O'Brien,
Peg McKenna,
Ann Heskin.
Seated, L–R:
Zelie Fallon,
Oonagh Heskin (captain),
Girlie Hegarty.

had won eight of the previous ten finals. It was not until 1993 that another Douglas player, Eavan Higgins, again won the title.

In 1969 Douglas again won through in Munster, and met Woodbrook in the final at Ballybunion. The same team as 1968 played in the preliminary rounds, but Zelie Gaynor was involved in a car accident en route to Ballybunion, and missed the final matches. Her replacement, Rosemary O'Regan, played well but the supreme skill and experience of Zelie Gaynor was missing, and Woodbrook defeated Douglas in the final 3 to 2.

At international level, five Douglas ladies won caps at different times during the 1960s. The Home Internationals are held annually, and teams of eight from Ireland, England, Scotland and Wales compete over three foursomes and six singles matches. Zelie Fallon (Gaynor after 1967) was on the Irish team in the Home Internationals every year from 1952 to 1965, and again in 1968 an 1969. Girlie Hegarty won international caps twice in the 1950s, and captained the Irish team for the Home Internationals in 1964 that were played at Royal Troon. Anne O'Brien was a reserve for the Irish team in 1964, 1966 and 1968, and she was on the Irish team at the European Championship at Tylosand in Sweden in 1969. Oonagh Heskin was a reserve for the Irish team in the Home Internationals in 1963 and 1968, but was a full team member in 1967. She was selected to play again in 1969 but had to cry off for personal reasons, but did play

at the European Championship in Sweden that year. Oonagh's sister Ann won her first Irish cap in 1969, and was capped four further times in the 1970s.

In the 1960s the Munster Senior Championship, which had been inaugurated in 1949, was won by Douglas ladies on four occasions: Zelie Fallon in 1961, Anne O'Brien in 1963 and 1967, and Oonagh Heskin in 1969. The Irish Ladies' Golf Interprovincial Series was first played in 1964, and with the exception of 1969, when the series was not played, a number of Douglas players were on the Munster team each year. Zelie Fallon, Anne O'Brien, Oonagh Heskin, Ann Heskin, Ide O'Riordan and Tess Hennessy played with their province on different occasions in those years, all six being on the team in 1964.

New Facilities

The purchase of the course in 1960 and the continuing financial health of the club also enabled the committee to look at upgrading the course and its facilities. The first phase of work was undertaken in 1962, and consisted of a new pro shop and caddie-car shed, and the surfacing of the carpark. There was some debate as to the siting of this new building, and eventually, having taken an architect's advice, it was decided to locate it near the twelfth tee. The work was completed by the end of the year and cost almost £4,000. 'The striking modern building that houses an attractive shop for professional John McKenna, as well as a spacious caddie-car store' – as reported in *Irish Golf* – is still (2009) serving the needs of club members.[24] The corrugated-iron structures in the carpark that had housed the pro shop and caddie-car store were removed.

The confidence that the committee and members at Douglas were feeling in the early 1960s led to the development of a driving range, a facility rare in Ireland at the time. At a meeting of the general committee in July 1962, the president, J P Ryan, suggested that a driving range would be a good source of revenue for the club as well as being beneficial to members.[25] A sub-committee was formed to look into the matter, and much advice was given by the Elm Park club in Dublin, where a successful driving range had been developed. It was decided to locate the driving range behind the newly built pro shop, and a modest tender of £320 for the work was accepted.[26] The range was officially opened on 2 February 1963; the president, J P Ryan, the captain, J J Kelleher, Irish internationals Bill Kelleher and Zelie Fallon, and club professional John McKenna were the first to drive off. Douglas members were initially charged 2s 6d for fifty balls, while members of other clubs paid three shillings. The range proved to be very popular, and *Irish Golf* wrote: 'It is grand to see golfers, male and female, ranging in handicap from scratch to the limit, bashing away, happily yet seriously, under the floodlights.'[27] It was soon found that the four bays were insufficient. Extra mats were placed outside the covered area to increase capacity. Over the following ten years or so, the driving range was a good source of revenue for the club, but by 1974 its continuing viability was being questioned. Usage had dropped and a storm had destroyed the roof. It was decided to replace the roof at a cost of £340, but by 1978 it was considered 'no longer a viable proposition'.[28]

The club bar had been the subject of frequent complaint by members. It was regarded as unattractive and unsuitable. At an AGM, one speaker said: 'it is the most uncomfortable bar I ever sat in, where one cannot hear what the person next to me is saying.'[29] The debate about improving the bar reflected what was happening in the changing society outside. Publicans were upgrading their bars and adding 'lounges' to cater for more demanding consumers and for the growing number of women who increasingly felt more confident about frequenting places that were traditionally the preserve of men. The bar at Douglas was for men only, women being served through

John McKenna at the driving range.

a hatch from their own lounge. At a committee meeting in 1962 that discussed possible improvements, one member suggested that 'it would be a help to allow mixed drinking'.[30] The bar was redecorated as an interim measure in 1963, and the suggestion by a committee member that 'the advice of a lady expert on colour schemes etc could be freely procured' shows the persistence of the old attitudes.[31] Ladies were permitted in the bar on the weekly bridge nights and 'on definite occasions'.[32] A committee meeting in December 1964 decided that the question of giving women full access to the bar would be put to a ballot of members, and four days later – at an EGM called to approve planned clubhouse improvements – the proposal was approved on a show of hands.[33]

In March 1964 a sub-committee was appointed to look into the matter of a major refurbishment of the clubhouse, and a firm of architects was engaged to prepare plans. In July a proposal was put before the committee for an upstairs bar, costing approximately £15,000. This was rejected in favour of a ground-floor scheme. New plans were presented to the committee in October, and put before an EGM on 18 December 1964. Ninety-four members attended, and a lively discussion followed President J P Ryan's presentation, which stressed the need for modernising and having clubhouse facilities in keeping with the high standard of the course. While it was generally felt that improvement was necessary, there were dissenting voices whose objections caused one member to remark: 'I have no time for those who go around complaining.' A member who asked if there would be a reduction in the annual subscription if the new bar proved very profitable was told he had 'a child's mind'! Sixty-one voted in favour of the general proposal, while thirty-two voted against.[34]

A special committee meeting decided on the specifics of the alterations, and tenders for the work were examined in July 1965. Three tenders were submitted, and that of Coveney Bros. – being the lowest at £11,583 – was accepted. Thirty-two weeks were allowed for the work. A week or so later, the committee agreed to an extra £1,200, as the building firm had neglected to include costs associated with a heating system. At the AGM in February 1966, some dissatisfaction was expressed with the cost of the building works, as the original estimate had been exceeded by more than £2,000. It was explained by the president, J J Condon, that the plans had been changed somewhat and that extra costs were thereby incurred. He added that going back to members for approval would have delayed matters.[35] The newly refurbished bar was officially opened on 11 June 1966. The total cost of the work was £15,000.

In another concession to modernity, the club acquired its first television set in late 1962. At a committee meeting in May 1960 – some eighteen months before Telefís Éireann began broadcasting – a member suggested that the club should install a television as 'the time was near at hand when such things would be in general use'.[36] The matter was deferred. In November 1962 it was decided to get a television 'with a view to improving social amenities or attracting more people to the clubhouse'.[37] A set was first rented, and in March 1963 a Pilot television set was purchased for £81 8s 0d. The set was initially located in the billiard room, and moved to the bar some months later, but it was reported that it did not bring in the expected extra income.

Finances and Membership

Shortly after he was elected president of the club, J P Ryan proposed that a finance committee be set up – reporting to the general committee – so as to better enable the club plan and manage its finances. While club finances were in a very healthy state in the early 1960s, the level of expenditure on improvements up to 1965 changed matters somewhat. Over £29,000 was spent on the purchase of the course, carpark surfacing, a new pro shop and caddie-car store, and a new bar. An EGM was held in December 1966 to approve an increase in the annual subscription of £2 to £18 for full members and pro rata for other categories. This was to cover higher staff wages, increasing insurance costs and the repayments on loans taken out to fund development work. Some members expressed anger at the proposal, and pointed out that the subscription had already been increased by £2 at the beginning of the year. The underestimate for the cost of the clubhouse was also criticised, as was the £13,000 overdraft, more particularly as the 1965 balance sheet had shown a surplus of £2,400. The proposal was defeated by a large majority.[38] This made things difficult for the committee during 1967, and at the AGM in February 1968 a proposal to increase the subscription by £3 to £19 was approved by a comfortable majority, the reality of the difficult financial situation having been effectively communicated to the membership. A proposal from the floor of the meeting that lady associates pay a disproportionately higher subscription was not put to a vote, one speaker saying 'we should not put a burden on the ladies who brought home the Senior Cup'.[39] By the beginning of 1970, the club was in a much stronger financial position, and only £4,000 was still owing to the bank.[40]

The popularity of golf in the 1960s began to put increasing pressure on the club. The growing suburbs of Douglas, Ballinlough and Blackrock were home to a large population, many of whom wished to play golf and become members of Douglas Golf Club, whose course was conveniently located nearby. Prior to 1963, the general committee dealt with all matters relating to membership, and the policies and procedures for admitting new members were often decided on an ad hoc basis, resulting in frequent confusion. In September 1961, for example, a waiting list for proposed new members was established, but the relatives of existing members and those with low handicaps were excepted. It was also decided that an entrance fee of £5 would apply for ordinary members and £3 for ladies. The entrance fee was deferred the following month, and less than a month later reimposed at the rate of £3 for men and £1 for ladies. It was also decided that 300 would be the maximum number for all categories of male membership, and 160 for ladies.[41] Arising from objections to the entrance fee expressed at the AGM in February 1962, it was decided to discontinue the fee, effective from 1 January 1962.[42] By October 1962 the question of closing the club to all new members was raised, and one committee member proposed that 'we should be careful and selective from now on'. It was decided not to issue any further proposal forms, and to establish a waiting list.[43] As much of the general committee's time was being taken up with debate on membership issues, the president, J P Ryan, asked: 'can we get a small committee to consider and recommend who should be elected in all categories?' Following this, a membership sub-committee – later a committee in its own right – was formed, and began to function from the beginning of 1963.[44]

While this initiative dealt more effectively with membership issues, the problems associated with the selection and election of members continued, and became a perennial feature of club business, leading occasionally to controversy and acrimony. The club had to limit its membership numbers, and then balance the demands of individual members for the admission of family, friends and business associates against the needs of the club as a whole. The officers and committees had to act in a way that would sustain the club, not just as a social club but also as a sports club that would attract and nurture new golfing talent and field teams capable of success in competition. This balancing act became increasingly difficult.

Douglas had a student category of membership since 1950, and students paid a reduced subscription – usually about a third of that for a full member. There were about twenty students in the club, but it was sometimes felt by ordinary members that they did not deserve what was perceived as special treatment. At an EGM in 1962 a number of complaints were made that students were using the course more than full members and that they should consequently pay a bigger subscription. It was also said that they frequently held up play. One member spoke on behalf of the students, and said that slow play was not the fault of the students 'but that of older members who treated them with contempt and gave them no encouragement'.[45] At the AGM in February 1964, similar complaints were again made, and one speaker felt that, at twenty-three, the club had too many student members, especially as there were so many on a waiting list for full membership.[46]

Some members paying the full subscription also took exception to the concession made to members under twenty-five years of age. From 1960 their subscription was half that of a full member, and the concession was a cause of annoyance to some full members, especially when an increase in the subscription was being proposed. At a special committee meeting in December 1962, a committee member objected to the under-twenty-fives having to pay only half the increase being applied to the full members: 'some of those young fellows are earning as much as men a good deal older and without the same responsibilities.'[47] A proposal that members of at least fifteen years standing and who were over sixty-five years old be given the same concession as the under-twenty-fives came before the AGM in 1963. The debate became heated, and again some full members strongly objected, the minutes noting that one speaker felt 'most of the people in question were well off and many of them had their own business', while another said 'it galled him to hear those who proposed and seconded the motion. They were the people who opposed the motion giving a concession to the under 25s and also restricted their numbers.' The proposal was carried.[48] The under-twenty-five category was abolished in 1967; from then on, members over twenty-one years of age paid the full subscription.[49]

The membership committee – first set up at the end of 1962 – slowly found its feet, and gradually formulated its criteria for the selection of members to be recommended to the general committee for election. Pressure from an increasing number of applicants continued, however. In July 1964 there were thirty-nine on the waiting list, and the membership committee suggested an entrance fee of £10 for the nine they recommended for election. By the following month, the number on the list had increased to sixty, and the general committee decided to apply the £10 entrance fee 'as a way of finding out who is really serious'. The committee also decided that the president and captain would be 'active members' of the membership committee.[50] During 1965 sixty-three members were elected to various categories of membership, and in January 1966 it was decided that only the sons and daughters of existing members could be elected as student, juvenile or junior members. A proposal in 1968 that applicants with a low handicap be given preference for membership – with a view to improving the club's competitive record – was strongly opposed by members of the general committee, who pointed out that some people had been over two years on the waiting list and 'would have a genuine grievance if elections were made as suggested'.[51] In 1969 the membership limit for men was increased by fifteen to 340, and it was decided to raise the limit on ladies to 170. Within months, the quota for men had been exceeded.[52]

The annual subscription in 1960 was £12 for ordinary members and pro rata for the other categories. During the following ten years, there were five increases, bringing it to £26 for 1971, an increase of 117 per cent. Douglas Golf Club continued to be the club of first choice of so many in succeeding years that it was never without a waiting list. This continued until 1981, when the waiting list was discontinued in favour of an alternative method of selecting members for election. This thorny issue of the selection and election of new members grew more contentious, and eventually led to threats of legal action and a consequent reappraisal of procedures in the 1990s (see chapter 9).

Air Disaster, 1968

On Sunday morning 24 March 1968 an Aer Lingus Viscount aircraft on a flight from Cork to London crashed off the Tuskar Rock with the loss of all those on board. The disaster shocked the country and more especially the Cork region, as most of the passengers were from the area. Three members of Douglas Golf Club were amongst those killed: Noel Mulcahy, Noel Nunan and Gus O'Brien. All three were active and well-known members of the club, and Noel Nunan and Gus O'Brien were committee members. The minutes of a special meeting of the committee held the following day record the following:

> The President said we were gathered here under very sad circumstances to pass a vote of condolence to the relatives of three valuable members of our Club who lost their lives in the tragic air disaster yesterday. He paid tribute to each of the deceased, two of whom he said were members of our Committee.

This meeting was particularly difficult for the president, Miah Heffernan, as his nephew had been co-pilot on the ill-fated plane. The minutes continue: 'Mr Sheehan said we should all join in a vote of sympathy to the President who lost his nephew and other friends in the disaster … Before the close of the meeting a minute's silence was observed, all present standing.'[53] On the following 1 December, a silver memorial plaque to the three club members who died was officially unveiled in the clubhouse.

Bill Kelleher

Bill Kelleher was born in 1934, and came from St Columba's Terrace in the heart of Douglas village. He was one of Ireland's finest pitch-and-putt players while still in his teens, and won the pitch-and-putt Matchplay Championship of Ireland in 1954 and 1959. Like Tadg Higgins some five years earlier, Bill Kelleher's supreme natural talent at the shorter game attracted the attention of those who saw a potential that could be adapted and developed for the related sport of golf. Bill Kelleher became a member of Douglas in 1959, and within a year the golfing press was noting his talent: 'Bill Kelleher ... a young man with a great future at the game ... he has now added power from the tee to guile on the greens'.[1] John Heffernan, writing in *Irish Golf*, recounted a story of Bill's first days at Douglas:

Bill Kelleher with the South of Ireland Championship trophy, J J O'Hea, captain (left) and G F Thompson, president (right), 1964.

Some five years ago at Douglas Golf Club three very average golfers in search of a fourth asked a strong-looking young man to join them. The young man confessed that he had not yet been given a handicap but that he'd be delighted to make a fourth. His companions, who doubtless felt that they had not been as hard-up for a fourth as all that, smiled bravely nevertheless and conceded him the limit of 18, whereupon the young man protested that as he had played quite a bit of pitch and putt, if they wouldn't mind, he'd play this match off 8 or less. They settled for eight handicap, and set out prepared to spend much of the afternoon fagging the new member's ball from various roughs. His partner on that occasion still speaks with immense satisfaction of how this young man proceeded to give the three of them a lesson in power golf, hitting the ball great distances, if somewhat erratically, with the woods, but always landing on the green, where the putts invariably dropped. The new member, whose name was Bill Kelleher, was subsequently given a handicap of eight.[2]

This handicap stood at scratch by June 1961, two years later, when Bill won the Joe Morrissey Memorial Trophy at Muskerry. In August of the same year, he went to Lahinch to play in the South of Ireland Championship, acquitting himself well by reaching the quarter final, where he was beaten by John Fitzgibbon. In spite of this defeat, the commentators again saw his potential:

The name of Bill Kelleher will be one to conjure with in Irish golf before very long. The critics were loud in their praise for the form and power revealed by this sturdy newcomer, exactly two years in the game ... It will be a serious crime against the fair cause of Irish golf if the Kelleher talents are allowed to wither and die for want of advice, help and opportunity.[3]

In 1962 Bill Kelleher began to achieve the success many had been predicting for him. In May of that year, he was a member of the Douglas team under Tadg Higgins that reached the finals of the Senior Cup. In July he played in the Irish Amateur Close at Baltray, losing his quarter final on the nineteenth to David Sheahan of UCD, the reigning champion. Kelleher, 'the best putter in the field', had been three up with four to play, and 'his defeat was nothing short of tragic', as one newspaper put it. He played for Munster in the Interprovincials at Portrush in July, and was beaten only once there. Bill Kelleher won his first international cap in September 1962, and had a dream debut.

International Debut, September 1962

The Home Internationals were played at Porthcawl in Wales that year, and Bill Kelleher stunned players, spectators and commentators by winning all of his six games over the three days. Joe Carr, quoted in a *Cork Examiner* report, said of Kelleher: 'We have been looking for a hero for a long time and here's our man!' He was paired with Tom Egan of Monkstown in the foursomes, and on the first day against England they beat D W Frame and B Critchley 3 and 2, while Kelleher beat Critchley 2 and 1 in the singles. England beat Ireland on that first day, but Ireland had an easy victory over Wales on the second. The final day for Ireland against Scotland proved to be most dramatic, and the two countries were tied on 8 apiece when Bill Kelleher went out against M C Black in the last match. As the *Irish Independent* wrote: 'the whole burden of responsibility rested on the inexperienced but broad and capable shoulders of Kelleher'. A win for Kelleher would result in a three-way tie for victory between Ireland, England and Scotland.

Kelleher was 3 up after seven, but had lost his lead by the tenth. He rallied again, and was 1 up after sinking a 10-foot putt on the sixteenth, and was still 1 up playing the last hole, which he had to halve to ensure a victory for Ireland and the three-way tie with Scotland and England. Kelleher's drive hit heavy rough and he had to play out well short of the green, with Black already on the green after 2. As P A Ward-Thomas wrote in *Country Life*: 'The situation, stirring enough in all conscience and well nigh unbearable for the supporters of three countries, was further spiced by the fact that this Kelleher had been pitching and putting people to death throughout the meeting.'[4] Kelleher's 70-yard third shot landed 12 feet from the hole. Black got his 4, and now Bill Kelleher had to sink his 12-foot putt to win. N J Dunne wrote in the *Irish Independent*:

> This is the kind of situation that makes a golf hole seem like a mere pin-prick, but Kelleher, who says he always putts to win, stroked it straight and true into the centre of the hole, and the resounding cheers of the Irish contingent must have startled the occupants of the nearby rest-home for miners.[5]

Kelleher had won, and Ireland shared the title. The *Cork Examiner* noted that 'it seemed almost incredible that only twelve months ago he had not even made the Munster team, and even stranger still, that four years ago he was not even playing golf'.[6]

Bill Kelleher had arrived. The press in Ireland and Britain lavished praise on him: 'He swings the club with an effortless rhythm, foundation enough for a remarkable talent', 'his putting had to be seen to be believed', 'the greatest performer of the week', 'Like a figure from a fairytale, Bill Kelleher rose to dreamy heights at Porthcawl' are typical of what was written. When he and his playing partner Tom Egan returned to Cork airport, several hundred people turned out to meet them, including Douglas president, J P Ryan, club captain, J J Kelleher, and ladies international, Zelie Fallon.

Despite his remarkable successes in 1962, Bill Kelleher was not invited to play in the Walker Cup trials at Turnberry in 1963, a decision that disappointed many. However, he continued to make golfing headlines. In April 1963 he won the Castletroy Scratch Cup by 1 stroke, with a total of 142 for the thirty-six holes. As at Porthcawl the previous year, he finished dramatically, having an eagle 3 on the eighteenth to win. Bill Kelleher was on the Irish team that played the Home Internationals at Lytham & St Anne's, but not with the success of the previous year.

Bill Kelleher (left), winner of the South of Ireland Championship, 1964, with John Nestor, runner-up.

South of Ireland, 1964: 'The greatest final'

At Easter 1964 Bill Kelleher was beaten in the final of the West of Ireland Championship by Brian Malone of Portmarnock, but at the South of Ireland in August, he hit the golfing headlines once again. On this second visit to Ireland's longest established provincial championship, he was a more mature and experienced golfer, and played steadily through the preliminary rounds on the famous Lahinch course. In the quarter finals, he beat Martin O'Brien (New Ross) by 3 and 2 (O'Brien later won the Irish Amateur Close title in 1968 and 1975). In his semi-final, Kelleher had a comprehensive victory over Greg Young (Kilrush), winning by 5 and 4. In the final, Bill Kelleher met John Nestor of Milltown, the last time the final of this championship was played over thirty-six holes. Recalling this match, an obituary of Bill Kelleher in the *Evening Echo* in 1997 noted: 'This has been recognised by all as the greatest final in the history of the oldest of the provincial championships.'[7]

Nestor had the better of the morning's eighteen holes, and was 1 up at the break, having gone round in 68. Bill Kelleher was playing catch-up through the first eighteen, and time and again was holing out for a half. 'Not that Kelleher looked as if he needed pity, for he was quite unperturbed by the succession of long putts that continued to rob him of holes almost won, and put him in danger of losing them', wrote John Heffernan in *Irish Golf*. He continued:

> But the afternoon round was Kelleher's, though he lost the first hole
> of it to a possible eagle. Two down now, he was really in trouble and
> his opponent kept up the pressure relentlessly. Yet Kelleher matched
> Nestor's birdie and par at the next two holes and then stole a hole
> at the 22nd with a brilliant birdie. At the 25th he drew level but at
> the next Nestor was in front again, and he was still 1 up at the turn.
> Here the new Champion produced some super golf, which Nestor just
> could not equal, winning the 28th with a birdie four and then having

a run of three threes which Nestor just could not match. Kelleher was now two up with 5 to play. The next three holes were halved, two of them with birdies, and now the Douglas man was dormie two. At the 35th Kelleher put his tee shot 50 yards or more in front. Nestor's second found the green nicely but his opponent's iron-shot stopped two yards from the pin, and when the Dublin man's long putt just stayed out it was all over, and Bill Kelleher had brought the South of Ireland Championship to Douglas ... Not since Redmond Simcox's win in 1926/27 had the men of Douglas won a Championship.[8]

Apart from his wonderful debut at Porthcawl in 1962, this was Bill Kelleher's finest hour, and it earned him a place in the annals of Irish amateur golf. A month later, in September 1964, he played for Ireland at the Home Internationals at Carnoustie, having held his place on the international side since 1962. In the singles matches, he won one, lost one and halved one, and had the same results in his three foursomes. That was Bill Kelleher's last international outing. In his three years as an international (1962–64), he played seventeen matches, winning ten and drawing two.

In February 1965 at its AGM, Douglas Golf Club marked the achievements of Bill Kelleher, its most successful golfer, by making him an honorary life member. *Irish Golf* reported on the event as follows:

> The acclaim of the members and the many eulogies [*sic*] expressed on this happy occasion give testimony to the popularity of this great golfer on his home course ... Not since the hey-day of Father Daniel Fitzgerald has Douglas produced a golfer like Bill Kelleher, whose epic battle with John Nestor at Lahinch last summer has already passed into golfing history. In his short career in golf Bill's fame has spread far and wide but he himself remains unchanged. He is a fine sportsman and it would be difficult to find a more unassuming golfer.[9]

He continued to play with some distinction on the Munster interprovincial side until 1966. In all, he played thirty times for Munster over that five-year period, winning fifteen matches and drawing five. While Bill Kelleher did not again attain the heights of those years, he continued to play competitive golf with some success, and was a regular member of Douglas Senior Cup and Barton Shield teams. He was always a loyal Douglas man, and he enjoyed his golf and cards in the company of his many friends up to his death in 1997.

9 *1970s*

Douglas Golf Club came of age in the 1960s, and developed a confidence that put it to the forefront of the game in Ireland. The club had produced players like Bill Kelleher, who not only won tournaments like the South of Ireland but who also represented his country with distinction. The Douglas ladies became a golfing power in Ireland, and won four Senior Cups while also having players on the Irish team in every year of that decade. The ladies maintained much of that winning energy in the 1970s, and although their male counterparts did not excel to the same extent, young players like John McHenry and John Morris junior were being nurtured, and made a national and international impact in the following decade. The 1970s saw the club continue a process of modernisation as new committees were formed to facilitate long-term planning and development, while new officer-ships were created to aid administrative continuity. The clubhouse

was extended, and new land acquired as the club sought to secure its boundaries and give the opportunity for course development. The world outside of golf impacted on the club as rampant inflation saw the annual subscription rise from £26 in 1971 to £134 in 1981, a rise of over 500 per cent. The cost of running the club greatly increased also, and the growing need for good financial control saw the reintroduction of the position of honorary treasurer in 1975. Douglas hosted the Dunlop Irish Professional Golf Tournament in 1971 and 1977, and hosted the Carroll's Irish Matchplay Championship in 1972, an indication that the course was still of championship standard.

Golf

In the early 1970s Bill Kelleher was still golfing to a high standard and competing regularly on Douglas teams. In 1971 he was joined by his brother John, Robin Turnbull and John C Morris on the Barton Shield team. (John C Morris had, like Bill Kelleher, been a champion pitch-and-putt player, and had won the Irish Matchplay title in 1958.) They beat Tipperary in the Munster final, but in the national semi-finals were beaten by Malahide (Malahide went on to win). Bill and John Kelleher lost by four holes to Raymond Kane and Tom Craddock, while John C Morris and Robin Turnbull lost by three to Paddy Caul and Michael Craddock.

The Pierce Purcell Tournament was first played in 1970, and

Facing page:
1971 Barton Shield Munster champions.
Standing, L–R: W A Kelleher, R A F Turnbull, J C Morris, J Kelleher.
Seated: J M O'Connor (president; left), and P R Elwood (captain).

1976 Pierce Purcell Munster champions.
Standing, L–R: B Waters, D Olden, C Buckley, B Cunningham, S O'Donoghue, S Mackey, G Mills, M Mullin.
Seated, L–R: F O'Brien, R Elwood, D Barry, R J Magnier (president), D V Collins (captain), J J O'Hea, T O'Halloran, A Madden.
Inset: F McQuillan.

was established to provide a national and provincial competition for higher-handicap players who would not be selected for Barton Shield, Senior Cup or Junior Cup competitions. Teams consist of ten players who play by foursomes, and players cannot have a handicap lower than 12, while each pairing is allowed a maximum combined handicap of 27. In 1976 the club enjoyed some success in this tournament, and won the Munster final at Lahinch. In the national semi-finals at Tramore on 24 September, Douglas was beaten 3½ to 1½ by Roscommon, the eventual winners of the competition. Finnian McQuillan and Dan Olden won their match, and Tadgh O'Halloran and Con Buckley halved theirs. The other Douglas pairs were Bernie Waters and Dermot Barry, Ray Elwood and Jim O'Hea, Michael Mullin and Seán Mackey. Brian Cunningham had played in place of Seán Mackey in earlier rounds. Success in the major competitions eluded Douglas for the rest of the decade.

While the 1970s were relatively lean years for the men of Douglas, the ladies picked up the slack somewhat, and won the Senior Cup in 1973 and 1978. In the Munster section of the competition, they continued their dominance, winning the final every year from 1964 to 1983. In 1973 they beat Castletroy in the Munster final, and defeated County Sligo 3 to 2 in the national semi-finals at Bundoran. In the final, they beat Milltown by the same margin. The Douglas team was led by Ann Heskin and the other players were Girlie Hegarty, Zelie Gaynor (formerly Fallon), Anne O'Brien, Rosemary O'Regan and Margot Murphy.

In 1976 and 1977 the Douglas ladies were beaten in the national final of the Senior Cup by Royal Portrush. In 1978, however, they denied Royal Portrush their three-in-a-row, beating them 4 to 1 in the final at Grange. The Douglas number-one was Rhona Hegarty, and the other team members were Ann Heskin, Anne O'Brien, Eavan Higgins, Mary Sheehan and Nuala Horan.

Zelie Gaynor played for Ireland in the Home Internationals for the last time in 1970, having won her first cap in 1952. She was non-playing captain of the Irish team in the Home series in 1972. Ann Heskin won caps in the Home Internationals in 1970, 1972, 1975 and 1977, and was a reserve in 1971 and 1979. Eavan Higgins did not win her first cap until 1981 but was a reserve on the Irish team in 1976, 1978, 1979 and 1980. Douglas ladies continued to play on the Munster team through the 1970s. Zelie Gaynor, Anne O'Brien, Ann Heskin, Oonagh Heskin (Fitzpatrick) and Eavan Higgins all played on the interprovincial side, and Girlie Hegarty was non-playing captain in 1971.

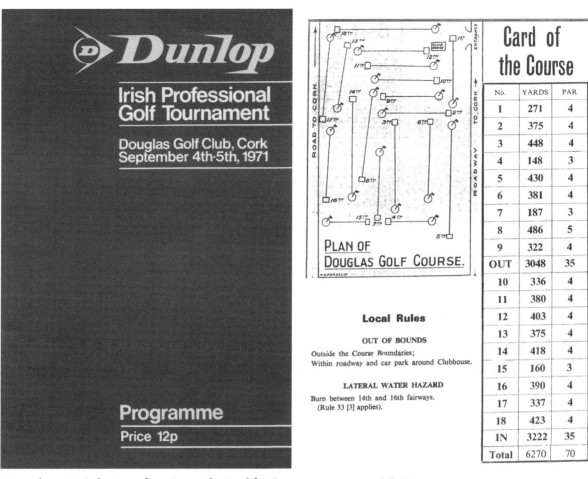

PLAN OF DOUGLAS GOLF COURSE.

Local Rules

OUT OF BOUNDS

Outside the Course Boundaries;
Within roadway and car park around Clubhouse.

LATERAL WATER HAZARD

Burn between 14th and 16th fairways.
(Rule 33 [3] applies).

Card of the Course

No.	YARDS	PAR
1	271	4
2	375	4
3	448	4
4	148	3
5	430	4
6	381	4
7	187	3
8	486	5
9	322	4
OUT	3048	35
10	336	4
11	380	4
12	403	4
13	375	4
14	418	4
15	160	3
16	390	4
17	337	4
18	423	4
IN	3222	35
Total	6270	70

Dunlop Irish Professional Golf Tournament, 1971

In September 1971 the Irish Dunlop Professional Golf Tournament was staged for the second time at Douglas, and had a prize fund of £2,000. On Friday 3 September Ireland's first professional putting championship took place for a £50 first prize and the title of Dunlop Pro Putter of the Year. All fifty-four professionals played in the new event, which was won by Eddie Polland (Balmoral). The two-day championship proper began the following day, with the first thirty-six holes of seventy-two being played, twenty-four qualifying for the final rounds. Hugh Jackson (Knockbracken) was favoured to win, but at the end of the first day's play, he was well down the field. John O'Leary (Foxrock) and Christy Greene (Milltown) were joint leaders on 138 going into the second day's play. Jimmy Kinsella (Castle) began to challenge in the third round, and with a 2-under-par 68 he led by 3 from John O'Leary going into the final round. Kinsella was never really challenged in the final round, and shot a 71, giving him 279 for the seventy-two holes, a winning margin of 4. Paddy Skerritt (St Anne's) and Jimmy Martin (Pine Valley) were joint second, and John O'Leary was third. In addition to the £500 first prize, Jimmy Kinsella was invited to play in the Dunlop Masters held later that month. Coincidentally, 279 was also the winning score when the tournament was first held at Douglas in 1963. The club made £566 profit from the tournament.

Carroll's Irish Matchplay Championship, 1972

In October 1972 another prestigious tournament was held at Douglas, the Carroll's Irish Matchplay Championship. It was planned as a three-day event for Friday, Saturday and Sunday 27–29 October, but due to bad weather and fading light on the third day, the final was held over to Monday. While fifty-nine professionals played in the tournament, there was some negative comment in the press about the absence of some of the top names: Christy O'Connor senior, John O'Leary and Peter Townsend were playing in Spain, and Jimmy Kinsella, who had won the Dunlop Irish Professional Golf Tournament at Douglas a year before, was travelling to Australia.

On Friday the preliminary round of twenty-seven-holes strokeplay was played, with the leading sixteen qualifying for the matchplay stages of the event. As the *Cork Examiner* correspondent put it, 'That's what makes it all the more interesting. The really big guns may be missing, but the man-for-man combat will still be fascinating.'[1] Only one of the qualifiers, Tommy Halpin (Naas), beat the par of 105, with a 103 – 3 strokes ahead of the next best. Fifteen players qualified on 109 or better, and with six finishing on 110 a sudden-death play-off was held to decide the final qualifying place. Three went out on the first tie hole, another faltered at the fourth, and the final qualifier, Paul Leonard (Whitehead), took the last place after winning the fifth tie hole.

Hugh Jackson (Holme Hall), Leonard Owens (Killiney), Tommy Halpin (Naas) and Roddy Carr (Sutton) won through to the semi-finals, which were played in atrocious weather conditions on Sunday 29 October. Dermot Russell of the *Cork Examiner* wrote:

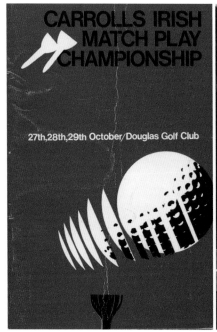
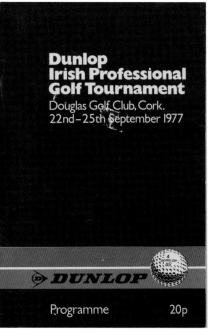

Dreadful it was … with a gale lashing the merciless rain horizontally across the course and every green showing some flooding. Not a shot could be played without the ceremony of drying the hands and the grip of the club. Between them the four semi-finalists used up some twenty towels on this procedure alone. Gripping the club was hazardous, swinging it was desperately difficult as the rain battered the face and the wind pulled at the body.[2]

Owens beat Jackson 4 and 3, while Carr beat Halpin by one hole in the more exciting of the two matches. The conditions persuaded the organisers to postpone the final until Monday morning, when Owens beat Carr 4 and 2 and took the £500 first prize. The final was unusual in that only two holes, the eleventh and twelfth, were halved.

Dunlop Irish Professional Golf Tournament, 1977

In 1977 Douglas hosted its third Dunlop Irish Professional Golf Tournament from 22 to 25 September. The prize fund was a very attractive £5,000, with £1,000 going to the winner. Amongst the seventy-five competitors were all the big names in Irish professional golf: Eamonn Darcy, the title holder and Irish Ryder Cup player, Jimmy Kinsella, Liam Higgins, Paddy Skerritt and Christy O'Connor junior. Eddie Polland withdrew the day before the tournament began, to the annoyance of the Irish PGA and the sponsors. The very popular putting championship was held on Wednesday 21 September, and was won by Jimmy Martin. Retired Douglas professional John McKenna came joint second.

After the first day's play in the four-round tournament proper, the top places were held by the form players: Hugh Jackson on 67, Eamonn Darcy on 68, and Christy O'Connor junior and Peter Townsend on 69. John McKenna shot 74, while his replacement at Douglas, Gary Nicholson, had 75. The weather deteriorated on the second day, and the competitors had to contend with gale-force winds. Peter Townsend was the only player to break par, with a 69 that gave him a 2-stroke lead at the halfway stage of the tournament. Hugh Jackson was second, and Christy O'Connor junior shared third place with four others, 5 strokes off the lead. Eamonn Darcy was a stroke further back, having had a 76 for his second round.

Peter Townsend maintained his lead through the third day's play, and shot 66 for his final round to win on 276, 3 strokes ahead of the field. Eamonn Darcy came in second, with 64 for his final round, the lowest tournament score in Ireland for fifteen years. Liam Higgins, who came third on 281, was the most disappointed player as he had been leading the field by 2, with eight holes to play, but Darcy's record-breaking 64 and Townsend's methodical and steady 66 left him trailing as he dropped shots over the last holes.

The tournament drew large numbers of spectators over the five days, and the final day's play – with Townsend, Darcy and Higgins jostling for the lead – had given the galleries a thrilling finish. Having now hosted three major professional tournaments since 1971, the club and its course had garnered much positive press coverage, and the officers, members and ground staff had shown that they were well capable of preparing for and organising such events. Scores of volunteers acted as stewards, while the greenkeeper, Paddy Keogh, and his staff had managed to maintain the course to an exacting professional championship standard. The ladies section of Douglas organised the catering for the spectators, making a profit of £107 45*p* from their tea-and-coffee stall at the event.[3]

Land

The 1960 purchase of the course secured the future independence of the club. Once that deal was complete, a sense of insecurity then grew in relation to the lands that bounded the course along most of its perimeter. As the 1960s advanced, the building of suburban housing estates at increasing distances from the city began to threaten the club, and it was felt that the land bounding the course would eventually be developed to the detriment of the club. Over a thirty-year period, beginning in the 1960s, the club was involved in attempts to acquire tracts of land on its boundaries, most especially to the left of the first fairway, to the right of the fourth and fifth, and to the left of the seventeenth and eighteenth.

In 1967 an approach was made by the club to John P Saunders regarding the land to the left of the first hole, which was considered ideally located to be developed as a carpark. The land was not for sale, but the club asked to be given the first option on it if it were to be sold.[4] The following year, some of Saunders' land to the left of the eighteenth was offered for sale, and the committee decided to make an offer on it. In November 1968 it was decided to offer £3,000 per acre for the field, but the club's solicitors advised that an offer nearer to £7,000 would be more realistic.[5] The committee decided to make an offer for the land adjacent to the first and fifth fairways in addition to that by the eighteenth – an area of about fifteen acres. An offer of £30,000 met with the reply, 'Our clients instruct us that they would not be interested in selling at anything like the price offered.'[6] The committee continued in its attempts to negotiate a satisfactory price, and in July 1969 was informed that the asking price was still £3,000 per acre, and that Saunders wished to sell all his land bounding the course – twenty acres in all – as one package.

While this negotiation was continuing, the president, J J Heffernan, was making approaches to Larry Cotter with a view to buying a parcel of almost fifteen acres adjacent to the fourth fairway. The ongoing wrangling over land prompted the committee to explore the possibility of the club moving to a new location, and enquiries were made about the possible purchase of lands at Old Court near Rochestown, which could be developed as a new Douglas golf course. A sub-committee investigated the proposal, but it came to nothing.[7] The growing uncertainty about the future of the club in an area of potential housing development caused the president and Joe O'Donovan – who had successfully negotiated the course purchase in 1960 – to hold discussions with the county manager about the possibility of housing being built in the vicinity of the course, 'and were told that it would be about 15 years before planning permission would be granted in this area'.[8] At a committee meeting following these discussions, the president said 'that it should go out from this meeting that a long term plan must be considered', and at the club AGM in March 1970, the new president, Hedley Graham, repeated the need for such a plan. Many speakers from the floor were also in favour, and suggested the formation of a planning committee. In June a special meeting of the committee was held to address the issue, and, agreement having been reached that 'we stay and develop this place', a land committee was formed.[9] Eventually, a decision was taken to buy approximately four acres of land to the left of the eighteenth, and a small strip 40-feet wide as a passway forward of the first tee. This was approved by the membership at an EGM, and the deal was finally agreed in August 1971, at a price of £12,300.[10]

The acquisition of the larger plots of Saunders' land adjacent to the first and fifth holes continued to be an issue for the club, and a deal was not finally agreed for their purchase until 1989, approval having been given by an EGM in 1988 (see chapter 9). In 1973, however, a developer proposed building a number of houses on the sixteen acres of Saunders' land by the fifth fairway. This alarmed the committee, and a series of meetings was held with the developer to register the club's concerns about possible trespass on the course, especially by children, and the danger of stray balls causing injury to residents if the building went ahead. Agreement was reached about the building of a wall to protect the course boundary, but the development failed to get planning approval and did not go ahead. While discussions were underway about this proposed development, another development company, Windsor Estates, approached the committee with an offer of £550,000 for the course, which was declined.[11]

The Cotter land to the right of the fourth fairway continued to exercise the committee through the 1970s, 1980s and 1990s, and many approaches were made to Cotter over a period of almost thirty years with a view to purchasing it, but a deal was never agreed. Larry Cotter died in 1996.

Building and Improvement Works

During the 1970s a number of building and improvement works were undertaken at the club. In 1970 £6,000 was spent on improvement works to the kitchen and men's locker rooms. The following year, a further £6,000 was spent on an extension to the bungalow occupied by the club steward, and in 1974–75 the carpark was properly surfaced and the entrance to the club from Maryborough Hill was rebuilt. In November 1975 it was proposed that the lounge be extended and refurbished, and that a new office be built for the secretary-manager. Architect and club member Brian Wain drew up plans for these works, and the proposed cost was estimated to be about £25,000. At the AGM of 27 February 1976, it was decided to postpone the building work, and to concentrate on redecorating and improving the bar instead. This work was complete by August 1976.

The question of a major extension to the clubhouse was revisited in October 1976, and a detailed report by Seán Jordan and Conor Clune on the need for such an extension was presented to the committee. A large extension costed at £117,000 had been recom-

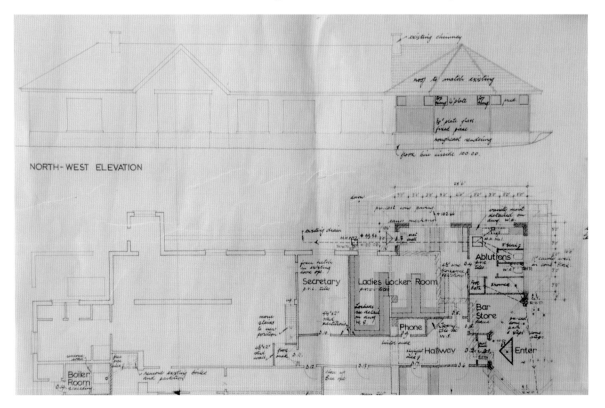

NORTH-WEST ELEVATION

mended in 1970 by a house sub-committee, but, because of soaring inflation, by 1976 the equivalent sum would be in the region of £300,000, a figure considered far too high for the resources of the club. A modified version of that plan was decided upon, whereby a second storey built on the existing walls would be added to the clubhouse, thereby providing the additional space needed. This modified proposal was costed at £70–75,000.[12] Brian Wain drew up plans for the work, and presented them for committee approval in January 1977. The plan proposed a large extension to the dining room on the ground floor, as well as a second-floor area for offices, billiard room, meeting room, and other facilities. This plan was presented to members at the AGM in February 1977. The cost was estimated at about £80,000, and it was proposed to finance this with a £25 levy on full members and pro rata for other categories, in addition to electing an additional twenty-five new members. The issue was hotly debated, a number of members expressing the opinion that the course should be improved rather than the clubhouse, while others objected to paying an increased subscription. The proposal was carried on a vote of 121 to 47.[13]

Tenders for the work were examined in September 1977, and the lowest of £77,192 was accepted. Work began on 27 September, immediately after the Dunlop Irish Professional Golf Tournament held that year at Douglas. As the project advanced, there were some changes to the original plan that added to the costs. By April 1978 it

Plans for extension to the clubhouse, drawn by Brian Wain (captain, 1982).

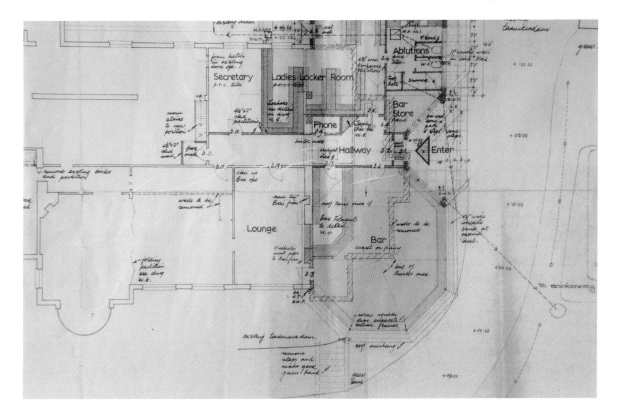

was reported to the committee that the building cost had increased by over £20,000 to £97,765, while the cost of furniture, billiard table, decoration, drapes and so on would bring the total cost to £122,089.[14] This did not unduly concern the committee, as rampant inflation had become a feature of everyday life in the 1970s. The new extension was officially opened on 15 July 1978.

During 1971 a watering system for the greens was installed at a cost of about £8,000. The system began to give trouble within a short time, and remedial work was eventually carried out in 1975 at a cost of £2,500. No major work was carried out on the course itself during the 1970s, but in 1974 the greens committee made a strong recommendation that a golf-course architect be engaged to inspect the course and suggest improvements. The committee agreed to the recommendation, but it is not recorded whether or not the matter was pursued any further.[15] As it was, the course met with the requirements of the Irish PGA for the holding of the Dunlop Irish Professional Golf Tournament in 1977. The only work on the course recorded in the minute books at this time is the removal of bunkers from the eleventh and twelfth holes, the extending of some tees, and alterations to the practice area near the eighteenth on the land acquired in 1972.[16]

Administration

At the club AGM held on 28 February 1969, a motion was passed to create the position of vice captain. The club captain, F C McGrath, chose Des Barry as the first vice captain in May 1969, and he then joined the general committee. He resigned in January 1970, and the position remained vacant until Pat Barry was chosen by 1971 captain, Ray Elwood. From 1976, the vice captain was elected at the AGM. The office of vice-president was created by decision of the AGM in February 1979, and the first to hold the position was F C McGrath.

The financial affairs of Douglas Golf Club were becoming more complex as the 1970s advanced. There was much expenditure on building and other improvement works, and with the impact of soaring inflation and rapidly increasing costs, it was proving quite difficult to plan and exercise proper financial control. Between 1970 and 1975, for example, the club had spent £41,000 on improvement works, and there were plans in the making to spend a lot more in the coming years on a major extension to the clubhouse. A new secretary-manager, T D Coffey, had been appointed in 1974, and the committee took advantage of the change to introduce new accountancy arrangements and to update the administration of club affairs. At the AGM in March 1975, it was decided that an assistant would be employed to aid the secretary-manager. In 1975 the position of honorary treasurer was reintroduced after a gap of forty-four years with a view to improving planning and control in financial matters; the honorary treasurer was to present a monthly statement of revenue and expenditure in all areas of club activity to the general committee. Seán Cody was the first to hold the new position. Through the second half of the decade, costs continued to rise, and there were increases in the annual subscription every year, taking it from £26 to £134 for 1981. While inflation, borrowing for building projects, high interest rates and occasional deficits all caused difficulties during the 1970s, the improved financial management introduced in 1975 enabled the club to continue to prosper and meet the challenges successfully.

From 1931 the minutes of the AGMs were typewritten, but the minutes of other meetings continued to be handwritten. It was not until 1954 that a typewriter was purchased for the use of the secretary, Patrick Corrigan. The matter was discussed on a number of occasions at committee meetings from late 1953, but it was April of the following year before it was eventually decided to purchase a second-hand portable machine. The minutes of committee meetings were typewritten from March 1975, the last handwritten minutes being those of 5 March 1975.

Membership

The continuing popularity of Douglas Golf Club resulted in a constant pressure from aspiring members. The membership committee, under the chairmanship of Joe O'Donovan, continued to wrestle with the difficulties presented as the number of those seeking membership continued to increase while the number of vacancies in any one year remained relatively constant. In September 1975 the club had 351 ordinary members and 181 lady associate members, but the waiting list for those seeking membership had grown to 329 men and 143 ladies, a level that rendered the idea almost useless for most of those on the list.[17] The waiting list seemed to be the only option open to the club as it endeavoured to be seen to be fair to all. The intractability of the problem was discussed at the AGM in February 1976, with the president, Jim O'Hea, saying that 'The membership position continued to be a mighty problem, with an enormous waiting list and no solution in evidence'.[18] Length of time on the waiting list was not the sole criterion for selecting new members; golfing ability, relationship to existing members and one's potential contribution to the club were also taken into account. It was not until 1981 that the problem of waiting lists was addressed.

The greatest difficulty in relation to the election of new members arose when people who were not related to existing members were elected ahead of the wives or children of members. This issue arose, for example, in relation to the selection of juvenile members. The committee had proposed a juvenile category of membership for twenty-five boys and twenty-five girls in 1925. At an EGM called to formalise the proposal, the committee's motion was defeated in favour of a motion that the sons, daughters, brothers or sisters of members under the age of nineteen would be allowed play the course on the payment of reduced green fees.[19] At the AGM in February 1950, it was carried that a juvenile category of membership be created open to children under eighteen years of age, paying ten shillings per year, while those between eighteen and twenty-one would be classed as junior members and pay £2 2s 0d.[20] In 1956 the age range for juveniles was set as twelve to sixteen years, and in 1966 it was decided that only the sons and daughters of members could be elected as juvenile, junior or student members.[21] The club had encouraged juveniles to join during the 1950s and 1960s, and special efforts were made to encourage young golfing talent, Gerry Roseingrave being particularly active in this area at the time. As these juvenile and junior members became adults, they had an understandable expectation that they could automatically become full members, and thus large juvenile and junior sections could potentially create problems for the future. This difficulty was debated at the AGM in 1974, and it was decided to have a maximum of forty-five in the juvenile section, the vast majority of whom would be the children of members, in addition to four children with no familial connection to the club.[22] The general committee discussed the issue subsequently, and was of the opinion that accepting 'outside' juveniles could deny membership to some children of members, even though it was proposed to take in only four from outside the club 'family'. On reflection, however, the committee accepted the recommendation of the AGM.[23]

John McHenry

John McHenry is the third generation of his family to have an association with Douglas Golf Club. John's grandfather and namesake joined the club in the early 1930s, his grandmother was lady captain in 1959, and his parents, Seán and Patsy, are long-time and active members of Douglas: Seán was captain in 1965 and president in 1979 and again in centenary year, 2009, while Patsy was lady captain in 1977. It was natural, if not preordained, that John would play golf, and he joined Douglas as a juvenile in 1977 when he was thirteen years old.

As a boy, John McHenry was involved in many sports, and his natural talent coupled with a determined will to achieve gave him an early taste for winning. While he enjoyed team games, such as rugby, it was in individual sports that he excelled. He played tennis at interprovincial level, was a successful competitive swimmer, and was a scratch pitch-and-putt player as he entered his teens.

When John began playing golf at the age of thirteen, he had a handicap of 18. Within eighteen months, he was playing off 3, and by the age of sixteen he was playing off scratch. He made his first senior team appearance at fifteen when he played on a Douglas team that came second in the Kinsale Scratch Cup in 1979. At the same time, he played with more youthful golfers – his contemporaries on the Christian Brothers' College inter-schools golf team.

As soon as John had the golf bit between his teeth, he did everything possible to progress: he practised daily, going to the course in the early morning and again in the evenings, and often broke club rules and etiquette by playing out of hours and sometimes playing more balls than he should. This youthful enthusiasm occasionally landed him in hot water, but as he explains: 'If I was to progress, I simply had to do those sorts of things … I simply had to be out there more.' In those early years, John was coached by his father and by retired club professional John McKenna, whom he found tough and authoritarian, but a gentleman. McKenna helped with the technical elements of his swing, and Gary Nicholson – who had come to Douglas in 1977 – enhanced those elements as well as giving John an understanding of the competitive side of the game. 'I found Gary to be a huge part of my life then, giving support, being there to tweak a club, play nine holes with me or have a putting competition,' John recalls.

In June 1980, at the age of sixteen, John McHenry won the first major championship of his amateur career, the Youths' Amateur Open Championship of Ireland, played that year at Clandeboye. According to a newspaper account, 'he shattered the field' in the first round with a 5-under-par 67. While the scoring in his subsequent three rounds was less shattering, he still won the event by 2 strokes from Philip Walton, then a senior international. The win gave John confidence and an understanding of his talent and potential: 'I suddenly had an appreciation of where I was, my status in Irish golf.' That winning way continued through the rest of that summer as John won the Kerry Boys' Open at Ballybunion and the Connacht Open Youths' Championship. He won his first international cap when he was selected for the Irish team for the European Youth Championship played in Dusseldorf, where Ireland finished third, and played in the Junior World Cup at St Andrews with Kevin McDaid, getting to the semi-finals. John McHenry had arrived as a serious amateur golfer, and in August 1980 the *Cork Examiner* called John 'one of the most exciting golf prospects in his native city since the pre-war days of the late, legendary James Bruen'.

John McHenry maintained his form through 1981, comfortably retaining his Irish Youths' Amateur title, playing for Ireland at boy and youth level, and making his debut on the Munster junior team that won the interprovincial title. At club level, he played in the final of the Senior Cup, and was the only Douglas player to win his match when Douglas went down to Bangor 3½ to 1½. He was also a member of the Douglas team that won that year's Kinsale Scratch Cup.

In 1982 John finished secondary school, and was awarded a scholarship to study for a degree in business at William and Mary University in Virginia, US. At this time, Philip Walton – his friend and rival on the amateur circuit – was studying

Left, Winner Youths' Amateur Open Championship of Ireland, 1980.
Right, 1984 Irish youths' international team, winners of the European Championship.
Standing, L–R: J Morris junior, J McHenry, E O'Connell, J Carvill. *Seated, L–R:* P Murphy, W J J Ferguson (president, GUI), F P McDonnell (non-playing captain), J Farrell.

at Oklahoma State University on a golf scholarship. Reflecting on the choice he made at the time, John believes that, from a golf perspective, Walton made the better choice as his university was more focused on golf whereas William and Mary was strong academically but with golf secondary to that. 'If I was ruthless about my game I would have gone to a far higher pedigree of golfing college,' he says, 'but there was more than golf in my life, and the US was a great experience. Those were the best four years of my life in terms of growing up, understanding who is John McHenry and so on … I progressed as an individual, but I don't think my game progressed as it should have.' In making his choice, John had hoped to keep options open – progressing academically in tandem with improving at golf – and while not regretting the decision, he can now see that his game needed something more: 'My talent brought me to where I was when I was eighteen, but what I needed between eighteen and twenty-two was a structure, a golf tuition package that would fine tune and hone my game, that would enable me to understand why I play good shots and why I play bad shots. In other words, I would have been almost converted into a machine in that period of time.'

John returned to Ireland every summer during his studies, and continued to impress as an amateur. He won the Muskerry Scratch Cup in 1983 and 1984, and won the Waterford Scratch Cup in 1984, 1985 and 1986. In September 1984 he was on the Irish team for the European Team Championship held at Hermitage Golf Club, and made a key contribution to Ireland's victory. In September 1985 John McHenry won his first senior international cap when he played in the Home Internationals at Formby, playing six matches and winning three.

In 1986 John completed his studies at William and Mary University, and returned

THE EIGHTY-FOURTH
SOUTH OF IRELAND
Open Amateur Golf Championship
26th - 30th July 1986

Bank of Ireland

Top: John McHenry, (right), with the 1986 South of Ireland trophy, and Liam McNamara, runner-up. *Below:* 1986 South of Ireland programme cover.

to Ireland to enjoy what was the best period of his golfing life. Having won the Waterford Scratch Cup for the third time, and after winning a quadrangular international tournament with Ireland against France, West Germany and Sweden, John went to Lahinch in July to play in his fifth South of Ireland Championship. It was a strong field that included all the Irish international players of that year. John won through to the semi-finals stage without undue difficulty, and there met the championship favourite, Garth McGimpsey, whom he beat 3 and 2. He played Liam McNamara of Woodbrook in the final. One of the newspaper accounts of that match noted that 'the difference in the match was that McHenry's work on the greens won the day'. He single-putted six times in the opening twelve holes, was 2 up after fourteen, and as good as clinched the match with a memorable par 4 on the fifteenth:

> It was straight out of the book of Seve Ballesteros – McHenry seemed doomed when he pulled his drive into the rough. It meant he could do no more than hack the ball safely onto the fairway. Still, he had 145 yards to go to the green. His line to the flag was obscured by a high mound, yet he drew gasps of disbelief from the huge gallery when he smacked the ball to within eight feet of the hole and slotted the putt for one of the best conceived pars ever witnessed at that hole.

John won 3 and 2. John Redmond wrote in the *Irish Press* that John McHenry was 'an exciting young golfer who, on the strength of this breakthrough, now seems to have the potential to flower into one of Ireland's great players'. That win was one of the highlights of his career – Ireland's oldest provincial championship, played in a magnificent arena, a title won in the past by two other Douglas greats, Redmond Simcox and Bill Kelleher.

Less than a week later, John won the Mullingar Scratch Cup, and then travelled to Royal Dublin

for the Irish Amateur Close Championship, beating Paul Rayfus of Trim in the final 4 and 3. Speaking to reporters, he said: 'The past fortnight has been like a dream come true. To have won three major events in the space of fourteen days is a great thrill.' Following those victories, John McHenry was presented with the Willie Gill Award by the Golfing Union of Ireland for being the year's highest achieving amateur. He also played for Ireland in the Home Internationals at Harlech in September, and again showed his mettle when he beat England's Peter McEvoy 2 and 1 in the singles – only the second time McEvoy was defeated in fifty-one Home International singles matches. Ireland came second in the series.

In December 1986 it was announced that John McHenry had been chosen to play for the Britain and Ireland Walker Cup team in the 1987 meeting with the US, the first Corkman to be chosen since Jimmy Bruen had played for the Walker Cup in 1951. This was seen as a just and deserving reward for a young golfer who was not only talented but who worked hard to achieve to the limit of his potential. Charlie Mulqueen wrote in the *Cork Examiner*: 'This modest young man has achieved a unique distinction and his dedicated and hard-working approach to the game must surely mean he has an even more glittering career in prospect.'

The Walker Cup was played for at Sunningdale in May 1987, and a large contingent of Douglas members provided a very supportive gallery for the British and Irish team, and for John McHenry in particular. The US, however, had a convincing 16½ to 7½ win. On the first day, John and his playing partner Paul Girvan lost in the foursomes 3 and 2, and John lost his singles match by one hole. Things went somewhat better for him on the second day when he won his foursomes match

A group of John McHenry's supporters at the Walker Cup, 1987.

with Jeremy Robinson 4 and 2, and also won his singles against Bill Loeffler 3 and 2. While this was a highlight in the history of Douglas Golf Club, John has mixed feelings about the occasion. It was undoubtedly an honour for him personally to be chosen to play, and he acknowledges the justifiable pride that the members of the club felt, but, in retrospect, he regrets that the team was not better prepared. They arrived at Sunningdale almost a week before the event, and practised every day to such an extent that the players were tired by the time competition began, and not in the best physical or mental state to do battle in what is the ultimate challenge for an amateur golfer.

A month later, in June 1987, he played for the last time as an amateur inter-national at the European Team Championship at Graz in Austria. It was one of John McHenry's most satisfying performances as he won 5½ of his six matches, and contributed significantly to Ireland's overall victory. 'I stepped up to the plate as number one and delivered as number one,' he remembers. He had announced that he would turn professional after the championship, and that he would make his professional debut at the Carroll's Irish Open at Portmarnock in July. The *Cork Examiner* said, 'McHenry leaves the amateur game on the highest possible note, for he was the inspiration behind the victory in Austria.' In a hundred years of Douglas Golf Club history, no player achieved as much as John McHenry did in the ten years since he had joined the club as a thirteen-year-old juvenile in 1977.

Turning professional was a logical next step for John McHenry. He was twenty-three years of age, had completed his university education, had achieved almost all that was possible for an amateur, including selection for the Walker Cup team, and had an attitude and ability that promised much. As he himself said: 'I achieved all

I set out to achieve as an amateur, and I needed a fresh challenge. I feel that I had nothing left to prove as an amateur.' He was invited by the sponsors to play at the Irish Open at Portmarnock, but his first outing as a professional was a chastening experience: he shot an 11-over-par opening round of 84, and while he had a much better 74 on the second day, he did not make the cut for the final two days.

In December 1987 John went to La Manga in Spain to the qualifying school for the European tour. Over six days of competition, players competed for the fifty cards that would give access to the European PGA tour. On the final day of competition, he won the forty-ninth of the fifty cards after a sudden-death play-off. During the 1988 season, he would have to finish in the top 120 in Europe – winning at least £20,000 – to qualify automatically for his tour card the following year. John McHenry began his first full year as a professional in Africa, playing on the Safari Tour before returning to Europe. On the European tour, the harsh reality of life as a professional golfer hit home. Being a rookie, virtually unknown in many European countries, it was difficult to get invitations to compete in tour events, and it was difficult to maintain a consistently high standard of play. In thirteen tournaments, John made the cut in only five, and his highest finish in 1988 was twenty-second. He returned to the European qualifying school in December, and again won his card, this time improving to forty-fifth place. The 1989 tour was even more difficult, and having failed to finish in the top 120, John went again to the qualifying school but failed to win his card. During 1990 and 1991 he played on the European Challenge Tour – sometimes called the 'Satellite Tour', essentially the second division of European golf.

John McHenry enjoyed some success on the Challenge Tour. In May 1990 he had his first professional victory when he won the Boggia International Tournament at Monza in Italy. In August he won the £7,000 first prize in the Rolex Pro-Am in Geneva. These two wins came at a crucial time for John, and removed some understandable doubts he had about his decision to become a touring professional. He played again on the Challenge Tour in 1991, and played better and more consistent golf, winning the Open de Lyons in France, and finishing fourth in the Challenge Tour order of merit at year's end. This gave him his European PGA tour card for 1992. He retained his card for 1993 having come 117th in the European order of merit. At the Irish Open at Mount Juliet in July 1993, John won the cheers of the Irish golfing public when he had a dream start to the event, being in joint second place after two rounds on 137. He maintained that standard on the third day, shooting another 70, and went into the final round in joint first place with José María Olazábal, 2 ahead of the field. The home crowd was fully behind John as he played the final round, and an Irish victory seemed likely. But the dream died, and a round of 79 meant that he fell back and finished in joint fourteenth place. This was the most disappointing and cruel finish of his career to date. He said in a press interview afterwards: 'I think the reasons for what happened were … bad judgement and bad club selection.' John McHenry finished the year in eight-first place in the European order of merit, and automatically qualified for the 1994 tour.

His form in 1994, however, deteriorated, and he failed to win his card at

the European Tour qualifying school held that year at Montpellier. This again caused uncertainty as John was now nearly thirty-one years of age and had been seven years on the professional circuit without making a significant breakthrough. The expense of touring was a constant concern. 'I was always asking: "Is there enough money to keep going?" There was never absolute security when you could turn around and say, "Well, I don't have to think about money."' He was also frustrated with his golf: 'I wasn't producing to my ability consistently. I was producing it in bursts. I wasn't doing it over four rounds of golf,' he says. 'I felt I was always fundamentally messing up two or three shots and that was the difference ... I never felt that nerves got in my way. It was more a case of – I wasn't consistent enough.' Despite the doubts, John toured again in 1995, and began the year with a confidence-boosting second place in the South African Players Championship and a prize of £14,000. In November he won his full European PGA tour card when he finished sixteenth at the qualifying school at San Roque, one place ahead of a new Irish professional, Pádraig Harrington. The years 1996 and 1997 were again frustrating one for John McHenry: a broken bone in his hand prevented him playing for over six months, and the top finishes and lucrative purses still proved elusive. It was increasingly likely that he would retire from the tour.

In 1998 John McHenry was given a sponsor's invitation to play in the Irish Open at Druid's Glen. He began well with a first round of 70, and was joint leader at the end of the second day with an aggregate 138. As had happened five years before at Mount Juliet, there was a distinct possibility that an Irishman would be in contention for the title as a 70 in the third round had John McHenry in second place going into the final day. The consistency that had so often eluded him previously was maintained, and although he did not win the title, a final-round 72 gave him joint third place and a career best prize of £53,996. David Carter won the title after a play-off, having tied with Colin Montgomerie on 278, 2 strokes ahead of McHenry. He remembers the 'wonderful environment' of the Irish Open and the embrace of the audience as he played well and stayed in contention with Europe's best: 'There's nothing better in golf.'

It was very fitting that Jim McCormack had caddied for John at Druid's Glen. Jim was a long-standing member of Douglas Golf Club, had caddied for John throughout his amateur career, and had the greatest influence on him as a person and as a golfer outside of his immediate family. 'I connected with him on the golf course as someone to talk to, someone to beat things off in a non-parental role. Jim was never judgemental, he listened to what I'd say and come back and talk to me. He brought a balance to me, he could read me, press the buttons. Ten minutes with him and I could walk away refocused.' Jim had last caddied for John on his professional debut at the Irish Open in 1987, and now, eleven years later, he carried his bag again on what was his most satisfying professional finish. The reunion had a poignancy in that Jim McCormack died four months later, in November 1998.

After the vicissitudes of eleven years on the European circuit, it was felt that the Irish Open finish could potentially transform John McHenry's ailing career, but it was not to be. John McHenry decided to retire in 1999 after making the cut in only four of his twenty-three starts. As Eamonn Sweeney wrote in a profile at the time: 'Still only 35 he has come to realise that while he is a good golfer, in the cruel world of the professional he is just not good enough ... he is remarkably honest and clear-eyed about his inability to make the jump into the top flight.' John vividly expressed the reality of life for many golf professionals when he said: 'If you're outside the top twenty or thirty and you're not winning big cheques, you end up on your own in the hotel cheesed off with your performance ... and after a period of time you wonder if you can face another year.' The uncertainty and insecurity was not conducive to playing golf of a sufficiently high standard to compete consistently at the very highest level. 'You have to have flow in golf. There has to be an element of, okay, you've done the work and now you just have to think about putting the ball in the hole,' John says. But it was not as simple as that for him. He remarks: 'I am an analytical person and that did not serve me well ... I reflected too much on everything.' He was married and had a young family, and, as he says, 'there was more than golf in my life.' He was not financially secure as a touring golf professional, and at thirty-five he was still young enough to embark on a new career.

Since retiring from competitive golf, John McHenry has made a new career in the world of golf. He was head professional at the K Club for a number of years, and was director of golf at that club when 'the most commercially successful Ryder Cup to date' was held there in 2006. In 2007 he set up his own golf consultancy business, and currently advises mobile-telephone company 3 on its strategy for golf sponsorship. He is also a regular contributor as a golf commentator with RTÉ and other media channels.

Following John McHenry's retirement as a touring professional in 1999, Charlie Mulqueen wrote in the *Cork Examiner*: 'everybody agrees that he remains as personable and likeable an individual to have walked the fairways of Europe in the last decade', while another sports writer, Eamonn Sweeney, summed him up thus: 'never less than honest and hard-working on the golf course, McHenry was a credit to his sport'.

10 *1980s & 1990s*

Douglas Golf Club had much to celebrate in the 1980s. John McHenry and John Morris junior won top amateur honours and represented their country with distinction, John McHenry playing on the Walker Cup team in 1987. The Douglas ladies won four Senior Cups, and Eavan Higgins began to make headlines as one of the country's most promising lady golfers. The club celebrated its seventy-fifth birthday in 1985 (one year late!), and published a short history, while a significant land purchase in 1989 partly solved the perennial boundary problem. In the late 1990s the course was redesigned, and the club brought in a new constitution in January 2000 that fundamentally changed its management structure and gave women equal status. In the 1980s national titles continued to elude the men of Douglas as they were beaten in the finals of the Senior Cup in 1981 and of the Barton Shield in 1986. The 1990s were kinder, however, and the 1991 victory in the Barton Shield and the 1999 Junior Cup success restored pride.

Final Disappointments, 1981 and 1986

Success in national team competitions continued to prove elusive for the Douglas men in the 1980s, although young players like John McHenry and John Morris junior were establishing themselves as the most successful golfers in the club's history. The last win of significance had been the Munster title in the Pierce Purcell Tournament of 1976. In 1981 the Douglas Senior Cup team got to the national final, a first for the club. In the semi-finals, Douglas beat the Leinster champions Sutton 3–2; it was a tight encounter, and the hero of the day was seventeen-year-old John McHenry, who won the vital match on the eighteenth. Douglas players Donal O'Herlihy and Pat Kelleher also won. In the final, Douglas met Bangor, which, like Douglas, had never won a Senior Cup title. John McHenry played Brian Kissock in a match that 'held a remarkably large gallery enraptured', according to a newspaper account, and remained composed through to the eighteenth against the much older and more experienced Kissock, a former professional. McHenry eventually won by two holes, having gone around in 65, prompting Kissock to assert: 'If John McHenry

Facing page:
Jubilee Medal, 1985.

195

1981 Senior Cup
Munster champions.
Standing, L–R:
P Kelleher, J McHenry,
T J O'Riordan (selector),
J C Morris,
S Kelly (selector).
Seated, L–R:
D O'Herlihy, S Martin
(president),
J Brett (captain),
J Kelleher.

plays like this all the time, then he's as good as anybody in Ireland and in that I include Philip Walton and Ronan Rafferty.' Unfortunately, it was not to be Douglas' day – Donal O'Herlihy, John C Morris and Pat Kelleher were all beaten in their matches, and John Kelleher was 1 up playing the seventeenth when he was called in, giving Bangor a 3½ to 1½ victory.

In 1986 it was the turn of the Douglas Barton Shield team to lose a national final. In the Munster final at Little Island, Douglas met Limerick, and John McHenry with Kieran Barry crushed their opponents by six holes, while brothers John and Peter Morris halved their match, giving Douglas a six-hole victory. The strong Douglas team, managed by Jim McCormack, was confident going forward to the national finals in Galway, and 1986 was proving to be a lucky year for the club – John McHenry had won the South of Ireland and the Irish Amateur Close titles, John Morris junior had won the Munster and Irish Youths' Open Championships, and the Douglas ladies had taken another Senior Cup title. In the semi-finals, Douglas beat Athlone by five holes, John McHenry and Kieran Barry winning by two, and Peter and John Morris junior winning by three. In the final against Woodbrook, Douglas did well initially and had an overall lead of three holes in both matches at the fourteenth, but things went wrong from there, and Douglas lost the final by one hole, John McHenry and Kieran Barry winning their match by 1, but Peter and John Morris losing theirs by 2. As Charlie Mulqueen wrote in the *Cork Examiner*: 'Douglas made the long trek home last night regretting several missed opportunities and unnecessary errors that eventually proved their downfall'.[1]

1986 Barton Shield
Munster champions.
Standing, L–R:
J McHenry, J Morris jun.,
J McCormack (team
captain), K Barry,
P Morris.
Seated:
J Ruby (president; left),
F O'Sullivan (captain).

Juvenile Heroes

The time and effort put into the coaching and encouragement of juveniles at the club began to pay dividends in the 1980s as Douglas began to produce a number of young and gifted players who won many honours. Some years earlier, in 1971, Robin Turnbull had played on the Irish team in the Home Internationals Youths' Team Championship, but through the 1980s there was hardly a year that did not have a young Douglas player on the Irish boys' and youths' teams, and John McHenry and John Morris junior also made an impressive mark on the national scene, winning a number of national and provincial titles. John McHenry won the Youths' Amateur Open Championship of Ireland in 1980 and 1981, and John Morris junior won that title in 1984 and 1986, along with the Munster Youths' title in 1986. At international boys level, John McHenry was on the Irish team each year from 1980 to 1983. At international youth level, he played in the Home Internationals every year from 1980 to 1984, and played in the European Team Championship from 1981 to 1983. John Morris junior played for Ireland's boys' team in 1982 and 1983, and at youth international level he played for Ireland from 1984 to 1986. They both played at senior level also, John McHenry playing in the Home Internationals in 1985 and 1986, and in the European Team Championship and Walker Cup in 1987, and John Morris junior playing in the Home Internationals from 1993 to 1998, and in the European Team championship in 1995. John McHenry's amateur career ended in 1987, when he turned professional (see feature, pp. 185–93)

While the names of McHenry and Morris dominated the scene in

John Morris junior,
1986 Munster and Irish
Youths' champion,
with J Ruby (president;
left), and F O'Sullivan
(captain).

those years, other young players also prospered: Ken Spillane won a
cap for Ireland playing in the European Boys' Team Championship in
1986, while John Paul Hughes won his Irish boys' cap in 1993 when he
played in the Home Internationals. John Paul won the Munster boys'
title in 1990. The Douglas youth team won the Munster section of the
Aer Lingus Youths' Club Championship in 1984 with John McHenry,
John Morris junior, Ken Spillane and Don Coughlan. In 1994 Douglas
again won the Munster section of this competition, now called the
Irish Club Youths' Championship, with David Connolly, John Paul

1984 Aer Lingus Youths'
Club Championship,
Munster winners.
Standing, L–R:
D Coughlan, J McHenry,
J Morris junior,
K Spillane.
Seated, L–R:
S Hurley (selector),
T O'Brien (captain),
S Treacy (president),
T Floyd (selector).

Hughes and Niall Hogan on the winning team. In 1995 the competition for the Fred Daly Trophy was inaugurated. This is an inter-club team competition for players under eighteen years of age. In 1996 the Douglas team of David Connolly, Anthony Gaffney, Mark Mythen, Ciarán Nicholson, John O'Mahony and Philip Quinn won the Munster section of the competition. In the national semi-finals at Galway, the Douglas team beat County Sligo 3½ to 1½, but were beaten 4 to 1 by Malahide in the final.

Walker Cup, 1987

The selection of John McHenry in December 1986 to play on the 1987 Walker Cup team was a cause for celebration for John himself, for his family and for the members at Douglas. John had experienced a glittering 1986, winning the Waterford Scratch Cup for the third time, the South of Ireland Championship, the Mullingar Scratch Cup and the Irish Amateur Close title. Many were comparing him to the legendary Jimmy Bruen, who in 1951 was the last Cork golfer to have played on a Walker Cup team. Club morale was high at the end of 1986 as, in addition to the achievements of John McHenry, the club had won the Munster final of the Barton Shield and had only narrowly lost the national final. John Morris junior had won the Munster Youths' Championship and was a youth international, and Ken Spillane had played on the Irish boys' team in the Home Internationals. The ladies of Douglas had won their tenth Senior Cup title in 1986, and Eavan Higgins had reached the final of the Irish Ladies' Amateur Close Championship as well as playing on the Irish team.

A large number of Douglas members led by the president, Tadgh O'Halloran, and club captain, Val O'Mahony, travelled to Sunningdale for the Walker Cup in May 1987, and over 150 people attended a reception held at the nearby Wentworth clubhouse to mark the occasion. Over the two days of competition, John McHenry had a large gallery of supporters, and 'the green army' of Douglas made its presence felt. Unfortunately, the British

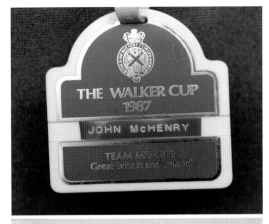

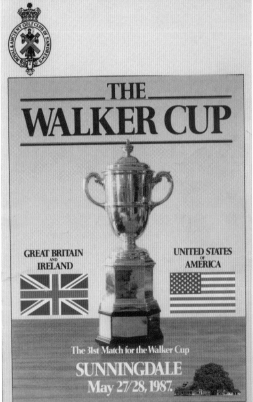

'The Green Army': Douglas supporters at the Walker Cup at Sunningdale, 1987.

and Irish team, under captain Geoff Marks, lost to the US, but John McHenry's play on the second day gave his supporters much to cheer about, as he won both his foursomes and singles matches. At the club AGM the following January, the outgoing president said that 'the members of Sunningdale, who probably never even heard of Douglas Golf Club, were left in no doubt as to who we were and who we had come to support ... [and] it was great to see the Douglas Club colours displayed in the hallowed halls of Wentworth.'[2]

Barton Shield Victory, 1991

In 1991 the men of Douglas came up trumps at last, and won their first national title in thirty-six years when they won the Barton Shield at Malone in September. In Munster, Douglas had victories over Cork and Tralee before beating Tramore in an exciting final at Little Island. They played Hermitage in their national semi-final. Peter Morris and Derek Maguire did not get off to the best start in their match, and were 3 down after four holes. However, they won six of the next ten, and eventually had a three holes win over their opponents. The other Douglas pairing of Don Coughlan and Denis Dudley had a one-hole victory in their match. Their opponents in the final were County Sligo, who, like Douglas, had never won the title. Charlie Mulqueen of the *Cork Examiner* described the final:

> ...it was real nailbiting stuff for both sets of supporters over the closing holes. In the end, it was all decided on Malone's splendid 428 yards lakeside 18th hole. Morris

200

1991 Barton Shield champions.
Standing, L–R: D McFarlane, K Canty, D Dudley, P Morris, D Maguire, S Curtis. *Seated, L–R:* D O'Herlihy (team captain), D Canty (president), R Langford (vice-captain), D Coughlan. Inset: J Scanlan (captain).

and Maguire [Douglas] arrived there one up against Francis Howley and Stephen O'Donovan and were able to win the hole with a bogey five when the luckless O'Donovan pushed his seven iron approach to the right of the green where it kicked into the water. Even then, Douglas had their work cut out, for Maguire had to hole a very nasty four-footer with a left to right break for a win in bogey.

That two-hole win for Maguire and Morris left Coughlan and Dudley with a comforting cushion and the latter, whom I saw to play several superb shots through the afternoon, knocked an extremely sensible five iron to the 'fat' side of the green. Young Gerard Sproule took on the flag for Sligo, but cut his shot to the right from where his partner Serryth Heavey pitched ten feet past.

When Sproule missed, Douglas were worthy champions and the celebrations began. In their hour of triumph, every Douglas member present spared a thought for the late John Scanlan, who died earlier this year in his captaincy, and who would have dearly relished the occasion.[3]

The Douglas team captain was Donal O'Herlihy, and his team was Don Coughlan, Derek Maguire, Peter Morris and Denis Dudley, with substitutes Seán Curtis, Kieran Canty and Don McFarlane, who was abroad and not available to play in the finals.

The minutes of the next meeting of the general committee at Douglas record the president, Dave Canty, as having said that 'he was a proud man having witnessed at first hand the excitement of the great victory in the Barton Shield at Malone Golf Club. He said that this was the most historic and best thing that had happened to Douglas Golf Club … They were a credit to the club and to themselves.'[4] As mentioned in the *Cork Examiner* account, the Douglas captain, John Scanlan, had died the previous April, and his loss was still keenly felt by all at the club, adding a note of poignancy to the win. As was said by the vice captain, Dick Langford, 'the victory would have gladdened the heart of the late John Scanlan.'[5] A victory dinner was held on 19 October, and at the AGM the following January, the president, Dave Canty, remarked that the night 'can only be described as one of the greatest nights in the history of the club.' He went on: 'I cannot find words to adequately describe the scenes in Malone. The incredible tensions during the matches, the pride at the way the squad represented Douglas and the release of emotions to total euphoria when the last putt was taken. It was complete ecstasy and a moment I will cherish for the rest of my life.'[6]

Senior Cup & Barton Shield, 1995: Munster Success

While Douglas did not win national honours in 1995, a little history was made when the club qualified for the national finals of both the Senior Cup and Barton Shield that year for the first time. The Munster finals of the competitions were played at Little Island, and in the Senior Cup semi-finals, Douglas played Killarney, winning 3½ to 1½, and then met Castletroy in the final. John Morris junior of Douglas beat Tom Corridan by 3 and 2, and Karl Bornemann beat his opponent, Stephen Moloney, by the same margin. Derek Maguire also had a win, and Kieran Canty and Don Coughlan halved their matches, giving Douglas a 4 to 1 victory. In the Barton Shield Munster semi-finals, Douglas beat Limerick by two holes, and met Killarney in the final. John Morris junior and his partner Karl Bornemann trounced their opponents, and were nine holes ahead when they were called in at the seventeenth. The other Douglas pairing of Kieran Canty and Derek Maguire were two down after fifteen, but the Douglas victory was assured by then.

The national finals were held at Portstewart on 14–15 September. The Douglas team was confident, and there were strong hopes of a unique Senior Cup and Barton Shield double. Bill Kelleher was the Douglas team captain, and he chose John Morris and Karl Bornemann, and Derek Maguire and Kieran Canty as his pairings for the Barton Shield. He had Don Coughlan, Denis Dudley, Donal O'Herlihy and Peter Morris in reserve, an indication of the strength

1995 Senior Cup and Barton Shield Munster champions.
Standing, L–R:
D O'Herlihy, K Bornemann, P Morris, D Coughlan.
Seated, L–R:
W A Kelleher (team captain), D Whelan (captain), S Coughlan (president).
Insets, L–R: K Canty, D Maguire, J Morris junior.

of the team, and Donal O'Herlihy was to join the first four for the Senior Cup semi-finals. Ardglass were the opposition in the Barton Shield semi-finals, and after a bad start, Morris and Bornemann came back and won their match by one hole. However, things did not go so well for the other pairing of Maguire and Canty, and they were beaten by three holes, giving Ardglass a two-hole victory and a place in the final, which they lost to County Sligo.

For the Senior Cup semi-final against County Sligo, Bill Kelleher chose his four Barton Shield players and Donal O'Herlihy, but, as the *Cork Examiner* noted, 'A dismal couple of days concluded for Douglas at Portstewart yesterday when they were demolished by a rampant County Sligo'. Douglas had banked on Morris and Bornemann to do well, but they both suffered at the hands of their opponents, Morris losing by 6 and 5, and Bornemann going down by 5 and 4. Kieran Canty and Derek Maguire halved their matches when they were called in, and Donal O'Herlihy was beaten by 4 and 3. Douglas lost by 4–1, and never really came close to taking the potentially historic double.

Junior Cup Victory, 1999

The victory in the 1999 Junior Cup was the clubs' third success in that competition, having won it previously in 1930 and 1955. It was a pleasing finish to a year that saw Douglas complete the redesign of its course on its ninetieth birthday. Douglas won the Munster final by beating Castletroy 3–2 in a thrilling match, and went forward to play in the national finals at Royal Portrush in September. The Douglas

1999 Junior Cup
champions.
Standing L–R:
G O'Herlihy, D Collins,
D Byrne, T Collins,
M Crowley, J Treacy,
G Adare, K O'Sullivan,
D Murray.
Seated, L–R: D Hurley,
B O'Donoghue (lady
captain),
D Thomas (president),
M O'Donovan, T Grealy
(president, GUI),
L Connolly (vice-
president).

team captain was Michael O'Donovan, assisted by Donal Hurley. In their semi-final, they met Galway and beat them 3–2, even though in the early stages of the encounter Galway looked the better prospect as seventeen-year-old Gary O'Herlihy of Douglas was beaten by Daire Loughnane and his team-mate Denis Collins lost his match to Ger O'Farrell. However, Derek Byrne gave Douglas a boost when he won his match, and that left Tom Collins and Michael Crowley having to win theirs to secure victory. Crowley won his on the eighteenth, and Collins halved on the eighteenth, leaving the sides level. On the first tie-hole 'the Douglas nerve held in exemplary fashion … Collins hit a drive and six iron to the heart of the green and Conroy [Galway], whose approach pitched on the green and spun back, was unable to match his opponent's fine par four'.[7] Douglas were through to the final against Warrenpoint.

In the first match of the final, Gary O'Herlihy more than made up for his heavy defeat in his semi-final match when he 'hit a succession of great shots and none more important than the five iron which he rifled onto the putting surface at the 18th to clinch his success.'[8] Denis Collins halved his match, and Derek Byrne was declared to have lost his 2 and 1 on the seventeenth as the final result had been decided in favour of Douglas due to the excellent play of the fourth and fifth Douglas players, Tom Collins and Michael Crowley. Tom Collins had fallen behind his opponent early in his match, but recovered well and won 4 and 3. Michael Crowley decided the outcome when he won 5 and 3. Tom Collins and Michael Crowley were unbeaten through the Junior Cup campaign, Tom winning six and halving two, and Michael winning eight and halving one of his matches. Douglas

Irish Club Youths'
Championship: Munster
winners, 1994.
Back, L–R:
David Connolly,
John Paul Hughes,
Niall Hogan,
Michael Ryan.
Front, L–R:
Tom McCarthy (team
manager),
Richard Lonergan
(captain),
Captain Frank Troy
(president).

had beaten Warrenpoint 3½ to 1½, and had won the Junior Cup for the third time in the club's history, and for the first time in forty-four years. As Charlie Mulqueen wrote in the *Examiner*: 'By any standards, this was a highly impressive performance by Douglas, and hardly surprisingly they went close to lifting the roof off the magnificent new Portrush clubhouse with their own special rendering of "The Banks"'.[9] The full Douglas team of players was Tom Collins, Denis Collins, Michael Crowley, Gary O'Herlihy, Derek Byrne, Kevin O'Sullivan, John Treacy and Donal Murray. The victory was especially pleasing to the two survivors of the victorious Douglas Junior Cup team of 1955, Éamonn McSweeney and Niall McNamara.

Winning Ladies

The Douglas ladies continued to achieve through these years also. They won the Munster section of the Senior Cup every year from 1980 to 1992, with the exceptions of 1984 and 1988, and won the national title in 1980, 1985, 1986, 1987 and 1990. In winning the three consecutive titles in the mid-1980s, Douglas joined an elite group of clubs – only Milltown, County Louth and Royal Portrush had previously achieved that distinction, with County Louth going one better with four consecutive wins between 1946 and 1949. In the 1980 Senior Cup final at Lahinch, Douglas beat their old rivals Milltown 3–0, with two matches called in. The team was Ann Heskin, Rhona Brennan (Hegarty), Eavan Higgins, Clare Keating, Pat Desmond and Ann Moran. In 1985 they won the title again, the first of a three-in-a-row; the team was Eavan Higgins, Clare Keating, Ann Heskin, Mary Harnett, Pat Desmond and Helen Elwood. At the

AGM of the Ladies' Branch the following February, there was an understandable pride in the achievement, and it was noted that

> ... it is obvious that we ladies have been on the golf scene here from the beginning. For three quarters of a century Douglas ladies have been contributing in a spectacular fashion to Munster golf. Indeed their influence has spread far beyond the province, to the country as a whole, many of them gaining International honours.[10]

In the 1986 victory at Castlerock, the team again had the Senior Cup experts Eavan Higgins, Ann Heskin, Clare Keating and Mary Harnett, joined this year by newcomers Ann Hegarty, Eileen Rose McDaid and Aoife Lane. The following year, the hat-trick of Senior Cup victories was completed under team captain Angela Lane, the team being Eavan Higgins, Clare Keating, Eileen Rose McDaid, Ann Heskin, Mary Mackey (Harnett) and Ann Hegarty. The ladies then had to endure two years without a Senior Cup title before winning again in Dundalk in 1990 for a record-breaking twelfth time. The winning team was Eavan Higgins, Eileen Rose McDaid, Clare Keating, Aoife Lane, Mary Mackey and Ann Hegarty. Ann Heskin did not play in the finals at Dundalk, but had played in place of Ann Hegarty in the Southern Division final.

While John McHenry and John Morris junior were blazing a trail on behalf of the Douglas men in the 1980s, Eavan Higgins was the highest achieving lady golfer at Douglas from 1980 until her retirement from competitive golf in 1996. She joined the club in 1974 and was playing on the Senior Cup team by 1976, winning six national titles with the team. She won her first senior international cap in 1981, and played on the Irish team in the Home Internationals from 1981 to 1995, with the exception of 1985, and played in the biennial European Team Championship from 1981 to 1995, again with the exception of 1985. Eavan won the Irish Amateur Close title in 1993, the first Douglas player to do so since Zelie Fallon in 1964, and won four Munster Senior Championships. Eavan was also a member of the Munster team that won five interprovincial titles between 1980 and 1993. Ann Heskin continued the form she had first shown in the 1960s, and having played for Ireland in the Home Internationals between 1969 and 1977, she captained the Irish side in 1982 and 1983, and captained the victorious Irish team in the European Team Championship in Belgium in 1983.

Facing page, top:
Douglas Golf Club
1910–1985, jubilee history, 1985.

Bottom:
Piaras Ó Dálaigh,
bunathóir na Seanóirí
Órga.

Jubilee History

For many years, 1910 had been regarded as the foundation date of Douglas Golf Club, and in 1984 a jubilee committee was formed to plan the celebrations for the club's seventy-fifth birthday in 1985. A short history of the club was written by Charlie Mulqueen, and twelve special monthly medal competitions were held during the year. The twelve silver medals and one gold were purchased with part of the proceeds of a fund-raising auction held in November 1984. In 1985 Cork city celebrated the eight-hundredth anniversary of the granting of its first charter, and as part of the year-long celebrations, a series of special competitions was organised for the four Cork clubs in August.

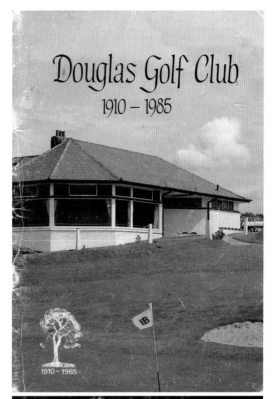

Na Seanóirí Órga

Sa bhliain 1987 d'iarr Piaras Ó Dálaigh cead ar Uachtarán agus ar Chaptaen an Chumainn, Tadgh O'Halloran agus Val O'Mahony, grúpa a bhunú laistigh den gCumann a thabharfadh deis do shean-bhaill, nó doibh siúd a bhí ag dul in aois beagáinín, leanacht ar aghaidh go gníomhach lena gcuid ghailf. Tugadh an cead agus baisteadh 'Na Seanóirí Órga' ar an ngrúpa. Bhí Galf-Chumann na Dúghlaise ar an gcéad chumann sa tír a raibh a leithéid de ghrúpa aige. Ó bunaíodh na Seanóirí Órga ar an 24 Aibreán 1987, tá cuideachta, comhluadar agus iomaíocht curtha ar fáil do an-chuid bhaill shinsearacha agus anois is gné lárnach é de shaol an Chumainn. An-sheans gur tháinig iarracht d'éad ar mhná an Chumainn, mar laistigh de chúpla bliain bhunaigh siad a ngrúpa féin, na Ladybirds, agus tá an grúpa sin anois ag freastal ar riachtanaisí na mban sinsear. Múinteoir agus Gaeilgeoir ab ea Piaras Ó Dálaigh agus shocraigh sé go mbeadh teidil na n-oifigeach as Gaeilge – Uachtarán, Rúnaí agus Cisteoir. Chomh maith leis sin déantar gnó oifigiúil na Seanóirí Órga tré Ghaeilge. Ba Rúnaí agus Cisteoir an ghrúpa é Piaras ó 1987 go 1995 agus bhí Seán Ó Cionnaith ina chéad Uachtarán. Bhí Tadhg Ó Súilleabháin ina Uachtarán ar na Seanóirí Órga do Chomóradh an Chéid, 2009.

Land

Douglas Golf Club purchased the land of the course in 1960, and thereby secured its future. In 1971 a parcel of about four acres to the left of the eighteenth was purchased, and developed as a practice ground. A large parcel of land to the left of the present first fairway and to the right of the fifth (where the carpark and practice ground are now located) was always coveted by the club as its acquisition would secure the boundary on Maryborough Hill; any housing development on that land could threaten the first and fifth holes. In addition, this land would provide space for a much-needed larger carpark and a safer entrance from the road outside. The landowner, John Saunders, was first approached by the club in 1967 with an offer to purchase those lands, but it was not until 1988 that final agreement was reached. In 1973 the land was offered at £75,000, in 1974 the price had risen to £85,000, and by 1977 the asking price was £200,000.[11] In the 1970s a planning application for a development of houses on the land was refused. Approaches continued to be made by the club to Saunders, but it was 1988 before the two parties began to make ground and approach agreement, and a committee was formed to plan fund-raising for the purchase. Seán Cody and Felix O'Sullivan concluded the negotiations on behalf of the club, and eventually a price of £250,000, exclusive of legal fees and other costs, was agreed for the sixteen acres of land, the house and outbuildings. Under the terms of the agreement, John Saunders was to have a life tenancy of the house.[12] An EGM of members, attended by 166, was held on 19 December 1988 to seek approval for the purchase and for the fund-raising necessary.

It was proposed to raise £120,000 from a draw, with 3,000 members paying £100 each. It was also proposed that a category of corporate membership would be introduced at the rate of £4,000 for a five-year term. With twelve or thirteen corporate members, £50,000 could be raised from this source. A further £50,000 was to be taken in from offering long-term membership to existing members. Increased green fees and interest-free loans from members would also contribute. There was also a proposal that planning permission would be sought for six half-acre sites to the rear of the eighteenth green, with an entrance from Maryborough Hill, and that these would raise about £60,000. This latter proposal was not proceeded with.

Having set out the plans for fund-raising, the minutes of the meeting record that 'the President [Seán Kelly] said that we now have an opportunity which we never had before and may not have again and that we owed it to ourselves and to future members to avail of it and he appealed to members to support the motion'.[13] Club captain Pat Harrington also spoke strongly in favour of the motion

to purchase, and concluded his appeal for the support of the meeting with the following: 'The Saunders family have tolerated for many years balls from the first tee into their property and even through their kitchen window, and that if anybody else occupied the property there would be a grave danger that they would get an injunction and we may lose our first hole as we know it.' The motion was passed unanimously. After some delays caused by a claim by a third party to have an option to purchase the lands, the deal was concluded on 14 April 1989. The minutes of the general committee meeting of 24 April record the club's debt of gratitude to Seán Cody and Felix O'Sullivan for their work in bringing a twenty-two-year campaign to acquire that land to a satisfactory conclusion.

In 1985 a land swap between Douglas Golf Club and Gortalough Holdings Ltd, the land-holding company of the Horgan family of Douglas, was first proposed. In exchange for a piece of ground – a little over two acres to the left of the eighteenth – Gortalough would give the club a plot of about three acres that would facilitate the extension of the seventeenth hole at the north-western corner of the course. Gortalough was proposing to seek planning approval for a housing development to the north of the eighteenth hole, where Maryborough Woods now stands, and the club plot would facilitate

The signing of the documents concluding the purchase of the Saunders' property in April 1989.
Standing, L–R:
J O'Donovan (trustee),
J J O'Hea (trustee),
D Barry (trustee),
S McHenry (trustee),
J Sheehan (trustee).
Seated, L–R:
D Hurley (captain),
W O'Mahony (trustee),
W J Scannell (president).

The Douglas Spirit! Members reinstate the course after the installation of a new watering system in 1990.

access to the site and enable the club to build a new, safer entrance from that northern side. Guarantees were given that any housing development would properly respect the course boundary, and that houses would be sited at an appropriate distance from that boundary. The swap was approved by an EGM of the members.[14] The proposed swap was not completed as problems arose with the County Council's plans for the widening of Maryborough Hill, which would necessitate the acquisition of a strip of land up to ten metres wide along the course boundary. It was not possible to come to an agreement with Gortalough Holdings Ltd regarding changes to the land-swap proposal, and the club decided to rescind the 1985 agreement at an EGM on 19 December 1988. At that meeting, the proposal regarding the purchase of the Saunders land was approved, and the swap that would enable the extension of the seventeenth hole had a lesser priority.

The swap proposal was revived in April of 1989, and Gortalough now offered the three acres or so at the seventeenth in return for a smaller 1.75 acres north of the eighteenth.[15] The new housing development was to be low density, and the nearest house would be at least 80 feet from the course boundary. The acquisition of the land at the seventeenth would enable the club to lengthen that hole and make it a par 4. The proposal had an added attraction in that a cash payment of £50,000 would be made to the club, and a considerable saving would accrue to the club through obtaining a connection to the sewage system of the proposed housing development. An EGM, attended by 116 members, was held on 13 October, and the new swap was approved, with only ten voting against the proposal. The legal documents relating to the swap were signed in the spring of 1990, but the lands were not exchanged until 1998. Planning permission for the Gortalough lands had been refused in 1991, which postponed the completion of the deal, but permission for building was eventually received in 1998, which enabled the swap to be finalised, and the land in the vicinity of the seventeenth hole was acquired by the club.

Finances

Club finances were in a relatively healthy state at the beginning of the 1980s in that the club showed a small surplus one year, balanced by a small deficit a year or two later. A small surplus of £3,000 at the end of 1980, for example, had grown to £18,300 by the end of 1982, but increased expenditure in 1983 led to a deficit of £4,500 at year end, followed by a modest surplus for 1985. At that time, the club budgeted for a break-even situation, and did not plan for surpluses that could be set aside for future investment in development projects. Major items of expenditure, such as land purchase, were financed on a case-by-case basis. In 1988 about £9,000 was spent on an extension and improvements to the pro shop, and £4 of the £12 increase in the annual subscription for 1989 was to partly fund this expenditure. In 1988 also, when the purchase of the Saunders land by the first and fifth holes seemed imminent, a finance sub-committee was set up to plan the fund-raising for the purchase price of over £250,000. As part of this scheme, a monthly 'super draw' for twelve monthly draws was established. It was planned that after allowing for the substantial prizes, about £120,000 could be raised by the project. A committee led by Seán Kelly and Jack Harrington took on the task of promoting the draw, and members were encouraged to support the draw by selling tickets and also by buying them themselves. After a slow start, the venture took off, and well in excess of the budgeted 3,000 tickets were sold by the time of the first draw in June 1989. After the twelve monthly draws, the profit was £176,048, almost fifty per cent ahead of budget.

The other innovation that proved very successful from a financial point of view was the introduction of corporate membership. The proposal was approved by the EGM of 9 December 1988, and introduced formally following the AGM of January 1989. Five-year corporate memberships were offered at £4,000 each, and by July of 1989 the target of £50,000 had been reached, with twelve male and one female memberships taken up. At that time, the annual subscription for an ordinary member was £255 50p. This new source of revenue was used the following year when it was proposed to install a new course-watering system at a cost of £40,000. It was decided that £8,000 of the cost would be funded by the admission of two new corporate members. It was reported at the AGM in January 1991 that the draw and corporate memberships had funded the lion's share of the £300,000 or so spent by the club on the Saunders land and the new watering system. By 1992 there were twenty-four corporate members in the club, and concern was expressed by some committee members at this growing number. It was pointed out that such members were a financial boon, and 'that as many of these people did not play actively that he felt that the number should be left open'.[16] This category of membership had not been created to further the playing of golf amongst the corporate class; rather, it was a device used by many golf clubs to boost their finances. Corporate members had most of the rights of ordinary members but could not vote at either AGMs or EGMs, and could not become committee members. In 1993 the cost of this membership was raised to £5,000 for a five-year term, and by 1994 there were thirty-one members in this category and the sum of £47,500 had been credited to the Capital Development Fund, set up in 1993, from those subscriptions.

At an EGM in December 1986, the honorary treasurer, Val O'Mahony, pointed out to members that in its budgeting, the club made no provision for capital items, and that no reserve had been built up. In 1992 club president Jack Harrington proposed the setting up of a finance sub-committee as part of his programme for long-term planning. This sub-committee reported in August 1992, and amongst other recommendations suggested the establishment of a capital development fund as a means of building up a reserve that could be used to fund large items of capital expenditure. It was suggested that the club budget for an annual surplus that would be credited to the fund, and details of how a surplus could be raised were set out. This was a new departure for the club, and proved to be a success: by the end of 1994, £75,245 had been credited to the fund, and it grew over subsequent years and was key to funding projects such as the course redesign in 1997–99.

Membership

Issues relating to the selection and election of new members continued to cause controversy in the 1980s and 1990s. At the club AGM in February 1981, a speaker from the floor expressed strong dissatisfaction with the waiting-list system then in operation as he felt it was open to abuse in that length of time on the list was not the only criterion for selection. While this point of view was understandable, the membership committee and the general committee of the club had a virtually impossible task as there was only a very limited number of vacancies in any one year, and only a small fraction of the demand for places in the club could be satisfied. The membership committee for 1981 again looked at the situation, and reported to the general committee in October. It was decided that a waiting list would not operate any further, and that when vacancies arose they would be advertised in the clubhouse. It was also decided that prospective members would have to be proposed and seconded by three members of at least five years' standing, and that such proposers or seconders may be required to appear before the membership committee. The report stressed that the final election of new members was in the hands of the general committee as stated in the club rules.[17] At the end of 1981, there were 569 males and 262 females in total in the various categories of membership in the club.

In spite of the best efforts of the committee members and officers, the difficulties with the admission of new members persisted. In 1988, for example, an issue arose with the position of junior members who had reached the age of twenty-two, as even those who were of a high golfing standard no longer had an automatic right to full membership. It was decided to admit in any one year up to five such members with handicaps of 10 or under.[18] The introduction of the category of corporate membership in 1989 also caused some unease. Although this category was created primarily as a means of raising finance, some felt that it could be used as a 'back door' for achieving eventual election to full membership. A membership sub-committee – set up in 1992 to examine all aspects of the membership situation as part of a long-term planning initiative – confirmed in its report in November 1993 that corporate members had no preferential rights in converting to full membership, and would only be considered on the same basis as other applicants, as set out in the club rules.[19]

In 1990 a sub-committee of the membership committee consisting of its chairman, the president, the captain and the secretary-manager was appointed to shortlist the applications to at least double the number of vacancies before they were put before the general committee for election. Complete confidentiality was essential to such a delicate process, but given that the supply of vacancies was but a small fraction of that demanded, and with great pressure often being brought to bear on committee members by applicants, it was not surprising that there was a leak. When the first shortlist came before the committee for a vote, great disappointment was expressed that the list had been discussed openly some days before at the club, and one speaker 'knew of a situation when a non-club member was given sight of the actual lists by a committee member'.[20] This led the president to suggest that a new system for the election of members should be introduced – something that did not happen for a number of years.[21] Meanwhile, the issue of whether all student and junior members would automatically progress to full membership arose again in 1991–92. At the end of 1991, there were nine in these categories seeking to progress to full membership, and the committee decided to facilitate all nine. It was felt by one member that this could create problems in the future in that there would be an understandable expectation of automatic progress to full membership by students and juniors. Another speaker was harsher in his comments, saying that such new members 'would only clutter up the course even more than heretofore'![22] At the following month's meeting, the matter was again discussed, and it was pointed out that a precedent had been set in admitting the nine, as in each of the following five years there would be up to fifteen such members expecting full membership. One committee member commented: 'We may have opened the floodgates as a result of the decision taken, as we have set a precedent.'[23]

The pressure continued into 1992, and a motion was put before the members at the AGM in January that proposed that the family members of a club member or of a deceased club member would be given preference over other applicants in seeking membership. The chairman of the membership committee pointed out that such a rule would greatly restrict the general committee, especially with regard to low-handicap applicants. It was also pointed out that the families of members were always treated sympathetically in the admission process. The motion was defeated, but its proposal and the debate that followed highlighted again the perennial problem: balancing the valid demands of members' families for membership with those of others not so connected when so few vacancies occurred.

The membership committee was keen to ensure that the club would manage the issues in relation to membership in a way that would sustain the club in the long term as an active sports club – one that catered to the golfing needs of its members and competed to a high standard at all levels while also offering an appropriate level of social activity. In 1992 a detailed questionnaire was sent to all members to get as full a picture as possible of the membership with a view to making detailed projections as part of the long-term planning process instigated that year by club president Jack Harrington. The membership sub-committee charged with this task produced a thirty-five page report on membership issues, and applied actuarial formulae to its figures in arriving at future membership projections. The work showed, for example, that the club's age profile was changing, with a steadily ageing membership, and that within ten years there would be more members over sixty-five than under. The sub-committee made thirteen principal recommendations on membership issues, and proposed that the playing membership be maintained at its existing level. The fundamental problem of a constant demand for membership far in excess of the availability of places could not be solved.

It was not a surprise that issues relating to the election, and, indeed, non-election, of new members eventually led to discord and acrimony. At a committee meeting in April 1995, one member resigned having expressed his great disappointment at the failure of a specific applicant to be elected to membership, and voiced strong objections to the manner in which members were being elected. He later withdrew his resignation, and returned to the committee as he felt that his dissatisfaction reflected the attitude of many club members who wished him to continue to represent that point of view.[24] Over the following weeks, a number of letters were received on the issue, a frequent complaint being 'that applications from family members and existing members have for various reasons been passed over in favour of applications for membership from individuals who had no club connection whatsoever.'[25] Another letter questioned the validity of the process as the appointment of a sub-committee to shortlist applicants before they came before the general committee may have breached club rules in that there was no provision for such a procedure in the rules.[26] The committee felt that the matter required a legal opinion, and the election of any further members was deferred pending a clarification from the club's solicitors.

Until 1981 selected applications from waiting lists were submitted by the membership committee to the general committee for election. From that year, when the waiting lists were discontinued, a shortlist from the applications for advertised vacancies was drawn up by the membership committee, and submitted to the general committee for the election process. The legal advice was to proceed on that basis pending the amendment of the relevant club rule, but the general committee was concerned about the possibility that a disappointed applicant would take a legal action against the club. The question was hotly debated, and further legal opinions on the matter were received. A sub-committee was appointed to draw up a revised rule 10 that would be put to the members at the next AGM to regularise procedures relating to the election of new members. The AGM in January 1996 approved the revision of the rules, and, amongst other things, vested in the general committee the sole right to decide when vacancies were to be filled and the number of such vacancies. The election of new members was to be by secret ballot. While this change clearly set out the procedures for the admission of new members, it did not resolve the problem of club members being disappointed and often angry at the failure of family members to be elected. In 1999, for example, a member of long standing wrote to the general committee expressing 'dismay and disillusionment' at the outcome of a recent election in which a relative was unsuccessful. It was 'an insult to him and to his family' when others with no connection to the club were being elected over those with long and proven family connections. He believed that some on the committee were guilty of 'cynical cronyism' and of pursuing personal agendas.[27] Such is the passion aroused by the seemingly intractable problems that can arise when seeking membership of a club like Douglas!

A New Course

The Sports Turf Research Institute at Bingley in West Yorkshire has been advising the club on matters relating to the course since at least the early 1950s. In 1991 D S Wishart of the institute visited Douglas and carried out a detailed inspection of the course over three days. His subsequent report and recommendations were considered at an EGM in January 1992. While the majority of the report was principally concerned with proposals for new bunkers, recommendations were also made with regard to the improvement of fairways through strategic planting and varying their widths by different levels of mowing. He concluded his report with the following:

> The writer found Douglas Golf Club to be very exciting and an extremely pleasant oasis. Undoubtedly the character of the course can be improved by adjustment to bunkering and what is offered is frankly only minimal, bearing in mind that configuration of the land at some

August 1997. Course reconstruction begins on the eighteenth green. *L–R:* S Cody, P Stack, D Canton, J Harrington, H Lynch, M Coughlan.

holes presents a sufficient degree of difficulty for the moderate/average player.

Increased yardage, with present-day equipment and standard of play in mind, would be helpful, and to this end, should the club acquire adjoining land steps could be taken to achieve this.[28]

The bunker reconstruction programme was carried out over the following three years, and was completed early in 1995.

Towards the end of 1995, a number of problems with the greens – involving compaction and other issues – were becoming apparent, and it became clear that the only long-term viable solution was a complete rebuilding of the greens. This inevitably led to consideration of a complete reconstruction of the course. The course at Douglas had remained largely unchanged since the redesign by Alister MacKenzie in the mid-1920s, and in the eyes of many a more challenging layout was needed, given that improvements in club and ball design had put long hitting within the reach of the average player, and that the club had acquired some additional land. During 1996 proposals for a redesign of the course were invited from three course-design consultants, and that of Sporting Concepts Ltd was chosen in November of that year. The cost of the proposed reconstruction would be in the region of £1 million, and it was planned to have the eighteen-month programme of work commence in spring 1997.

This was to be the biggest and most costly programme of work ever carried out at the club, and the proposals generated some misgivings. Some members of the general committee had doubts about the suitability of the proposed sand-based greens, while others felt that decisions were being made too quickly, and that the reconstruction should be spread over a longer period.[29] A presentation on the proposed redesign was made to members by Peter McEvoy of Sporting Concepts Ltd at two information evenings in December 1996 prior to an EGM in January 1997 that would be asked to formally approve the proposal.

The EGM, attended by 219 members, was held on 3 January 1997, and was asked to approve the motion

that this meeting authorise the General Committee of the club to engage the firm of Sporting Concepts Ireland Limited to upgrade and re-model the Course in accordance with the plans, as displayed in the Clubhouse, at a cost of £673,000 + VAT together with possible additional expenses, to a maximum amount of £280,000, to cover cost of replacement of machinery, loss of Green Fees, loss of Bar Gross Profit and other necessary and ancillary costs attendant thereon.[30]

The rationale for the proposal, as well as details of the costs and financing of the project, were presented to the meeting. The ensuing debate was passionate and sometimes heated. A number of speakers expressed strong reservations about the proposal, feeling that not enough time was given to the planning of the reconstruction, others were against the specific plans for some holes, while more wanted extra time to make submissions. Strong support for the proposal was also expressed, the minutes of the meeting recording one accomplished golfer saying 'that the club had taken the best advice and unfortunately he had to say that if a person was driving well in Douglas that it was really only a Pitch and Putt course and he felt that what was proposed would make it a most interesting course for all handicap golfers.' The poor performance of club teams in national competitions was put down by some to the non-challenging nature of the course. The vote to approve the motion was carried by 117 to 90.

At a later general committee meeting, a sub-committee to oversee the redevelopment project was formed, its members being 1997 president and captain, John Sheehan, and Donal O'Herlihy, Fintan Sheehan, Pat Stack, Tom Linehan and 1996 captain, Kieran Barry. The sub-committee was to run for the duration of the project.[31] The contract with Sporting Concepts Ltd was signed on 24 March 1997, and ten days later, on 3 April, a letter signed by twenty-four club members, including ten past officers, was received by the committee calling for an EGM to rescind the agreement.[32] This EGM, held on 17 April, was attended by 257 members. The meeting was quite tense, and opinions on both sides of the debate were deeply held and passionately expressed. The proposer of the motion to rescind the agreement felt that the proposed project could be disastrous for the club, and he asked for more time for the members to consider it. The proposed cost was also a worry, and with increased maintenance on the new course, he felt that the annual subscription would greatly increase. The minutes of the meeting record his final point: 'he said that it was obvious where we were heading, we were heading for an exclusive country style club and he felt this was not what Douglas Club was meant for'.[33] The arguments in favour and against the project were then expressed by a number of speakers, many of whom voiced their worry that the club was being split. The meeting was adjourned indefinitely after Martin Langan, who had stood to speak, collapsed and later died.

The general committee had a special meeting a week later to review the situation, and it was clear that views on both sides of the debate had hardened. A delegation from the committee had met with a number of those seeking to rescind the agreement, but they were

The course
from the air,
2006.

not willing to withdraw their motion. The situation became potentially more perilous when the meeting was informed that Sporting
Concepts Ltd might seek a large sum in compensation for each week's
delay. The danger of a serious rift within the club was a concern to
all, and it was agreed that written submissions would be sought from
members on the proposed course redesign, and that these would be
considered at an open forum on 14 May before the EGM would be
reconvened on 26 May to consider the motion to rescind the original
agreement.

At the reconvened EGM, the written submissions by members and
the suggestions that were made at the open forum were outlined by the
president. An alternative proposal was then put to the meeting by a
member who outlined in detail a phased and less costly redevelopment
of the course that could be agreed with Sporting Concepts in place
of the original plan. The meeting approved of this proposal, and
adjourned pending discussions between members of the committee
and Sporting Concepts. Two days later, on 28 May, a delegation from
the general committee met with Paddy Governey, managing director
of Sporting Concepts Ltd, with a view to renegotiating the contract
to accommodate the new proposal from the EGM. The meeting
lasted four hours, and a compromise proposal was finally agreed.
Sporting Concepts would not alter its proposed design but would

agree to a two-phased redevelopment, completing nine holes in the first phase of work for half the contract price, and completing the second nine holes for a similar cost at a later stage if the club decided to finish the project. This would essentially mean a phased two-year redevelopment. Members were circulated with the new proposals, and the EGM convened for the third time on 16 June.

The president, John Sheehan, outlined to the meeting the somewhat tortured history of the project since it was first mooted over eighteen months previously, and said: 'I appeal not as John Sheehan but as President of Douglas Golf Club for sensible discussion on the motions … We are, after all, all members of the same Club, we may not agree with the actions of others but for the sake of the club we have to pull together.'[34] In the debate that followed, it was pointed out that a decision to rescind the original agreement could cost the club in excess of £200,000 in compensation and other costs, while the course would remain unchanged and with ongoing problems with the greens. It was felt by one speaker that 'there seems to be a great fear amongst the membership to move forward'; another said 'there was a danger that the club was going to self-destruct if it did not move forward'. A vote was eventually taken on the 17 April motion to rescind the agreement, and this was defeated by a large majority. The compromise two-phase project proposal agreed with Sporting Concepts was passed overwhelmingly, with only two

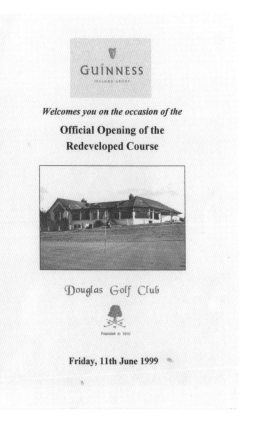

votes against, and a third vote approved an amendment that would facilitate the second stage of the project. At a subsequent EGM held on 18 August, there was unanimous support for the second phase of the redevelopment to go ahead. The EGM also considered the issues concerning the financing of the project. However, during this meeting, Jack Harrington, the 1992 president, was taken ill while speaking, and later died.

The controversies and tragedies associated with the course redevelopment made this a very trying and sometimes upsetting period for club members. The work on the course was carried out over almost two years from the summer of 1997. Eighteen new, large, sand-based greens were built, as well as new tees and bunkers. While all holes underwent some alteration, the first, fourth, fifth and seventeenth were changed most – the first and seventeenth, for example, being considerably lengthened. The work was completed in 1999, and the new course was officially opened on 11 June 1999. While there was general satisfaction with the new course, a number of players found it a little too challenging, and in 2004 golf architects Donal Steel and Jeff Howes were invited to inspect the course and suggest alterations. The submission of Howes was chosen, and his suggested alterations were presented to members at information evenings later that year. The 2005 AGM gave the go-ahead for his suggested work. The remodelling maximised the length of the course, with the construction of new tees on the first, second, fourth, fifth, sixth, eighth, ninth, tenth, thirteenth and seventeenth holes, and changes were made to the fairway bunkering on a number of holes. In all, twenty-eight bunkers were removed from the course by early 2008, and since then ten further bunkers have been remodelled. Changes have been made in the plantations on the course, and 300 trees were planted between 2007 and 2009. While the present course follows the general layout of the Mackenzie redesign of 1925, in that most holes still have their original orientation, the changes made in 1963, the major redesign of 1998–99, and the course work undertaken since 2005 have long since diluted the Mackenzie influence.

The course record of 63 is held (2009) by Peter O'Keeffe. He achieved this gross score when playing for James Doolin's Captain's Prize in 2007, scoring an eagle, eight birdies, eight pars and one bogey. A little bit of Douglas Golf Club history was also made on the course some years earlier, in 1992, when Jim Collins had two holes in one in the one round, on the fourth and on the seventeenth, while his brother Tom – centenary-year captain – also had a hole in one on the same day!

Douglas Golf Club Ladies' Branch

Women have been active golfers at Douglas from the club's foundation in 1909, and their affairs were initially looked after by the honorary secretary of the Ladies' Branch, Miss Amy Gregg. She lived at that time in Ballinlough House, and according to the 1911 census returns was the eldest daughter of Mary de la Cour Gregg, a widow. Miss Gregg partnered Mr Winder in the first reported competition on the new course at Douglas on 21 April 1910, a mixed foursome. Ladies' golf was well established in the Cork region by 1909, with ladies' branches at each of the other three Cork clubs and a number of inter-club competitions being regularly contested, in addition to the confined activities. The demand for golf by women in Cork is shown by the fact that the *Irish Field* reported on 18 December 1909 that the limit for lady members at the new Douglas club had almost been reached before the course first opened for play.

The Struggle

There was an unprecedented growth in the popularity of golf amongst both men and women in the latter part of the nineteenth century, but the women's game generally functioned in a secondary role to that of the men. An exclusively ladies' club was founded in Ireland as early as 1888 when the Hollywood Ladies' Golf Club was set up by fifteen women, only five of whom played golf![1] The vast majority of clubs, however, were founded and run by men in almost all cases, and the women belonged to a 'ladies' branch', a distinct group within a club with lesser rights and privileges. A very small number of early clubs did give equal rights to women. At Malahide, for example – founded in 1892 – women unusually had full access to the course, and could attend and vote at annual general meetings, but could not become members of the committee. The Curragh Golf Club also gave women full membership and full voting rights. These were very much the exception, however, and in the case of Malahide a ten-year controversy on the issue was not resolved until 1948, when women were relegated to associate membership within the club, the Curragh having brought their constitution in line with GUI demands in 1938. Given that women in general society did not enjoy equality of treatment and opportunity with men, it could be argued that women's golf had done well to have achieved the position it had by the beginning of the twentieth century.

Up until the later nineteenth century, golf for women was a relatively tame affair – more akin to a short version of pitch and putt rather than golf, in that it consisted of only chipping and putting. The customs of the time would not have allowed 'respectable' women to engage in the more vigorous strokes required for the longer game, and the restrictive nature of their clothing would in any case have militated severely against energetic swinging. As the nineteenth century drew to a close, women – especially those of the middle classes – enjoyed more emancipation in the area of sport as attitudes and customs became more enlightened. Outdoor exercise by way of swimming, cycling, tennis, hockey and golf grew more popular as their value in promoting good health was increasingly recognised. The wives and daughters of the professional and merchant classes had the leisure time and the opportunity to indulge their interest in sport, and the added benefit of appropriate social interaction with others of a similar background saw the growth of many clubs in a variety of sports. Golf for women in Ireland grew in parallel to that in Britain, and, indeed, Ireland was somewhat ahead of its neighbours when the Irish Ladies' Golf Union was founded in 1893.

May Hezlet, born in 1882, was a pioneer in Irish ladies' golf, and won the Irish Women's Close Championship on five occasions and the British Amateur title three times. In 1904 she wrote *Ladies' Golf* – essentially a guide to the playing of golf for women – in which she addresses the benefits of golf for women:

> It is essentially a game for women: the exercise is splendid, without being unduly violent, as is sometimes the case in hockey or tennis, and the life in the open air has a most beneficial effect upon both the mind and body. The game is, of course, not meant to be the sole object and aim of life, but as a relaxation and occupation for spare time it is better than any other sport of its kind. It has, indeed, proved a boon and a blessing to many women, who would otherwise be leading bored, aimless lives; and when one sees the numbers who frequent the links, one wonders how they managed to exist before they learnt to play golf.[2]

In the later nineteenth century, and indeed in the following century also, as more and more women took up sport, those who excelled, including golfers, were often lampooned and regarded as unladylike. This was a reaction to the growing emancipation of women, which was seen as a threat by many men, and it made it more difficult for women in sport to be taken seriously. An article in the *Cork Examiner* in 1911 by the newspaper's golf correspondent is not untypical of the attitude to women in golf at the time:

Flapping skirts and unsteady headgear were a hindrance to early women golfers.

We cannot, of course, expect from ladies the same rigid regard for the canons of sport which are held so sacred and so inviolable by mere man. We have got to consider the more excitable temperament of the lady competitor, for no matter how much they are associated with outdoor sport they will never be able to withstand the strain and excitement, and retain the clear mind to view everything in the proper perspective.[3]

In her 1904 book, May Hezlet took issue with those who belittled women golfers:

It is very unfair that a whole class of people should be judged by one or two unfortunate specimens, but that is what generally happens, and non-golfers are only too delighted to find something to criticise. They imagine a picture of the 'golfing girl', a weird and terrible creature clad in the most extraordinary garments, striding along with self-possessed walk, and oblivious to everything but her beloved game.[4]

The issue of comfortable and appropriate clothing for the golf course also exercised the early women golfers. Taboos in relation to women's clothing were relaxing a little as the nineteenth century ended, and the growth of women's golf was no doubt helped by the acceptance of less restrictive fashions, especially for the playing of sport. Until the 1930s women golfers wore, and were expected to wear, 'skirts of decorous length, sleeved upper garments, and hats or bandeaux'.[5] Trousers were still taboo. May Hezlet again articulated the difficulties faced a century ago:

For a woman it is one long struggle; not only has she to fight against the elements and expend her strength trying to get the ball to travel any distance, but she has also to battle with flapping skirts and unsteady headgear, making an effort through it all to keep neat and tidy.[6]

Things eased in the years after the First World War, and women's golfing attire gradually became more comfortable. A significant line was crossed in 1933 at the British Ladies' Championship at Westward Ho! when a Miss Gloria Minoprio appeared on the course wearing 'a pair of exquisitely-tailored trousers with knife-edge creases'. The reaction of onlookers 'ranged from admiration by males to scandalised consternation among competitors and officials'.[7] The LGU and most players objected, but a point had been made. Within a few years, trousers had become commonplace, and eyebrows were no longer raised as women opted in increasing numbers to wear them.

Restrictions on what women could wear on the golf course were but an element of the greater issue of gender inequality in golf. In the 1970s gender inequalities in broader society were addressed, and the equal status of women and their right to equal treatment with men in many areas of life and work was enshrined in law. The growing realisation and acceptance that women were entitled not to be discriminated against on the grounds of gender led to a demand by some within the world of women's golf that the lower status of women within golf clubs needed to be changed. This pressure for equality accelerated in the 1980s and into the 1990s. Within Douglas Golf Club, the issue was first looked at in a serious way in 1996, and although a new constitution was introduced in 2000 that allowed for gender equality in club affairs, it was 2002 before there was full agreement on how it was to be implemented (see chapter 11 for a detailed treatment of the topic).

Douglas Ladies

In the hundred years since golf was first played at Douglas, the club's Ladies' Branch, as it was known until 2000, has catered admirably for the golfing and social needs of its members. No doubt the pioneering Miss Gregg and her fellow golfers had also to deal with the slights and obstacles experienced by women golfers elsewhere, but they persevered and established an enduring tradition of participation, enjoyment and success that has been the hallmark of women's golf in Douglas for a century.

While the minute books of committee and annual general meetings of the Ladies' Branch at Douglas do not survive for the years before 1939, the branch was organised at the club and was quite active from the beginning. *Guy's Cork Almanac and Directory* for 1911 lists Miss A Gregg of Ballinlough House as the honorary secretary – a position she held for a number of subsequent years. The 1939 AGM of the Ladies' Branch is noted in the minutes as the twenty-seventh such meeting, indicating that the first AGM was held in 1912. This would suggest that the formal structures of the branch were set up in 1911. From 1939 – when the Ladies' Branch records begin – until the later 1960s, the minutes of meetings of the ladies' committee are quite short, rarely extending over one handwritten page. The committee meetings were mostly concerned with arrangements for competitions, and were held at Cork City Library initially, and later at the Green Door restaurant, which was owned by club member Mrs C J (Myra) Riordan, and occasionally at

Ladies of Douglas Golf Club, 1957.

the B & C, Pavilion and Thompson's restaurants. It was not until the 1960s that meetings were regularly held at the clubhouse, even though the first AGM to be held there was in 1946.

When the records begin in April 1939, Mrs M Murphy was lady captain, Mrs J Henchy was honorary secretary and Dr M Lucey was handicap manager. In addition to these officers, four others served on the ladies' committee at the time, giving a total of seven. From reports in *Irish Golf*, it can be established that for the years 1935 to 1938, the lady captains were Miss V Sullivan, Mrs C Murphy, Miss J McCarthy and Mrs J Henchy. In 1935 that magazine refers to a Miss K O'Mahony as 'ex-captain' of the branch, suggesting that she held office in 1934. It is quite likely that Miss Amy Gregg, honorary secretary in the early years, was honoured as lady captain at some stage before the mid-1930s. Miss Gregg was still involved with the club as late as 1940, when she is recorded as having presented a prize to the ladies.[8] Miss Eleanor Tivy was also lady captain some time in the 1920s or 1930s. She joined Douglas in 1922, and although she is recorded as having resigned her membership in 1935, she renewed it later and was clearly a devoted Douglas member: she was made an honorary member of the club for the years 1940–46 while she served as president of the Irish Ladies' Golf Union; in 1942 she presented a prize to the club 'which would be 18 holes stroke & not more than seven clubs to be carried as these were Miss Tivy's wishes';[9] she presided at the 1945 AGM of the Douglas Ladies' Branch, and is recorded as having sent her apologies for not attending the 1946 and 1947 meetings; in 1944 she offered a prize 'for a competition to help the professional';[10] in 1970 Eleanor Tivy attended the inaugural Past Lady Captains' Dinner. Miss Tivy was also a member of Cork Golf Club, and – like many others – probably maintained membership of both clubs simultaneously.

Left, Munster Junior Cup winners 1963. *L–R*: Mrs D Collins, Mrs J Cronin, Mrs J Horgan, Mrs K Spillane, Miss M Mackesy.
Right, Past lady captains 1998 at the Golden Jubilee Dinner in honour of Eileen O'Callaghan, lady captain in 1948. *Back, L–R*: Claire O'Connor, Mary Cody, Pat Desmond, Ann Heskin, Helen Elwood, Carmel Murphy, Ruth McGrath. *Middle, L–R*: Kate Cawley, Phyllis Harrington, Helen Hennessy, Marjorie Horgan, Ann Dorgan, Breda Treacy, Jo Lyden, Edie Scannell, Mary Collins, Clare Keating, Rena Jordan. *Front, L–R*: Zelie Gaynor, Jill Hornibrook, Eileen O'Callaghan, Betty Barrett, Mary Mackey, Helen O'Sullivan, Yvonne Crofts.

Up to the 1980s the Ladies' Branch at Douglas tended to have very long-serving honorary secretaries and handicap managers. Miss Amy Gregg was the honorary secretary from the branch's foundation for a number of years, and Mrs J (Aileen) Henchy held that office from at least 1935 to 1940, except for 1938, when she was lady captain. (It has not as yet proved possible to establish the names of the honorary secretaries between Miss Amy Gregg and Mrs J Henchy.) It is most likely that Mrs Henchy held the office for some years prior to 1935, as in February 1938 *Irish Golf* noted that in becoming lady captain, she resigned as honorary secretary 'after many years service'. Mrs Henchy was succeeded in 1941 by Miss Julianne McCarthy, who had served on the ladies' committee for a number of years prior to that. She held the post until 1961, with the exception of 1950, when Miss E T O'Callaghan held the office. When Julianne McCarthy died in 1961, the ladies' committee gathered subscriptions for a trophy in her memory, and it was first played for in July 1963. Julianne McCarthy achieved a legendary status within the club, and her name became synonymous with the office she held for twenty years. Her successor, Mary Horgan, became equally legendary and long-serving, and was honorary secretary from 1961 until her death in 1982. For those twenty years, she and Maureen O'Donovan – as handicap manager – maintained an iron grip on the affairs of the Ladies' Branch, and it was often difficult for committee members and lady captains to be innovative and to bring about change given the experience and knowledge of those formidable and long-serving officers. The branch was efficiently run through those years, and some changes *were* introduced. From 1966 the committee consisted of nine, including officers –an increase of two – and from 1970 there were eleven committee members. It was decided at the 1964 AGM that committee members would have to resign after three years' service, but that they could seek re-election after a lapse of one year. While this facilitated the introduction of new members to committee while also allowing a measure of continuity, no time limit was put on the length of service of the honorary secretary or handicap manager.

The 1980s saw the administration of the Ladies' Branch change and modernise as the old order that had served the ladies so well gave way to a newer approach. Mary Horgan, honorary secretary since 1961, died in August 1982, and was succeeded by Maureen Rose, who served until her death in 1985. Maureen O'Donovan had become handicap manager in 1952, following her term as lady captain in 1951, and ably served the ladies of Douglas in that capacity for the next thirty-two years. Following the death of Mary Horgan, the committee decided that Maureen O'Donovan needed the help of an assistant, and Helen Hennessy agreed to accept the position.[11] At the November committee meeting, a discussion was held on the appropriate term of office for the branch officers, and it was decided that the rules should be changed to read that the honorary secretary and handicap manager would not hold office for longer than three consecutive years; at the AGM in February 1983, this proposal was approved, despite some dissent.[12]

Maureen O'Donovan signalled her intention to retire as handicap manager towards the end of 1982, and in January 1983, 'A letter was read from M O'Donovan stating that she was resigning as Hon Handicap Manager. She thanked

Left, Maureen O'Donovan, handicap manager, 1952–84.
Right, Zelie Fallon with the 1964 Irish Amateur Close trophy, and the ladies' committee,
with club captain, J J O'Hea.

the committee for all their help during her years of office.'[13] Maureen O'Donovan
had joined Douglas in 1926, and was made an honorary life member of the club in
1980. She died in 2002 at the age of ninety-six. Helen Hennessy succeeded Maureen
O'Donovan in 1983; from then, three consecutive years is the maximum branch
officers have served. The resolution passed at the AGM in 1983 was observed, but
it was January 1986 before a branch EGM decided to amend the bye-laws and the
title honorary handicap secretary replaced that of honorary handicap manager,
while bye-law 12 was changed to read: 'The Hon Secretary, Hon Treasurer and
Hon Handicap Secretary must be Lady Associate Members of the club for five years
prior to election and may not hold office for more than three consecutive years.'[14]

For many decades, the ladies' committee principally concerned itself with the
organisation of competitions, and only occasionally debated matters such as the
secondary status of ladies in the club and the procedures for the admission of lady
associate members. In January 1942 the ladies' committee discussed the rights of
lady associates and 'their treatment in general' with a view to requesting the general
committee – or 'the men', as they are frequently referred to – to grant better playing
rights.[15] The following month, the ladies' honorary secretary was instructed to write
to the general committee asking for permission to hold competitions on Sundays,
'and pointing out that the majority of the members were business girls who cannot
enter for Tuesday competitions on the short days'.[16] The men's captain replied that
Tuesday would continue to be ladies' day, with right of way for ladies up until 6pm.
A small concession was made, with ladies having the first tee reserved for them
from 1–2pm on Sundays.[17] This continued to be an issue for the ladies, and a cause
of frequent annoyance.

The right of the general committee to select and elect lady associate members
also exercised the ladies' committee, especially from the 1980s. Equality for women

had been achieved in many spheres, and it is not surprising that the situation in golf clubs began to be addressed. In 1987, for example, the ladies' committee wrote to the general committee requesting an involvement in the selection of new lady members.[18] The following month, the lady captain received a list of potential new lady members from the general committee, with the request that the ladies choose 'a few names'. Four names from the list were chosen and recommended for membership. However, the lady captain informed the next committee meeting that none of the four had been elected by the general committee. The ladies accepted this rebuff but were not deterred, and 'agreed that our approach was the right one, and we should try again next year'.[19] The general committee placated the ladies somewhat in granting the lady captain the privilege of nominating one new lady associate member in her year of office, in line with the existing right of the president and captain. Even that concession met with objections from some members of the general committee, but the decision was carried on a vote. The inexorable progress towards equality had begun!

While there was subsequently some consultation with the ladies regarding the selection of new members, by 1992 it was felt to be unsatisfactory, and a letter was sent to the general committee outlining the reasons why the ladies should have an input into the selection of new lady associate members when vacancies arose.[20] It was reported in January 1994 that no progress had been made on the issue, and it was a growing cause for concern as the ladies wished to ensure an intake of 'a small number of lowish handicaps ... to replace the large number of elderly members who cannot play and have not played in some cases for years'.[21] This pressure from the ladies for what they saw as a proportionate input on a matter of fundamental importance coincided with the growing pressure on all golf clubs to address the matter of equality, and from 1996 this was formally addressed within the club, leading to the adoption of the new three-tier management structure in 2000, and an agreement two years later on the implementation of measures that gave the women at Douglas equal status with the men (see chapter 11).

The manner in which the names of lady captains are recorded on the club honour board reflects the change in attitude on the part of the ladies of Douglas as well as wider changes in the status of women in society. Up to 1995, married lady captains, with a small number of exceptions, are recorded under their husbands' names: Maureen O'Donovan, for example, is recorded as Mrs W J O'Donovan. Unmarried women are recorded as 'Miss' with the initial of their first name. In 1995 a long-established tradition was broken, and the lady captain for that year had her full name recorded without title – Pat Desmond. From 1999 this has become the norm for all.

Golf

The Douglas Ladies' Branch was always very active, and from its foundation regular reports appear in the local press of the various ladies' competitions at the club and about the involvement of Douglas ladies in inter-club events. In the mid-1930s Mrs D P McCarthy, whose husband was captain in 1933 and 1934, dominated club competitions. In 1934, for example, she won the Derby and Championship Cups, and the following year won the O'Regan Cup, the President's Prize for Ladies, the Lady Captain's Prize and the Championship Cup. Other ladies who were frequently mentioned in reports at that time were Miss M Howard, Miss K O'Mahony, Miss K O'Callaghan and Mrs P Coveney. In the early 1940s Miss E T (Eileen) O'Callaghan came to the fore, 'a young player at Douglas who shows very promising signs', according to *Irish Golf* in June 1940, and she was the club's most successful golfer until Zelie Fallon came on the scene later in the decade. John McKenna, the club professional from 1937, had a very significant influence on the improvement of golf at Douglas, especially amongst the ladies, and was regarded by all those he coached and mentored as a wonderful teacher. His wife Peg was a very accomplished golfer, also and was on five winning Senior Cup teams.

The big breakthrough for the ladies of Douglas came in 1952 with the first Senior Cup national title. The club had previously played in the competition, and had got to the national finals in Baltray in 1949, but the 1952 team, led by captain Peg McKenna, caused a sensation by winning the title and becoming the first club in Munster to do so since 1927. The other members of the team were Zelie Fallon, Madeleine Murphy, Eileen O'Callaghan, Mary O'Byrne and Myra Riordan. Eileen O'Callaghan had been attracting notice for her golfing prowess for over a decade, and the victory was a just reward for her dedication. Zelie Fallon had only been playing golf for five years, and having been chosen as a substitute for the Irish team in the Home Internationals in 1951, she won her first full cap in the summer of 1952, when she played for her country at Troon, becoming the first Douglas lady to win an international cap. Her performance in the Senior Cup finals merited special mention in the golfing press: 'The sweeping measure of her 6 and 5 victory over the Milltown top player [Miss V Hannin] pales almost into insignificance when compared to the shining glory of her thrilling win over Mrs Z Bolton, the British international and Curtis Cup player [in the semi-finals against Royal Portrush]'.[22] The 1952 triumph was the first of twelve Senior Cup victories won by the ladies of Douglas between that and 1990, a feat bettered only by Royal Portrush with twenty-three, and Milltown with fifteen. The club won the Senior Cup four times

in the following decade: in 1960, 1961, 1967 and 1968. In the 1980s Douglas won three victories in a row in the competition: in 1985, 1986 and 1987. Only Royal Portrush, Milltown and County Louth had previously achieved a three-in-a-row.

While Douglas lies third in the order of merit for Senior Cup wins, the club's record in the Munster section of the competition is second to none. Since 1952 Douglas have been Munster Senior Cup champions on thirty-nine occasions, including an unbroken run of twenty victories from 1964 to 1983.

The achievements of a number of individual Douglas ladies are also noteworthy:

Zelie Fallon (see feature, pp. 141–3) won the Irish Amateur Close title in 1964, and was an Irish international from 1952 to 1965, and again from 1968 to 1970. In 1972 she was non-playing captain of the Irish team. Zelie Fallon won the Munster Senior Championship in 1955, 1956, 1957, 1959 and 1961, played on the Munster interprovincial team many times, and played on six winning Douglas Senior Cup teams.

Eavan Higgins (see feature, pp. 234–7) also played on six winning Douglas Senior Cup teams, and won the Irish Amateur Close title in 1993. She won many international caps, and was on the Irish team every year from 1981 to 1996, except for 1989. She was Munster Senior Champion in 1982, 1988, 1990 and 1996, and also played for her province.

This and facing page, from left:
1973 Senior Cup champions. *Back, L–R:* Anne O'Brien, Girlie Hegarty, Ann Heskin, Margot Murphy. *Front, L–R:* Rosemary O'Regan, Mrs F Murphy (lady captain), Zelie Gaynor.

1978 Senior Cup champions. *Back, L–R:* Nuala Horan, Eavan Higgins, Helen O'Sullivan (lady captain), Rhona Hegarty. *Front, L–R:* Anne O'Brien, Ann Heskin, Mary Sheehan.

1980 Senior Cup champions. *Back, L–R:* Ann Moran, Clare Keating, Eavan Higgins, Rhona Brennan. *Front, L–R:* Ann Heskin, Jo Lyden (captain), Pat Desmond.

1985 Senior Cup champions. *Back, L–R:* Clare Keating, Eavan Higgins, Mary Harnett, Pat Desmond, Helen Elwood. *Front, L–R:* Angela Lane (team captain), Helen Hennessy (lady captain).

Ann Heskin (see feature, pp. 257–61) played on eight winning Senior Cup teams, and was Munster Senior Champion in 1970, 1971, 1974, 1975 and 1978. She gave sterling service to her province, and was a Munster team member from 1964 to 1984. She won international caps in 1969, 1970, 1972, 1975 and 1977, and was non-playing captain of the Irish team that won the European Ladies' Team Championship in 1983, as well as being non-playing captain of Ireland for the Home Internationals in 1982 and 1983.

Girlie Hegarty (see feature, pp. 144–5) was another of the Douglas greats, and won Senior Cup honours with Douglas in 1960, 1967, 1968 and 1973. She played for Ireland in 1955 and 1956, and captained the Irish team in the Home Internationals in 1964.

Oonagh Fitzpatrick (Heskin) was on the winning Douglas Senior Cup teams of 1967 and 1968, and won her first international cap in 1967 in the Home Internationals. She was chosen to play for her country again in 1969 for the Home Internationals, but had to cry off, and was also on the Irish team for the European Team Championship that year. Oonagh was Munster Senior Champion in 1969, and was on the Munster interprovincial side in 1966, 1968, 1970, 1971 and 1980.

Anne O'Brien was a member of six winning Douglas Senior Cup teams, and was Munster Senior Champion in 1963 and 1967. Anne was also a regular on the Munster team from 1964 to 1974. She won international honours in 1969 when she was chosen for the Irish team in that year's Home Internationals. In that year, four Douglas ladies were chosen to play for Ireland: Zelie Fallon, Ann Heskin, Oonagh Heskin and Anne O'Brien.

Eileen Rose Power (McDaid) has played Senior Cup with Douglas on a number of occasions, and was on the winning teams of 1986, 1987 and 1990. She won the Irish Close in 1990 and 1992, and played on the Curtis Cup team in 1994. She played for Ireland in the Home Internationals from 1987 to 1996, and was also on the Irish team in the European Ladies' Team Championship from 1987 to 1995. Eileen Rose Power was Munster Senior Champion in 1985, 1993 and 1994.

Rhona Brennan (Hegarty) was on the winning Douglas Senior Cup team in 1978 and 1980, and was Munster Senior Champion in 1976, 1979 and 1981. She played for Ireland in the Home Internationals from 1974 to 1979, and again in 1981. She also played for her country in the European Ladies' Team Championship of 1979 and 1981.

Clare Keating was a champion pitch-and-putt player, and had won fourteen national titles before she turned to golf, where she also excelled. Clare was Munster Senior Champion in 1986, and won five Senior Cups with Douglas. She was also a member of the Munster interprovincial side from 1980 to 1984, and again in 1987 and 1988.

Douglas and the Irish Ladies' Golf Union (ILGU)

Douglas ladies have served the ILGU at every level of the organisation. In 1940 Eleanor Tivy became president of the ILGU, and served until 1946. Girlie Hegarty was president from 1974 to 1976, and in 1982 was elected honorary life vice-president. She also served on the Southern District executive, the ILGU central council and the LGU executive council. Ann Heskin is the third Douglas member to have served as president, holding office for the years 2005 and 2006. Ann also served on the Southern District executive and the central council of the ILGU, and followed that with a term on the LGU executive council.

Rena Jordan has given long and dedicated to the ILGU, serving as a member of the Southern District executive as well as taking on the duties of assistant honorary secretary with responsibility for fixtures, including the various leagues and championships. Rena also served as chairman of the Southern executive, and on the ILGU central council. Maura Coffey and Ann Moran served as honorary secretary of the Southern District executive, and a number of other Douglas ladies have given of their time to serve as members of the executive, including Zelie Falon, Anne O'Brien, Clare Keating, Margaret Barry, Angela Lane and Helen O'Sullivan. The latter two have also served as chair of the executive.

Senior Foursomes, 2009

In September 2009 the ladies of Douglas provided their club with a significant highlight for centenary year when they won the All-Ireland Senior Foursomes at Royal Tara. Having beaten tournament favourites, Carlow, in the semi-finals, the pairings of Karen O'Neill & Deirdre M O'Hanlon, Eavan Higgins & Wendy Daly and Kate MacCann & Sabina Nagle went on to beat Ballycastle 2½ to ½ in the final (see p. 247).

Facing page, from left: 1986 Senior Cup champions. *Back, L–R:* Mary Harnett, Clare Keating, Eavan Higgins, P Turvey (honorary secretary, ILGU), Ann Heskin, Ann Hegarty, Eileen Rose McDaid. *Front, L–R:* E M Bruen (president, ILGU), E Duddy (Castlerock GC), Yvonne Crofts (lady captain), Angela Lane, D Nutt (Castlerock GC), A Tunney (honorary treasurer, ILGU).

1987 Senior Cup champions. *Back, L–R:* Mary Mackey, Clare Keating, Ann Hegarty, Ann Heskin. *Front, L–R:* Eavan Higgins, Angela Lane (team captain), Helen Elwood (lady captain), Eileen Rose McDaid.

Eavan Higgins

Eavan Higgins, winner of the 1993 Irish Amateur Close title.

'If I wasn't going to win then I wanted to come second, and if not second then third,' says Eavan Higgins as she explains how her competitive spirit drove her from an early age. As a schoolgirl in Clonmel, Eavan loved to compete, and she played tennis, table tennis, hockey, pitch and putt, golf and also rowed. After leaving school in 1974, she moved to Cork where she started work with an insurance company. Eavan remembers that on her second day at work, Girlie Hegarty, a long-time member of Douglas and an astute judge of golfing ability, called to the office to see her, told her that she was now a member of Douglas Golf Club, and that she was to use the membership and play! Eavan's father had been a member of Douglas in the early 1950s before the family moved to Clonmel, and he had spoken to Girlie about Eavan joining. Eavan had played golf in Clonmel and Tramore before coming to Cork, and unknown to her, Girlie had contacted Pat O'Sullivan of Tramore Golf Club, a former international and Irish captain, to establish her golfing bona fides. Satisfied that Eavan Higgins was a potential asset to the ladies of Douglas, the way was clear for Eavan to join. It was an astute move on Girlie's part as over the following twenty years, Eavan Higgins represented Douglas with distinction, and won a host of provincial, national and international honours.

Eavan Higgins first played Senior Cup with Douglas in 1976, and she has been a member of the team every year since, winning the national title in 1978, 1980, 1985, 1986, 1987 and 1990. She played for Ireland in the Home Internationals every year from 1981 to 1996, except in 1989, and played in the European Team Championship in 1981, 1983, 1987, 1989, 1991, 1993 and 1995. She won the Irish Amateur Close title in 1993, won the Munster Senior Championship four times, and was a member of the Munster team that won the interprovincial title in 1980, 1985, 1986, 1991 and 1993. In addition, Eavan has won innumerable scratch cups, open competitions and other local and club events.

In her first years at Douglas, Eavan remembers the friendship and help of Dick and Angela Lane, and of their daughter Oonagh. Amongst the ladies of the club at the time, Ann Heskin, Anne O'Brien and Girlie Hegarty stand out as formidable golfers and mentors who helped her settle in and had her playing on the Senior Cup team by 1976. This was Eavan's introduction to serious competitive golf, and through the decades since she has travelled with the Douglas team and supporters to most of Ireland's golf clubs, making long-lasting friends through golf in all four provinces. Eavan feels that her involvement with the Senior Cup team was the foundation for her later successes as she learned not only how to play at a serious level but, more importantly, how to compete. Eavan's first of six successes with the Senior Cup team came in 1978 when Douglas beat Royal Portrush in the final at Grange 4 to 1, and her last Senior Cup triumph came in 1990 when she captained the team. As her golf improved, and as her talent and potential to achieve at the highest level became apparent in the later 1970s, she found that the members at Douglas were keen to give her every possible support and encouragement in a very unselfish manner. 'It's what you do,' she explains.

As she developed as a golfer, Eavan wanted to be able to get distance from the tees as well as improving her short game. 'It's all about distance,' she says. 'I wanted to stand up there and hit it hard.' She found that playing with some of the better, big-hitting male golfers at Douglas helped her greatly. She played often with Bill and John Kelleher, John C Morris, Douglas professional Gary Nicholson, and later with John McHenry. She was given no shots, had to play from the men's tees, and had to stretch herself to keep up. Eavan played fourballs with players like these at least once a week, and on summer evenings often carried on for a further nine holes after playing a full round. This strengthened her game, and gave her a power that many women never achieve.

Eavan competed at the highest level from 1976 to her retirement from the competitive scene in 1996, and amongst many achievements her Irish Amateur Close title in 1993 stands out as a highlight. She had competed every year from 1975, and had disappointingly lost two finals, in 1986 and 1988. In 1993 the Irish Ladies' Golfing Union celebrated its centenary, and winning the title in that year would have an added historical significance. Eavan vividly remembers the event and her feelings as she won through to the final at Royal Belfast: 'I remember standing on the first tee in the final and thinking that losing just wasn't an option. I stood there and I knew I was going to win … It was nearly a scary feeling. It didn't make me nervous. It got me to the level I needed on the day.' After six holes, Eavan and her opponent, Aideen Rogers, were level, and she recalls the moment that she decided to up her game and go for the win: 'I remember going down the seventh and I just felt that we were ambling along. I remember saying to myself, "If I keep going like this I'm going nowhere." It was a case of "You need to do something."' She did 'do something', and went 3 up over the next four holes, but lost some of that lead over subsequent holes, and was 1 up playing the eighteenth. 'I remember standing on the eighteenth green – I had two putts for it. I said I'd take the two putts and not do anything dramatic.' She did take the two putts but did something dramatic by winning the title, the first Douglas winner since Zelie Fallon in 1964. Dermot Gilleece and John Redmond, in their *Irish Ladies' Golf Union: An Illustrated History 1893–1993*, wrote of her victory:

> And justice was seen to be done in this Centenary Year when Eavan
> Higgins was finally crowned. Defiantly overcoming doubts that she
> was fated never to win, Eavan put behind her the disappointment

of previous losses in the final, to housewife Therese O'Reilly, at Castleknock in 1986, and to Laura Bolton, at Tramore in 1988, when she finally triumphed in this special year's championship at historic Royal Belfast, over a fresh new face in Aideen Rogers of The Island, another youthful talent striking a resounding note to take us into the next generation.

The ILGU had long discontinued the practice of presenting the Irish Close champion with a replica trophy, but as it was centenary year Eavan was presented with a replica that had been acquired from Philomena Garvey, who had won the title fifteen times in her long career.

Eavan played on the Irish team in the biennial European Team Championship from her debut in 1981 until 1995. Ireland had a famous victory in the event in 1983 when it was held at Waterloo in Belgium. Ann Heskin of Douglas was the non-playing captain of the side, and Eavan Higgins played a vital role in Ireland's victory. In the quarter final against Scotland, Eavan played Pamela Wright in a pivotal match that finished dramatically on the nineteenth hole. After two shots, Eavan was off the green, 20 yards from the hole, while her opponent was on the green, 9 feet from the hole. The *Irish Times* described the finish:

> Irish hearts slumped and not for the first time during the day. But in deadly silence and watched by all her team-mates, Higgins stepped up and rolled her chip shot from 20 yards away into the hole for a birdie three. Irish cheers were heard all over this historic battleground. Little Miss Wright, not altogether unexpectedly in the circumstances, missed her putt and Ireland were through to meet Sweden in the semi-finals.

Ireland beat Sweden, and met England in the final. Eavan's partner in the four-somes match was Mary McKenna, and again Eavan played the game of her life, as they won in another dramatic finish on the nineteenth hole. Ireland led going into the afternoon singles, and needed to win only two of the five matches to take the title. Eavan again contributed, halving her match with Kitrina Douglas. Ireland took the title, and Eavan Higgins came through the championship unbeaten, having taken 5½ points out of 6.

Three years later, in 1986, Ireland had another historic win, this time in the Home Internationals, played at Whittington Barracks in Wales. Eavan Higgins was on the team, and was the top Irish performer, winning 5 out of 6 points in what was Ireland's second-only victory in the series. Her contribution on the final day's play against England was crucial to the victory, and as the history of the ILGU records:

> Indeed it was left to Miss Higgins at number five, to save the day. Admirably confident of beating Julia Walter, the Douglas player drove the ball superbly and her four-holes lead at the turn included two winning birdies. She finished the match at the 15th where she recovered from a greenside trap to two feet for a winning par.[1]

The international victories in 1983 and 1986 are especially memorable for Eavan as in each case her performance was crucial to the win.

1990 Senior Cup. *Back, L–R:* Ann Heskin, Ann Hegarty, Clare Keating, Mary Mackey, Aoife Lane. *Front, L–R:* Tim O'Sullivan (president), Eileen Rose McDaid, Eavan Higgins (team captain), M Collins (lady captain), Dan Thomas (captain).

Eavan retired from the competitive scene in 1996 after over twenty years in the top flight of ladies' amateur golf in Ireland. She remembers previewing her very full golfing schedule at the beginning of that year and thinking: 'Why exactly am I doing this?' She felt that she was, to an extent, just doing it out of habit. It was becoming difficult to maintain the will and the need to win: 'I realised that I didn't care as much when I lost, which was hugely important because that is what made me win … and I really didn't care enough when I won either.' Eavan could not, however, abandon the Senior Cup. That had been her introduction to serious competition, and given the Douglas record in the event, abandoning that would have been tantamount to abandoning golf itself.

It took Eavan two to three years to come fully to terms with her retirement. When she was competing, she practised constantly at every aspect of her game, and when she cut back on this, she found that it was difficult to play the shots that had come so easily to her in the past. The technique of visualisation – where she could see the shot as she stood to take it, where she could see where the ball would land – eluded her now. Eavan remembers playing at Lahinch a few years after her retirement, and recalls: 'I stood up on every tee and I had no idea where it was going to go. When I was in total control I did know where it was going every time.' She is quite happy now playing off 2, and has retained her competitive instinct: 'I still just want to win. I still prepare. Even with a fourball it's still important to win.'

Eavan Higgins now gives time to the coaching and management of Douglas teams, has served on committees at the club, and was lady captain in 2000. 'I feel I owe Douglas a huge amount,' she says. 'I don't think I could ever repay them for what I got out of it. I owe them more than they owe me.' When asked what part Douglas Golf Club played in her life, Eavan replied: 'I just couldn't imagine being without it.'

Douglas Golf Club and the Golfing Union of Ireland

The Golfing Union of Ireland (GUI) was founded in 1891, and Douglas Golf Club became affiliated to the Union in 1911. Douglas members have served the Union at provincial and national level in a variety of capacities over the subsequent ninety-eight years. The Munster Branch of the GUI was founded in 1921, and Mick English – a founding member of Douglas and the club's honorary secretary from 1916 to 1922 and from 1925 to 1928 – was secretary of the branch from November 1921 until April 1926. R J McKechnie, captain of Douglas in 1921 and 1922, was the chairman of the branch from April 1925 until February 1927. J G Musgrave, Douglas captain in 1928 and 1929, also served as chairman of the branch, and held office from 1933 until his death in 1937. He was succeeded by J B Coghlan, also of Douglas, who served until November 1938, when he in turn was succeeded by another Douglas member, P J Collins. P J Collins served as chairman for ten years, until November 1948. From November 1959 until November 1966, Douglas W Loane, Douglas captain in 1952, was Munster Branch secretary, and followed that seven-year term with six years as branch chairman, serving until 1971. Frank Bowen was elected chairman in 1979, and served until November 1983. In 1985 he was president of the GUI, the first serving Douglas member to hold that office. John Brett of Douglas was elected chairman of the Munster Branch in 2000, and seved until his death in 2003. From 1922 until 1945, Fred W Lambkin of Douglas was honorary auditor of the Munster Branch of the GUI. A number of other Douglas members have also served as delegates to the Munster Branch, and also to the central council of the GUI. The GUI president from 1950 to 1952 was Redmond Simcox, who began his golfing career at Douglas, and was club captain in 1925.

Left: Frank Bowen.
Right: Presentation to John Brett on being made an honorary life member of Douglas Golf Club in 2001. *L–R:* Liam Connolly, John Brett, Fintan Sheehan, Eavan Higgins.

Frank Bowen joined Douglas Golf Club in 1952 as a juvenile shortly after his family moved to Cork and settled in Blackrock. Though modest about his golfing skill, he played on Douglas Junior Cup and Barton Shield teams in the 1960s. In 1968, when Seán Martin was captain, Frank first served on the executive of the Munster Branch of the GUI, and was later match and handicap secretary for Munster. In 1979 he was elected chairman of the Munster Branch, and served for four years. He was president elect of the GUI in 1984, and in 1985 Frank Bowen became president, the first Douglas member to hold the highest administrative office in Irish golf.

Douglas Golf Club has been part of Frank Bowen's life for over fifty years. He remembers the early 1960s – when he was finding his feet as a golfer – as a period of transition. The old order was slowly giving way to a more modern approach, and at Douglas this was led by officers like Joe O'Donovan and Jim Ryan. Frank's brother James, a senior Irish international in the early 1960s, also started his golfing career at Douglas, where John McKenna coached him. He later moved to Cork Golf Club.

John Brett grew up in Woolhara Park in Douglas, and joined Douglas Golf Club as a juvenile in 1952. After studying dentistry at UCC, John went to England in 1961 and worked there for a number of years, playing his golf at Cuddington Golf Club in Surrey. Following that, he spent some time in Belfast, where he played his golf at Belvoir Park Golf Club, before returning to England to work in Cambridge. On his eventual return to Cork, he took up an appointment with the Southern Health Board, and renewed his association with Douglas Golf Club. He served on committee, represented his club on Senior Cup and Barton Shield teams, and was club captain in 1981. In 1992 he was elected as a club delegate to the Munster Branch of the GUI, and in 2000 was elected chairman of the branch, a post he held until his unexpected death in 2003. Had John lived, he would have served as president elect of the GUI in 2005, and as president in 2006. In 2001 John Brett's contribution to his home club, to the promotion of the junior game and to the administration of golf in Munster was recognised when he was made an honorary life member.

John Brett was very committed to the promotion of the game at junior level, and was captain of the Munster boys' team in 1994 and 1995. He later captained the Munster youth team in 1996, and was captain of the Irish youth team from 1997 to 1999. In 2000 he managed the Irish international youth team, and from 1997 to 2000 was a member of the GUI's junior committee. Following his death in 2003, the GUI inaugurated a competition in his memory: the John Brett Trophy is played for annually by representatives of each of the four provincial branches. In 2009, Douglas Golf Club's centenary year, the event was held at Douglas on 21 September, an appropriate honour for the club, and a fitting memorial tribute to John Brett.

John Brett is fondly remembered by all at Douglas principally as a devotee of golf but also as one with a consuming interest in, and an encyclopaedic knowledge of, all sports. As Rory Conway, club president in 2005, remarked at the conclusion of his eulogy to John at his funeral Mass, 'Ní bheidh a leithéid arís ann.'

11
Towards a New Century

Equality and a New Club Constitution

In the late 1990s the question of gender equality in the club was finally addressed, and with the introduction of the new club constitution in 2000 a framework was put in place to give women the same status as men in the club, and to give them the option for the first time of becoming full and equal members. Gender equality in sports clubs and in society in general had become an issue for serious debate in the 1960s, and over time it became increasingly accepted and enshrined in law that women were entitled to equal treatment with men in matters of employment, pay, succession and a wide range

of other areas. In light of this increasing recognition and acceptance of the right of women to equality in all areas of society, the situation in most golf clubs – where women were associate members and not entitled to the same rights and privileges as men – was seen as outdated and unfair. In 1991 a letter was sent to golf clubs from the Oireachtas Joint Committee on Women's Rights stating that attention was being given to what was considered to be the unsatisfactory situation whereby most golf clubs in the country continued to discriminate against women in regard to membership and available facilities. This Oireachtas committee requested information regarding the facilities for women and the conditions of their membership of their clubs. The general committee at Douglas discussed the letter at its meeting in February 1991, but decided not to take any action on the issue.[1]

The matter was officially left to rest for five years or so, although members and lady associate members, as well as some in the media and the broader community, continued to debate the question. In 1996 a management and structures sub-committee was set up by the club to look at the future needs of the club at all levels, and members were invited to make submissions. This sub-committee reported in April of that year, and the issue of equality of membership was addressed:

Members gather at Douglas Golf Club, on 1 January 2009 to mark the beginning of centenary year.

Equality of Membership – This Club should be pro-active in this area and not wait for legislation. The implementation of this change would necessitate certain committee structures different to what we have, but not altogether in conflict with the general thrust of members' suggestions for committee restructuring.[2]

The general committee agreed that the management and structures committee 'would be asked to give equality of membership their priority'.[3] This they did, and although controversy about the redesign of the course occupied the attentions of many at the club through 1997, the management and structures sub-committee, chaired by Willie Scannell, examined the equality issue in some detail, and the 1998 AGM approved discussions with the lady associate members at the club with a view to progressing towards a solution.

Work on the new constitution and the issue of equality continued through 1998, and a number of meetings were held between repre-sentatives of the ladies' committee at Douglas and the management and structures sub-committee. The ladies were generally dissatisfied with these encounters, and felt that they were not being allowed have a meaningful input into a process that would fundamentally affect their status and position.[4] A number of information evenings were also held to inform members of progress, and to seek their views on the proposed new structures. At an EGM on 16 October 1998 the proposed new three-tier structure for the club was approved in princi-ple. This structure was based on a model that had the approval of the GUI and the ILGU, and consisted of a men's club affiliated to the GUI and controlled by a men's committee, a ladies' club affiliated to the ILGU and controlled by a ladies' committee, and a joint club of which all full members of the two affiliated clubs are members, managed by a management committee. The other motion before the EGM was more contentious, and concerned the proposal that women becoming members at Douglas would have the option of becoming ordinary members on the same terms and conditions as men. Some speakers felt that this would discriminate against men in that women would then have the choice of ordinary or lady associate membership, a choice that men did not have. The motion was passed, with the detail of specific terms to be decided later, and the members of Douglas Golf Club thereby agreed in principle to fundamental changes in the nature of the structure and membership of the club.

Following the EGM, the work on the details of the new consti-tution and management structures continued, and the issues around the terms and conditions applying to lady associates transferring to ordinary membership were also addressed. It was hoped to have the new structures in place in 2000. The proposal that lady associates would pay an entrance fee of £1,000 on transferring to ordinary membership was quite controversial, and strongly opposed by the Ladies' Branch. The ladies wished to have representation on the management and structures sub-committee that was drafting the new constitution, but this was resisted by the general committee, and a request to have the implementation of the new structures deferred until 2001 to allow further time for resolving outstanding issues for ladies was also refused.[5]

A decision at an EGM on 15 December 1999 paved the way for the proposed new constitution and club structure to be put to an AGM in January 2000. The text of the new constitution and bye-laws was circulated to members in December 1999, and the AGM was held on 21 January. A motion was put to the AGM proposing the deferral of the introduction of the new constitution and bye-laws as the ladies of the club had expressed strong reservations about some of its provisions, and were not happy with their level of involvement in its drafting. The motion proposed the setting up of a working party of three men and three women to draw up alternative proposals. The motion was defeated, and that concerning the approval of the new constitution was passed, putting in place the new three-tier structure.

The AGM of the Ladies' Branch was held ten days later, on 31 January, and dissatisfaction was expressed with the outcome of the men's AGM. Prior to that meeting, the equal status sub-committee of the ladies' committee had sought to yet again clarify its position, and 'to confirm that in the best interests of our membership we could not recommend that they [the ladies] accept this offer of full Ordinary Membership as it currently stands'.[6] The £1,000 was a major sticking point, and as one speaker said, 'It does not give full equality with our male members, charging us an entrance fee of £1,000 was not applicable in our situation, as we were already members of the club.' A motion was carried that no lady members would apply for ordinary membership for the time being. At the last meeting of the general committee, held on 21 February 2000, a letter from the Ladies' Branch was read out in which it was stated that no ladies would be seeking transfer to ordinary membership, and that any lady who would go on the new management committee would not represent the Ladies' Branch.[7]

The inaugural meeting of the new Joint Club was held on 25 February, and that of the new Men's Club on 10 March. The minutes of the last meeting of the general committee record the following:

> Mr Connolly [2000 President] said that the General
> Committees of Douglas Golf Club had over the years
> served the club extremely well and had in the main been

Last meeting of the general committee 21 February 2000.
Standing, L–R:
J McGrath, S F Cody, D Thomas, T Linehan, M O'Donovan, P Dempsey, J Magnier, D Murray, T O'Sullivan, D Collins.
Seated, L–R: B Barrett (manager), D Hurley (vice-president), L Connolly (president), F Sheehan (captain), E Kenny (vice-captain), J O'Leary (honorary treasurer).

very hardworking committees and that he personally had admired the work load of the committees for a long number of years. He said that the future was an exciting one for the club with the new structures and he wished everybody associated with them every success … The President then invited all members of the Committee to join the Captain and himself in the Bar for a farewell drink.[8]

Although the ladies at Douglas had not accepted the conditions of ordinary membership as offered to them, the new Ladies' Club came into being in 2000 also, and functioned in accordance with the terms of the new club constitution. In 2001 the Ladies' Club formed a new equality sub-committee, and following meetings with the management committee of the Joint Club, an agreed discussion document on all issues relating to equality and ordinary membership for ladies was circulated for comment. A working group was set up consisting of three representatives each from the Men's and Ladies' Clubs, and chaired by Liam Connolly of the management committee. This group began work in February 2002, and by August an agreement was reached that was acceptable to both the Ladies' and Men's Clubs. As lady captain, Mary Sheehan said at the AGM of the Ladies' Club in February 2003: 'It has taken five years of patient negotiations to reach this agreement regarding the terms of Ordinary Membership for ladies in Douglas Golf Club … I feel it is a good and fair outcome, and certainly the best it was possible to achieve without further, perhaps years, of delay.'[9] The agreement was approved by all, and the new constitution was accordingly amended. The membership categories of lady associate and five-day lady associate were closed to new members, who could now become either ordinary or five-day-plus members – the same arrangement as for men, who could no longer become five day members. Existing lady associates transferring to ordinary membership would now pay a transfer fee on a sliding scale based on years of membership instead of the £1,000 entrance fee, and ladies who were full members could now play on Saturday and Sunday mornings. The equality issue was now considered closed.

Golf

The youths of Douglas Golf Club enjoyed success again in 2002 when they won the Munster final of the Irish Club Youths' Championship. The team was Peter O'Keeffe, Aaron O'Callaghan, Denis J Collins, Aidan Uniacke, Craig Conway and Brian Cahill. They went through to the Irish final at Royal Tara, but were beaten in the countback by Banbridge.

In the same year, the foursome of Denis J Collins, Aaron O'Callaghan, David O'Leary and Brian Cahill beat West Waterford to win the Munster final of the Irish Junior Foursomes. Unfortunately, the team lost in the national semi-finals when they were beaten by six holes by Claremorris.

Aaron O'Callaghan has represented Douglas with distinction at international level on a number of occasions since 2003. Between 2003 and 2004 he played on the Irish boy's team in the Home Internationals and in the European Youths' Team Championship, winning eleven of his nineteen matches and halving three. In 2005 and 2006 he played for Ireland at youth level, winning four of his eight matches and halving one. Aaron won his first senior international cap in 2005 also, and played eleven matches in all between that and 2006, winning two and halving two. Peter O'Keeffe played for Ireland at youth level in the Home Internationals in 2002.

Douglas schoolboy internationals, 2003: Peter O'Keeffe (top) and Aaron O'Callaghan.

Pierce Purcell Shield, 2009

In the summer of 2009 Douglas had its most successful run in the Pierce Purcell Shield since 1976. In the Munster semi-final, Douglas played Shannon, and won 4–1, having won three matches with the final two called in. The pairs that played were Richard Lonergan & Kevin N O'Sullivan, Leonard Horgan & Kevin O'Sullivan, Eddie Cogan & Frank Walsh, Michael Lucey & Andy Herbert, and Brian Kenneally & John Mackey. In the final, played at Kenmare, Douglas met Ceann Sibéal, and won 3–2, Emmet Martin & Philip O'Driscoll, Eddie Cogan & Frank Walsh and Brian Kenneally & John P Ryan winning their matches. Brian Kenneally & John P Ryan had a nail-biting finish to their match, winning on the nineteenth having been one down playing the eighteenth. The pairings of Richard Lonergan

& Kevin N O'Sullivan and Tony Barry & Andy Herbert were unfortunately beaten.

The national finals were played at Tullamore in September, but the hopes of a centenary-year victory were dashed when Douglas were beaten in their semi-final, 3–2, by Corrstown. Michael Lucey & John Scannell, and Eddie Cogan & Frank Walsh were the winners for Douglas, but Richard Lonergan & Kevin N O'Sullivan, Tony Barry & Paul Herlihy, and Frank Mackey & Philip O'Driscoll were beaten in their matches. The Douglas team was ably managed by Mark O'Sullivan, assisted by Jim Collins, Greg Forde and Bart Kenny.

While a loss is always regretted, team members find a lasting solace in the friendships made during a long campaign and in the satisfaction of having represented their club at a national level. As one member of the team remarked: 'It has been one heck of a journey to reach the All-Ireland semis, made all the more special by the great friendships made and support we have received en route … It's been great to have been part of this experience.' Tom Collins, centenary-year captain and one of the team caddies, summed up the campaign thus: 'I think it is fair to say that we started out with a group who just paid their subs at the start of the year, and we have finished up with "members".'

Ladies' Golf

The ladies of Douglas have won the Munster section of the Senior Cup on three occasions since 2000. In 2000 team captain Ann Hegarty led Eavan Higgins, Aoife Lane, Grace Harvey, Mary Mackey, Clare Keating and Ailish Thompson to victory in Munster. However, Douglas were beaten by the Curragh in the national semi-finals played at Slieve Russell Golf Club in County Cavan. The team repeated their provincial victory in 2001 – with Kate MacCann in place of Mary Mackey – when they defeated Cork Golf Club at Thurles. The Senior Cup national finals were played at Douglas that year, but the home team was unfortunately beaten in the final by Royal County Down. In 2002 Douglas ladies completed a Munster three in-a-row with Clare Keating as captain and Mary Mackey back in the side. The national finals were played at Balbriggan that year, and Douglas beat Royal County Down in the semi-finals, but were unfortunately beaten by County Louth in the final.

In September 2009 Douglas won the All-Ireland Senior Foursomes, and brought a long-awaited and well-deserved national trophy to the club in its centenary year. The competition was first played in 2006, and in 2008 Douglas was beaten in the semi-finals. In August 2009 the Munster finals of the event were held at Douglas, and the home team beat Killarney in the final, two and one. The pairing of Karen O'Neill & Deirdre M O'Hanlon won on the sixteenth, while Kate MacCann & Sabina Nagle won on the fourteenth. Eavan Higgins & Liz O'Donnell were beaten in their match on the seventeenth.

The national finals were played at Royal Tara in September, and in the semi-finals Douglas met the favourites, Carlow. Eavan Higgins & Liz O'Donnell were beaten on the seventeenth, but victories for Karen O'Neill & Deirdre M O'Hanlon and Kate MacCann and Sabina Nagle ensured a place in the final for Douglas.

Douglas played Ballycastle in the final, and won emphatically, 2½ to ½. Karen O'Neill & Deirdre M O'Hanlon won 6 and 5, Eavan Higgins & Wendy Daly won 4 and 3, and Kate MacCann & Sabina Nagle halved their match. Aoife Lane had played in the early stages, and was a substitute for the Munster and national finals. The team was managed by Kate Cawley, and captained by Pat Desmond – a veteran of many Douglas campaigns – assisted by May Sheehan and Ruth McGrath. This was the club's first national title since 1999, and the victory was an appropriate highlight for centenary year. The loyal Douglas supporters, the 'Green Army', had followed their team from the start of the campaign, and their delight at the win reminded many of times past, when national titles seemed to come more frequently to Douglas.

A Decision to Move

In November 2004 John Barry of Castlelands Construction Ltd requested a meeting with Liam Connolly, then chairman of the management committee at Douglas. At that meeting, Liam Connolly was informed that Castlelands Construction was interested in acquiring the Douglas course for development purposes. The proposed deal would give Douglas Golf Club two new courses between Carr's hill and the Ballinrea road to the west – about 1.5 kilometres south of the present course – in addition to a substantial cash payment. At that time, the country was in the grip of an unprecedented property boom: houses and development sites were changing hands for ever increasing amounts, and a site like that of the Douglas course was considered a very desirable location for housing development. It was not altogether surprising that a serious offer would be made for the land. Sports clubs in Cork and in other parts of the country had made very lucrative deals with property developers whereby club lands in areas of high development potential were sold or part exchanged in deals that gave the clubs more extensive grounds and new clubhouse buildings in another location.

The outline of the Castlelands proposal was put to an EGM in late 2004, and at the AGM in January 2005, the incoming management committee, under chairman Donal Hurley, was tasked with further investigating the proposed deal. A task force under Pat Desmond was set up, and in conjunction with the club solicitors, Barry C Galvin & Son, detailed negotiations with Castlelands Construction were conducted, and the details of a proposed deal were worked out, worth in total just over €171 million. In return for all of the club property in Maryborough, Castlelands Construction would give the club 421 acres that would be developed as two championship courses, one an eighteen-hole parkland-style course, the other an eighteen-hole heathland-type course. The courses would be the first in Ireland to be designed by the Robert Trent Jones II team. The new facility would also have a short nine-hole course, a driving range, and putting and chipping greens. In addition, a 20,000-square-foot clubhouse of the highest standard would be built, along with tennis courts and a bowling green. Castlelands would also build two maintenance buildings, and provide the full complement of machinery and equipment necessary for the two courses. Over 2,500 semi-mature deciduous trees would be planted to give the whole development a mature appearance. The club would not have to vacate the existing facility until the new development was fully complete and ready for play, and, in addition, the club would then receive a cash payment of €50 million, indexed from October 2006. The proposed development of the club lands on Maryborough Hill would be dependent on the local authorities rezoning those lands for mixed residential use, and if this were to happen in the 2009 County Development Plan, the new courses and facilities could be ready for occupation by 2012.

Following the conclusion of negotiations, the details of the proposed relocation package were put to members at an EGM in March 2007, attended by over 500 members. Approving of the proposal would mean the end of over a hundred years of golf on the familiar course on Maryborough Hill, and a move to a more rural location, though still not too distant from the slowly spreading southern suburbs of the city. Reservations were expressed by a number of members about the advisability of breaking with tradition and abandoning the ancestral home, as it were, while there was also concern about the future cost of maintaining two high-quality courses to a high standard. The detail of the proposed new package seemed almost too good to be true to some more recent members who, understandably, do not feel the same sentimental attachment to the old course. When the proposal was put to a vote, it was carried by a substantial majority, approximately eighty-seven per cent to thirteen per cent. Following the vote to accept the deal, the club received €5 million from Castlelands Construction, bringing the total non-refundable payment to the club for agreeing to the deal to €6.4 million. The die was thus cast, and Douglas Golf Club may now spend its second century on the far more extensive lands in Ballinrea.

The proposed relocation generated some controversy in the greater Cork community and in the local media also. There was a feeling that the proposed development of the club lands on Maryborough Hill was a step too far in the inexorable loss of green space in the vicinity of the city. The lands to the west, north and east of the course have already been largely developed, and building on the course would mean the loss of about 120 acres of amenity land. Voices were also raised in opposition to a trend whereby sports fields were being pushed further from centres of population as the power of the property-development euro persuaded an increasing number of clubs to relocate to new sites. The members at Douglas were aware of these concerns and, indeed, shared some of them. However, their decision to agree to the deal was taken in the best interests of the club and its future members. There was a realisation that if the relocation proposal failed to get the approval of members, it would not be very long before a similar but possibly less attractive proposal would be forced on the club. The existing course cannot expand further, and the modern game of golf demands longer courses. Douglas Golf Club has not been able to satisfy the demand for membership since the 1930s, and the new development should relieve this pressure somewhat while also introducing greater numbers to the game. The new development

Charity Am Am Trophy
2002. *L–R*:
John Crowley (Heineken
Ireland Ltd), Ed Kenny,
Ray Murphy (president),
Declan Farmer,
Dave Canty.

also presents opportunities for developing the game amongst greater numbers of young golfers, and an imaginative approach to this could contribute significantly to the development of golf for Douglas Golf Club and for the game in general.

Charity Pro Am and Am Am

In 1981 Dave Canty, captain in 1983 and president in 1991, took on the organisation of an annual charity Pro Am at Douglas. It began as a one-day event, but such was its popularity that it was soon extended to two days. The Irish PGA supported the event, and a good rapport was established with Brian Campbell of that organisation in the early years, and later with Michael McComiskey. Up to forty professionals and assistant professionals played each year, and over the first two decades of the event many members and their guests had the opportunity of playing with players such as Christy O'Connor senior, Des Smyth, Philip Walton, Jimmy Kinsella, Paddy Skerritt, Christy O'Connor junior and many others.

In 2002 it became an Am Am, but has continued to be an attractive annual club event, with competitive golf and an enjoyable social element also. Since its inception, over €300,000 has been raised for a variety of charities. The custom is that each year, the three club officers – president, captain and lady captain – each nominate a charity to receive a share of the proceeds, ensuring a spread of benefit. Dave Canty is now joined by Declan Farmer and Ed Kenny, captain in 2001, in organising the event, which has become an attractive annual fixture on the Douglas calendar. A trophy, modelled on the Ryder Cup and presented by Ed Kenny, is played for each year, and Heineken Ireland Ltd has been generous in its support since 1998.

More than Just a Golf Club

While a review of 100 years of any club would necessarily attempt to record the achievements of individual players and teams at provincial and national levels, and to celebrate national and international success, it is the ordinary members – those who play golf as a leisure activity at a relatively benign competitive level – who are the life of a club. So it is with Douglas. The club plays in all the national competitions – the Senior and Junior Cups, and the Barton, Jimmy Bruen and Pierce Purcell Shields – but at a local Cork level, there are a number of events that are specifically for those who have not represented their club in national events. The Senior and Junior Leagues are the longest established of those local competitions, and are played for by the four old Cork clubs – Cork, Muskerry, Monkstown and Douglas. In more recent years, four more competitions have been added to the programme: the Summer Shield for handicaps of 13 and over, the Topmost for 16+ handicaps, the Utmost for the over-sixties with 18+ handicaps, and the Mixed Most. The competitions are concluded over a two-week period, and while preliminary rounds are shared between the four clubs, the finals are all staged at one club on a Sunday, with a total of thirty-three matches being held on the day. These competitions are as keenly contested as any national event but have the added spice of intense local, but good-humoured, rivalry. It is customary for the losing club captain to present the relevant trophy to the winning club captain – always an occasion for well-meaning banter! In 2006 Douglas had the distinction of winning five of the six local tournaments, failing only to win the Junior League.

The club is justly proud of its heroes, but the principal achievement of a century at Douglas Golf Club is the opportunity given to thousands of members over those years to play the game they love and to interact socially. The club has developed an atmosphere and traditions over time, and many members of long standing see

2006 The combined Senior League, Summer Shield, Topmost, Utmost and Mixed Most victorious teams with 2006 President Val O'Mahony, centre front.

their club as a second home. Like family photographs, the pictures of winning teams from the past adorn the walls of the clubhouse, and the honour boards record the names of past officers, presidents, captains and lady captains who have led and served their club.

It is an annual tradition at Douglas that the past presidents and captains gather to play eleven holes of golf for the honour of winning the Silver Salver before adjourning for a celebratory dinner. The deceased members of the club are remembered at an annual Mass celebrated at the clubhouse, and at the funerals of past officers it is customary for a guard of honour of club officers, past and current, to be present. It is also a tradition that the men of the club gather for an annual dinner in honour of their president and captain, and the toasts and responses have often become the stuff of legend. The club ladies hold an annual dinner in honour of their captain also, and the after-dinner entertainment is generally more creative and theatrical than that put on by the men! The Bridge Club at Douglas has been an integral part of the social life of the club for decades, and was run most efficiently for many years by Bill O'Mahony. He is remembered for being quite impatient with those who did not play with what he considered to be appropriate care and concentration! 'He was a bit of a martinet when it came to bridge,' as one member described him. The rivalries within the Bridge Club can be as intense as those on the course.

The past 100 years have seen Douglas Golf Club grow and endure, sometimes against seemingly impossible odds. Within six years of its foundation, the club came close to extinction, but the indomitable spirit of the early members saw it survive that first crisis. In 1921 the club again suffered a potentially fatal blow when the club-house was destroyed in an arson attack, but the members came up trumps a second time, and oversaw the building of a new clubhouse. That is the spirit of Douglas. The club has been excellently served by its officers and committee members through the years. Hundreds of people have given voluntarily of their time to serve the club in a variety of capacities in what can often be thankless and unnoticed work. Unpopular and controversial decisions have sometimes been taken, but doing what is best for the club as a whole in the long term is always the guiding principle. In 2009 the club is again at a cross-roads as a decision has been taken to relocate to a new site where two courses and a state-of-the-art clubhouse and facilities are to be built. The challenge will be to bring the club spirit and traditions, 100 years in the making, to wherever Douglas will play its golf.

Centenary year, 2009.
Seated L–R:
Seán McHenry (president), Deirdre Buckley (lady captain), Tom Collins (captain), with visiting club officers.

Top:
2009 management committee.
Standing, L–R:
Donal Barry, John Sheehan
Martin Hayes.
Seated, L–R: Clare Keating,
Paul Clune, Jim O'Shaughnessy.

Centre: Top: Men's Club
committee, 2009.
Back, L–R: Seán Ó Caoimh,
Shane Scanlan, Ray Barry,
Ger Coyne.
Front, L–R: Seán Murphy,
Ger Lonergan, Paul Herlihy,
Emmet Martin.
Inserts, Back, L–R: John Treacy,
Tony Barry, Kieran Canty.
Inserts, front, L–R: Kieran Barry,
Seán McHenry, Tom Collins.

Bottom: 2009 Ladies' Club
committee.
Back, L–R: Aoife Lane,
Mary Mackey,
Deirdre O'Sullivan,
Mary Costello,
Ann Hanley.
Middle, L–R: Joan Slattery,
Sue O'Connell.
Front, L–R: Patsy Hurley,
Deirdre Buckley (lady captain),
Ursula Morris.
Inserts, L–R: Sinéad O'Sullivan,
Deirdre M O'Hanlon.

Facing page, top:
Chairmen of management committee,
2000–09. *L–R:* Pat Dempsey,
Donal Murray, Liam Connolly,
Donal Hurley, Paul Clune.

Facing page, centre:
2009 trustees. *Standing, L–R:*
Seán Kelly, Seán Cody,
John Sheehan.
Seated, L–R: Seán McHenry,
Helen Hennessy, Tom Linehan.

Facing page, bottom:
2009 centenary year committee.
Standing, L–R: Declan Farmer,
Ed Kenny, John Keating,
Teddy O'Donovan, John Sheehan.
Seated, L–R: Helen Hennessy,
Seán McHenry, Val O'Mahony,
Phyllis Harrington.

Top: 2009, past lady captains.
Back, L–R: Mary Sheehan, Chris O'Herlihy, Patsy Hurley, Hilda Whelehan, Jill Hornibrook, Maeve Buckley, Kate Cawley, Ruth McGrath.
Middle, L–R: Grace Harvey, Angela Lane, Valerie Whelan, Eileen O'Leary, Helen O'Sullivan, Helen Hennessy, Margaret Barry, Helen Elwood, Mary Mackesy, Phyllis Harrington, Claire O'Connor, Clare Keating.
Front, L–R: Patsy McHenry, Marjorie Horgan, Mary Cody, Carmel Murphy, Deirdre Buckley, Rena Jordan, Pat Desmond, Bonnie O'Donoghue.
Inserts, L–R: Oonagh Fitzpatrick, Ann Dorgan, Ann Heskin, Edie Scannell, Mary Collins, Yvonne Crofts, Eucharia Buckley, Eavan Higgins, Laura Sheehan.

Bottom: 2009, past captains and presidents.
Back, L–R: Tim O'Sullivan, Pat Dempsey, Fintan Sheehan, Tom O'Riordan, Bernard O'Shaughnessy, Felix O'Sullivan, Teddy O'Donovan, Frank Troy, Bob Casey, Dermot Costello, John Sheehan, David Lane, Donal O'Herlihy, Dick Langford, Richard Lonergan, Ed Kenny.
Middle, L–R: Michael O'Sullivan, Seán Kelly, Vincent Poland, Liam Connolly, Val O'Mahony, Dave Canty, Seán Coughlan, Liam Ahern, Frank McGrath, Michael O'Donovan, Kieran Barry, Donal Hurley, John Keating.
Front, L–R: John McGrath, James Doolin, Dixie Whelan, Brian Wain, Seán Treacy, Tom Collins, Seán McHenry, Geoff Thompson, Seán Cody, Tadgh O'Halloran, Mick Kenny, Ray Murphy.

My Memories of Times Past

by Ann Heskin

Having come to live in the Douglas area in December 1962, my sister Oonagh and I were delighted to accept the late Girlie Hegarty's suggestion that we join Douglas Golf Club. In those days, it was impossible for the working female to get any competitive golf in Cork Golf Club, where we were both members (and I am still lucky enough to be a member). However, Douglas did facilitate the working lassies, and, of course, it also had the highly renowned and well-respected John McKenna as its club professional. Our sister Mary joined us at the club some years later.

John McKenna's base in his early days at the club was a green shed in the middle of the carpark. He subsequently got a more permanent structure – where the pro shop is today – that consisted of a small shop and workroom at the back, where he made and repaired golf clubs. When Mr McKenna was out giving lessons – a wonderful teacher – his good wife, and no mean golfer herself, would often mind the shop for him. Later, a driving range was laid out at the back of Mr McKenna's

Irish ladies' team, winners of the Ladies' European Team Championship at Royal Waterloo Golf Club 1983, captained by Ann Heskin. *Back, L–R:* Geraldine Costello (vice-captain), Eavan Higgins, Mary Tinney (Irish ambassador to Belgium), Ann Heskin (team captain), Maureen Madill, Claire Hourihane, Mary McKenna. *Front, L–R:* Philomena Wickham, Carol Wickham.

shop, with balls being driven down the twelfth fairway each night (Monday to Friday) in the winter months. It was manned each evening by the late Bob Ryan, a nature's gentleman of a groundsman, who lived in a small house at the entrance to the club, roughly where the bungalows are today.

Mr McKenna gave his lessons either below the eighteenth green or at his favourite spot over in the corner, forward and left of the eighteenth tee, with shots being played towards the eighteenth fairway. Go for an hour's lesson with him and you would finish about an hour and a half or two hours later, or maybe longer, with Mr McK saying, 'The last three' about a half a dozen times! He was a wonderful player, teacher and friend. He coached five women internationals – Zelie Fallon, Girlie Hegarty, Anne O'Brien, Oonagh Fitzpatrick (née Heskin) and myself – along with many others in the club, not forgetting the men who gained from his expertise. As long as his players worked on their game, he was willing to help them fulfil their potential, whatever their level of expertise.

During the sixties, Oonagh and I spent most of our summer evenings up at the club, either having a lesson, practising or playing, maybe as many as twenty-three holes – as long as the light lasted – after our day's work. We used to have great fourballs with Zelie and Anne O'Brien. Oonagh, Anne and I travelled around together so much to championships and open days that Anne was quite often taken as one of the Heskin twins! We spent many an evening after our golf over a cup of tea in the dining room of the club listening to Eddie John O'Sullivan's yarns and ghost stories! Those were the days when members stayed on in the club after golf, more than they do nowadays … I guess folks lived a more leisurely way of life.

My initial memory of the clubhouse is that the ladies had a sitting room, with a fireplace, high fender, small couch and some easy chairs, with a rectangular bay window looking out on to the carpark. The bar was strictly members (men) only, with the ladies permitted to buy drinks through a hatch at the far end of the bar, opening into the dining room. The clubhouse was completely refurbished in the Sixties. However, I have no recollection of how the members coped during these renovations, nor when it had another revamp some years later, resulting in the fine clubhouse we have today, which is the envy of many of our visitors, particularly its panoramic view out over the city. In the early days, the lady members did the catering for all special occasions; I well remember turkeys being cooked at home for the club, not forgetting the provision of delicious desserts, along with linen table cloths and table appointments – such as candlesticks and so on – for all important social occasions. When Douglas hosted the Ladies' Munster Championship in 1967, the lady captain, Oonagh, and her committee ran a jumble sale in Paul Street in town to make money to cover the cost of hosting the usual buffet for the championships in the club – all highly successful.

While I realise it can be dangerous to mention some members of the club – both past and present – I feel that there are some who do deserve special mention. However, in doing so, that is not to say that others have not been loyal, supportive and fondly remembered members who each contributed in their own way to the welfare of the club over the years. The following were some of the staunch supporters, particularly of our Senior Cup teams of yore: the late Jim Ryan, who often slipped us some Dunlop 65s, the top golf ball of the day, on the 'QT' – think of how the top players are assisted nowadays! The late Jim and Pearl Sheehan; the late Gerry Roseingrave and his gracious wife Clare; our club trustee, Helen Hennessy and her late husband Dan; Patsy and Seán McHenry; Ruth and Frank McGrath; Phyllis Harrington and her late husband Pat; Yvonne and Michael Crofts; Eileen O'Leary; Helen O'Sullivan; Carmel Murphy; Angela and Dick Lane; and Marjorie Horgan. Maud O'Hanlon is another fantastic character in the club, who travelled to the most exotic parts of the world – a wonderful pianist, who often put her expertise on show for the enjoyment of the ladies, and who served as a renowned teacher in the Cork School of Music for many years. The late Myra Riordan of Green Door fame, the late Betty Barrett, who in her eighties considered it a waste of time to change her shoes for just nine holes, preferring to play the full eighteen! Eucharia Buckley, who was such a wonderful member of the club along with her late husband David, until she was struck down with a severe illness which has had her hospitalised ever since. The late Eileen (E T) O'Callaghan, one of the longest serving members of the club, who was a member of the Senior Cup team that brought the national trophy to Douglas for the first time in 1952. Eileen graced the fairways for many a long day, and helped me on numerous occasions by acting as my caddie – the only person, apart from John McKenna, who was able to get me back on track if and when my swing let me down. My sister Mary undertook the caddie duties subsequently, to the detriment of her own golf.

While I never knew the late renowned Julianne McCarthy, who had been ladies' honorary secretary for many a day, her name often came up in conversation. She was obviously quite a character, a wizard when it came to the stock market, I believe. Her successor as honorary secretary was the late Mary Horgan, who literally was a law unto herself. She ran the Ladies' Branch for years, with, I guess, due deference to the lady captain. The ladies' honorary handicapping secretary in those years was the late Maur (Maureen) O'Donovan. Maur retired from that post shortly after Mary Horgan died suddenly while on holidays in Schull one summer. They were both great characters and staunch members of the Bridge Club, as were many of the golfers, like the Butlers, Burkleys, Coulters, McHenrys and the O'Mahony brothers, to mention but a few.

The ladies in Douglas Golf Club brought great honour and glory to the club over the years, winning the Irish Ladies' Senior Cup – the premier national inter-club team event – on no less than twelve occasions, surpassed only by Royal Portrush and Milltown. Zelie Fallon and Eavan Higgins brought the Irish Ladies' Close Championship crown to the club in 1964 and 1993 respectively. Zelie Fallon reigned supreme in Douglas in the Fifties, Sixties and Seventies. She was ever present on the Irish ladies' international team virtually from 1952 to 1970, and non-playing captain in 1972. I think it would be fair to say that Eavan Higgins took over the mantle of top lady golfer in Douglas from Zelie in the Eighties and Nineties, when she was a regular on the Irish team. Other to grace the international scene and thereby bring extra glory to the club were Girlie Hegarty, Oonagh Fitzpatrick (née

Heskin), Anne O'Brien and myself, Ann Heskin, and our two Senior Cup players Rhona Brennan (née Hegarty) and Eileen Rose McDaid. A relative newcomer to the club, Kate MacCann, also played for Ireland earlier in her career, when a member of Headfort and Milltown, and has been a great addition to our Senior Cup team of late.

One of my proudest moments was leading the Irish team as non-playing captain to victory in the Ladies' European Team Championship at Royal Waterloo Golf Club, Brussels, beating England in the final by 5½ to 1½. Eavan Higgins played a truly exceptional part in that great Irish victory, gaining 5½ points out of a possible 6 in the matchplay stages of the tournament. Her chip in from the back edge of the nineteenth hole in the vital match against Pam Wright of Scotland was the shot of the tournament for me, ensuring an Irish win against Scotland. Ireland overcame Sweden in the semi-finals, and in the final Eavan again played a very important part – a true credit to her family, club and country.

The Douglas ladies have also been very prominent in the administrative side of the game – as, indeed, have the men. Many of its members have given of their time voluntarily and freely – sometimes to the detriment of their own playing of this great game of ours – so that it may be controlled and administered successfully for the good of all golfers in this fair land of ours. Three Douglas ladies have had the wonderful honour and great distinction of serving as president of the Irish Ladies' Golf Union: Eleanor Tivy from 1940 to 1946, Mrs J F (Girlie) Hegarty from 1974 to 1977, and I was deeply honoured to have been nominated and appointed to this high office in January 2005, serving for the two years 2005 and 2006. At that time, my good friend and loyal Douglas colleague, Rena Jordan, reigned as chairman of the ILGU's Southern District executive – a unique situation for the club that might have been even more unique had the good Lord not called John Brett home before his time, as he was in line to become president of the Golfing Union of Ireland in 2006. Another Douglas stalwart, Frank Bowen, ably filled that post some years ago. I was deeply grateful for the tremendous support and encouragement I got from all the Douglas members during my term in office, as indeed was Rena. We deeply appreciated and thoroughly enjoyed the wonderful celebration night held in our honour in Douglas Golf Club on 25 February 2005 – a night of great music and *craic* like various other celebration nights of old in the club. It was on such occasions that the various artistic and musical talents of the members were shared for the enjoyment of all. I am one of these lucky people who got an awful lot of fun, enjoyment and a certain amount of success out of golf during my playing career, and I count myself very fortunate that I have had the opportunity to put something back into the game on the administrative side, hopefully for the good of the game and its enjoyment by our ILGU members up and down this great country of ours. I am deeply grateful to Angela Lane, who invited me to follow in her footsteps as lady captain of Douglas in 1976, which, I guess, set me up for my long career in golf administration subsequently.

What have I got from nearly fifty years at Douglas Golf Club? Great enjoyment, friendship and comradeship. I wouldn't have lived without it.

Ann and Oonagh Heskin: Some of their Achievements

Ann Heskin was a member of the victorious Douglas Senior Cup teams in 1967, 1968, 1973, 1978, 1980, 1985, 1986 and 1987. She was Munster Senior Champion in 1970, 1971, 1974, 1975 and 1978, and was a member of the Munster team from 1964 to 1984. Ann was a member of the Irish team in the Home Internationals in 1969, 1970, 1972, 1975 and 1977, and was non-playing captain of the Irish team for that series in 1982 and 1983. In 1981 she was non-playing captain of the Irish team at the Junior Ladies' European Team Championship, and was also non-playing captain of the Irish team that won the European Ladies' Team Championship at Royal Waterloo in Belgium in 1983. Ann was an Irish national selector from 1984 to 1989, and again from 1991 to 1996, and an international (LGU) selector from 1991 to 1994. She was president of the ILGU for 2005 and 2006.

Oonagh Heskin was a member of the Douglas teams that won the Senior Cup in 1967 and 1968, and played for Munster in the inaugural Ladies' Interprovincial Series in 1964, rejoining the team in 1967, and playing each year until 1971. She played again for Munster in 1980, when Munster won the series for the first time. Oonagh was Munster Senior Champion in 1969. In 1967 she played for Ireland in the Home Internationals at Sunningdale, and was selected again in 1969 but had to cry off. She was on the Irish team for the European Team Championship in Sweden in 1969. Oonagh Heskin was an Irish national selector from 1990 to 1994, and again from 1996 to 1998, and was an international (LGU) selector from 1995 to 1998.

1968 Senior Cup champions.
Back, L–R: Ann Heskin, Anne O'Brien, Oonagh Heskin, Zelie Gaynor.
Front, L–R: Girlie Hegarty, Eucharia Buckley (lady captain), Peg McKenna.

The Positions of Honorary Secretary, Assistant Honorary Secretary and Secretary/Manager

Like all golf clubs, Douglas had an annually elected honorary secretary from its foundation in 1909. The first incumbent was Marshal William Litton, who worked as an insurance inspector in Cork and resided at the club; he served until 1912. In the absence of club records for the period up to 1921, one must rely on external sources (*Irish Golfer's Guide, Irish Golfing Guide, Irish Field*, etc.) for information on office holders at the club. Lieutenant-Colonel M J Carpendale, J D Hilliard, L A D'Obree, S G James and O C Barry succeeded Litton in turn between 1912 and 1916, and it would appear that Mick English became honorary secretary in 1916 following the dissolution of Douglas Golf Links Ltd and the establishment of Douglas Golf Club. He was still holding that office in 1922 when a joint honorary secretary, T S Sullivan, was elected to assist him.

This new arrangement only lasted a short time, and it was decided that paid help was needed for the honorary secretary. D J Callanan was appointed assistant secretary in July of that year in a part-time capacity at a weekly wage of fifteen shillings plus tram fares and teas! Callanan left in 1924 to take up a position in Tralee, and F Cussen was appointed in his place to assist the then honorary secretary, R McKechnie, who had been elected to the position in 1923. It would appear that Cussen and McKechnie did not enjoy a pleasant working relationship as in June 1925 the committee asked that Cussen give 'particulars of unpleasant incidents referred to in his letter of resignation of 9th inst'. At the same meeting, the committee accepted the resignation of McKechnie. At the August committee meeting, Mick English agreed to resume duty as honorary secretary, and F Cussen agreed to be assistant honorary secretary, unpaid. Three years later, at the 1928 AGM, F Cussen was elected honorary secretary, and J A Collins became his assistant, but by April 1931 dissatisfaction was being expressed with the honorary secretary's work, the committee feeling that 'he has been very lax in his duties in not making arrangements for the General Meeting, and that nothing has been done towards closing the books for 1930'. The following day, the committee met again as 'things were in a very chaotic condition owing to the neglect of the Hon Secy Mr Cussen to perform his duties'. The AGM was eventually held on 29 April in the absence of the honorary secretary, and it was decided unanimously

> that the interests of the club would be best served by obtaining the services of a paid Secretary, who would take over the work at present done by the Hon Sec, Assist Hon Secy, and Hon Treasurer ... that these latter three positions be abolished, and a paid Secretary be appointed to take their place.

At the committee meeting that followed the AGM, Mick English was appointed to the position of secretary at a monthly salary of £8 6s 8d, or £100 per annum. He was a senior club member, and had previously served as honorary secretary. Unfortunately, he died in May 1932 after serving barely a year as secretary – or secretary/manager, as the position became known later.

English was replaced by Maurice Reidy in July 1932, and he served until 1944. He was made an honorary life member of Douglas at the AGM in February 1945 'as a mark of appreciation of his exceptional services as secretary for a period of twelve years'. S J Murphy took over from Reidy in October 1944, and he served until September 1952, to be followed by Commandant Patrick Corrigan. By this time, the annual salary was £204, paid monthly. Patrick Corrigan was Douglas Golf Club's longest serving secretary/manager, serving for twenty-three years. He retired officially in February 1975, and was made an honorary life member of the club. He was followed by T D Coffey, who had begun work at the club in the summer of 1974 while Patrick Corrigan was ill. It was during T D Coffey's term at Douglas that the title secretary/manager was first used.

By this time, it was becoming increasingly difficult for one person to manage the affairs of a club as big as Douglas. The cost of running the club now ran to over £75,000 annually, and the duties of the secretary/manager were more akin to those of a manager of a small business than of a sports club. At the AGM in March 1975, it was recommended that the secretary/manager 'would take complete control of the management of the club and ... would issue directions to members of the staff on behalf of the president, captain and members of the committee. It was further recommended that new accountancy arrangements and books should be introduced to meet the modern demands'. After a further period of five to six months – during which the new accountancy system was being introduced – it became increasingly obvious that the secretary/manager, working as he was an average week of even fifty to sixty hours, could not cover the demands of the management of the club and supply adequate service to members. Accordingly, a part-time paid assistant, G P Whelan, was appointed to assist T D Coffey. In addition, the position of honorary treasurer was recreated after a gap of forty-four years, and Seán Cody was the first to be elected to that new position. T D Coffey left Douglas in August 1981, and Grace Buckley took over his duties, first in a temporary capacity, and from July 1982 as the permanent secretary/manager. She resigned in April 1986, and Piaras Ó Dálaigh acted as an honorary secretary until the appointment of G A Finn as Grace Buckley's replacement in May of that year. G A Finn left in October 1987, and was replaced by Brian Barrett, who served the club until October 2002. Brian Kiely took up duty as secretary/manager on Brian Barrett's departure, and left after less than two years in July 2004. Ronan Burke has been secretary/manager at Douglas Golf Club since March 2005.

Club Officers, 1909–2009

Year	President	Captain	Lady Captain
1910	W Guest Lane	R A Galwey	
1911	W Guest Lane	R A Galwey	
1912	Prof J P Molohan	J O'Callaghan	
1913	Prof J P Molohan	W V Pericho	
1914	A Mahony	C Blake	
1915	A Mahony	C Blake	
1916	J J O'Brien Snr	C Blake	
1917	Dr A Winder	R A Galwey	
1918	H Hitchmough	W Smith	
1919	H Nalder	J O'Brien	
1920	Dr H N Townsend	M English	
1921	Revd. R A O'Gorman	R McKechnie	
1922	Revd. M McSwiney	R McKechnie	
1923	Revd. M McSwiney	Dr J Murphy	
1924	C Blake	S J Morrogh	
1925	H Longfield	R Simcox	
1926	H O'Keeffe	V M Morrogh	
1927	W T O'Sullivan	V M Morrogh	
1928	W T O'Sullivan	J G Musgrave	
1929	J Maskill	J G Musgrave	
1930	P J Collins	T R O'Regan	
1931	P J Collins	T R O'Regan	
1932	J Crofts	M J Henchy	
1933	J Henchy	D P McCarthy	
1934	J Henchy	D P McCarthy	
1935	H Golden	J J O'Leary	Miss V Sullivan
1936	S F Whelan	Dr T Donovan	Mrs C Murphy
1937	M Roche	Dr T S Reynolds	Miss J McCarthy
1938	M Dorgan	J O'Driscoll	Mrs J Henchy
1939	J C Reardon	J Power	Miss M Murphy
1940	J Mountjoy	D Daly	Mrs J Halpin
1941	H St J Atkins	F V Mahony	Miss V Lynch
1942	C F Murphy	P J Collins	Mrs K Crean
1943	J G Munro	T Murphy	Mrs P Coveney
1944	Revd. R J Dalton	W J O'Mahony	Miss M Munro
1945	F J Bennett	J J O'Mahony	Dr A Stritch
1946	W E Williams	S M O'Sullivan	Miss G V Mahony
1947	T R O'Regan	S F Thompson	Miss A Dunne
1948	Dr T Donovan	R J Coleman	Miss E T O'Callaghan
1949	Prof C Boyle	F J Bennett	Mrs C J Riordan
1950	J Fallon	J K Coakley	Mrs F Horgan
1951	R M Cogan	D Barry	Mrs W J O'Donovan
1952	F V Mahony	D W Loane	Mrs J McKenna
1953	J J O'Mahony	G F Thompson	Mrs D O'Sullivan
1954	E F Butler	J J Moynihan	Mrs J Coulter
1955	J C Coulter	A W Stokes	Mrs E Rorke
1956	W J O'Mahony	J J Condon	Mrs S D Barrett
1957	T E Philpott	D A O'Connell	Mrs J Hegarty
1958	J E Murphy	E K Farrell	Mrs J P Ryan
1959	A W Stokes	C Brownlee	Mrs J J McHenry

Year	President	Captain	Lady Captain	Chairman Management Committee
1960	B G Burkley	J O'Donovan	Miss M Coffey	
1961	E Aherne	J O'Donovan	Mrs Z Fallon	
1962	J P Ryan	J J Kelleher	Mrs G Burkley	
1963	J P Ryan	J P McSweeney	Mrs J Reardon	
1964	G F Thompson	J J O'Hea	Mrs J Horgan	
1965	J J Condon	J F McHenry	Miss P Grant	
1966	W N O'Leary	S Treacy	Mrs K Magner	
1967	J Sheehan	E A O'Brien	Miss O'Heskin	
1968	J Heffernan	J Martin	Mrs D Buckley	
1969	J J Heffernan	F C McGrath	Miss M Mackesy	
1970	A H Graham	G F Roseingrave	Mrs S Treacy	
1971	J M O'Connor	P R Elwood	Mrs D K Spillane	
1972	D Barry	P C Barry	Mrs J Sheehan	
1973	P J Lonergan	E R Murphy	Mrs F Murphy	
1974	C F Clune	T O'Halloran	Mrs N Murray	
1975	J J O'Hea	B D O'Shaughnessy	Mrs R A Lane	
1976	R D Magnier	D V Collins	Miss A Heskin	
1977	S F Cody	S Jordan	Mrs J F McHenry	
1978	M F Crofts	W J Scannell	Mrs M T O'Sullivan	
1979	J F McHenry	S F Kelly	Mrs M Rose	
1980	F C McGrath	T J O'Riordan	Mrs B P Lyden	
1981	J Martin	J E Brett	Mrs F C McGrath	
1982	M N Conlon	B Wain	Mrs F P Dorgan	
1983	P R Elwood	D T Canty	Mrs W J Scannell	
1984	S Treacy	D A O'Brien	Mrs S F Cody	
1985	T J McHugh	R F Conway	Mrs H Hennessy	
1986	J A Ruby	F D O'Sullivan	Mrs M F Crofts	
1987	T O'Halloran	Val O'Mahony	Mrs R Elwood	
1988	S F Kelly	P J Harrington	Mrs P C Barry	
1989	W J Scannell	D A Hurley	Mrs J D O'Leary	
1990	Tim O'Sullivan	D F Thomas	Mrs D V Collins	
1991	D T Canty	J P Scanlon	Mrs R Jordan	
1992	J J Harrington	D Langford	Mrs J Keating	
1993	M C Kenny	Liam Ahern	Mrs P Harrington	
1994	Capt. J F Troy	R J Lonergan	Mrs F D O'Sullivan	
1995	S Coughlan	Dr D Whelan	Pat Desmond	
1996	John P Keating	K P Barry	Mrs T P F O'Connor	
1997	J C Sheehan	D A O'Herlihy	Mrs Kay Cawley	
1998	John McGrath	P G Dempsey	Mrs E A Hornibrook	
1999	D F Thomas	Tim O'Sullivan	Bonnie O'Donoghue	
2000	Liam Connolly	Fintan Sheehan	Eavan Higgins	Pat Dempsey
2001	Donal Hurley	Edward Kenny	Maeve Buckley	Pat Dempsey
2002	Ray Murphy	Joe Magnier	Mary Sheehan	Pat Dempsey
2003	Dermot Costello	Bob Casey	Hilda Whelehan	Donal Muray
2004	M T O'Sullivan	C V Poland	Grace Harvey	Liam Connolly
2005	R F Conway	Derek Maguire	Valerie Whelan	Donal Hurley
2006	Val O'Mahony	David Lane	Laura Sheehan	Donal Hurley
2007	Ted O'Donovan	James Doolin	Chris O'Herlihy	Donal Hurley
2008	C V Poland	M J O'Donovan	Patsy Hurley	Paul Clune
2009	J F McHenry	Tom Collins	Deirdre Buckley	Paul Clune

Greenkeepers, 1909–2009

John (or George) Henry 1909–1911
Maurice S Harris 1911 –?
Wiliam Magee pre-1921–1936
Robert Ryan 1936–1973
Patrick Keogh 1973–1979
William Scott 1979–1983

John C Morris 1983–1987
Robert Mackay 1988–1989
Gordon Bennison 1989–1989
Peter Baume 1990–1992
Peter Morris 1992–

Douglas Golf Club Members, 2009

Honorary Life Members

Bowen, Frank W
Fitzgerald, Daniel P, Fr
Heskin, Ann
Higgins, Eavan
McDaid, Eileen R
McHenry, John
Morris, John, Dr

Members: Male

Adair, Gordon V
Ahern, Barry
Ahern, Bryan
Ahern, John
Ahern, Joseph
Ahern, Liam
Ahern, Patrick
Ahern, Shane
Augustine's, St
Barber, Peter
Barrett, John V
Barrett, Richard
Barry, David
Barry, Des
Barry, Donal J
Barry, Greg
Barry, Jim
Barry, John
Barry, John P
Barry, Kieran, Dr
Barry, Kieran P
Barry, Niall
Barry, Norman T
Barry, Patrick
Barry, Ronan
Barry, Roy
Barry, Simon J

Barry, Tim
Barry, Tony
Barry, W Romauld, Revd.
Blower, Gavin
Boland, Cian
Boland, Killian
Boland, Liam
Bolton, Harry
Bornemann, Charlie
Bornemann, Karl
Bornemann, Robert
Boylan, John G
Boylan, John J
Bradley, William
Brett, John V
Brett, Patrick J, Dr
Brett, Peter R
Buckley, Aidan D
Buckley, Colin
Buckley, Con
Buckley, Conor
Buckley, David G
Buckley, Denis A
Buckley, Eoghan
Buckley, Eoin J
Buckley, Frank P
Buckley, John, Revd. Dr

Buckley, John G, Dr
Buckley, John M
Buckley, Richard
Buckley, Ted F
Buggy, Dan
Burke, Daniel T
Burke, James
Burke, John M
Burke, Michael
Burke, Pat
Burke, Paul
Burkley, Joseph
Burns, Bobby
Burns, Derek
Burns, Jack
Burns, Rory
Butler, Stan
Byrne, Dan M
Byrne, Danny J
Byrne, Derek
Byrne, James
Byrne, Jim
Byrne, Patrick J
Byrne, Peter
Cafferkey, Michael
Cagney (jun.), David
Cagney, Bryan

Cagney, David
Cahill, Bill
Cahill, Brian
Cahill, Ian
Cahill, John
Canniffe, Eoghan
Canniffe, Kieran
Cantillon, Gregory J
Cantillon, Jack
Cantillon, Shane
Cantillon, Viv
Canton, Declan J
Canty, Dave
Canty, Dave
Canty, David F
Canty, Justin
Canty, Kieran
Canty, Paul
Canty, Tony
Carey, Michael
Carmody, Stephen
Carrigy, Jack
Carrigy, Peter F
Carrigy, Seán
Carty, Ryan
Casey, Jack
Casey, Patrick J
Casey, Robert A
Casey, William (Billy) J
Cawley, Aidan
Cawley, Ray
Cawley, Shane
Clancy, Gavin
Clancy, Kieran
Clancy, Rory
Clark, Gerard
Clarke, Billy
Clarke, Ian
Clarke jun., Roy
Cleary, Noel D
Clehane, David
Clehane, Stan
Clifford, John
Clune, Conor S
Clune, Michael
Clune, Paul
Clune, Robert
Cody, Seán F
Cody, Stephen
Cogan, Edmund
Coleman, Alan
Coleman, Finbarr Barry
Coleman, John B
Coleman, Keith
Coleman, Kenneth

Collins, Brian
Collins, David J
Collins, Denis
Collins, Denis A
Collins, James M
Collins, John
Collins, John F
Collins, Thomas N
Colton, Adam
Colton, Andrew
Colton, Paul, Bishop
Condon, Kieran
Conlon, Michael N
Connolly, David
Connolly, Dermot
Connolly, Liam
Connolly, Raymond J, Dr
Connolly, Ronan
Conway, Bryan R
Conway, Craig
Conway, Dermot F
Conway, Rory F
Cooney, Alan
Corcoran, Daniel
Corrigan, Michael J
Corrigan jun., Michael
Costello, Dermot J
Cotter PP, John, Fr
Cotter, Eamon
Cotter, Edward
Cotter, Jack
Cotter, John A
Cotter, John S
Cotter, Sylvester
Coughlan, Daniel
Coughlan, David
Coughlan, Don
Coughlan, John J
Coughlan, Michael
Coughlan, Michael G
Coughlan, Noel
Coughlan, Noel
Coughlan, Seán
Coughlan, Thomas
Coveney, Kieran D
Cowhig, Jack
Coyne, Conor D
Coyne, Gerard
Creagh, John
Cremin, John
Crofts, Michael
Cronin, Jerry M
Cronin, Justin
Cronin, Kevin
Cronin, Michael G

Cronin, Stephen
Cronin, Terence
Crowley, Bryan T
Crowley, John
Crowley, Michael
Crowley, Michael, Revd.
Crowley, Michael J
Crowley, Michael P
Crowley, Pat D
Crowley, Tim
Cullen, Brendan
Cullen, Marc
Cummins, Pat
Cunnigham, Conor
Cunningham, Brendan V
Cunningham, Bryan
Cunningham, Mark
Curtin, Bryan R
Curtin, Dan
Curtis, Bryan
Curtis, Seán
Daly, Daniel
Daly, Frank
Daly, Jack
Daly, John
Daly jun., John
Daly, Rory
Daly, Tony
Davis, Joseph P
Dawson, Pat
Deasy, Killian
Deasy, Michael J
Deasy, Ronan
Dempsey, Darragh J
Dempsey, Kevin P
Dempsey, Pat J
Dennehy, Finbarr B
Dennehy jun., Finbarr J
Dennehy, Olan D
Dennehy, Paudie
Derham, Paul
Desmond, Kevin
Dillon, D Frank
Dillon, Joseph P, Dr
Dillon, Noel J
Dillon, Noel M
Dinan, Jack
Dineen, Denis
Dolan, Mark
Dolan, Eoin
Donovan, Bernard, Revd.
Donovan, Edmond, Dr
Donovan, Edward
Doolan, James
Doolan, Seán

Dorgan, Andrew
Dorgan, David J
Dorgan, Frank G
Downey, James
Dudley, Denis
Duggan, Conor, Dr
Dullea, Finian J
Dullea, Florence
Dullea, Gerard
Dunlea, Aidan
Dunlea, Dean
Dwyer, Jerry
Dwyer, Jim
Elwood, Kenneth
Elwood, Paul F
Elwood, Ray
Fahey, Liam
Fahey, Peter
Fahy, John P
Farmer, Declan K
Farmer, Kieran
Farry, Peter
Fenton, Rory
Field, Kevin P
Field, Patrick G
Finn, Cormac
Fitzgerald, Alan
Fitzgerald, Barry
Fitzgerald, Christopher, Revd.
Fitzgerald, Cyril
Fitzgerald, Declan
Fitzgerald, Don
Fitzgerald, Frank J
Fitzgerald, Ray
Fitzpatrick, John C
Flannery, Alan
Flannery, Brendan J
Fleming, Gerry
Floyd, Anthony M
Foley, Denis
Foley, John
Foran, Luke
Foran, Matthew
Forde, Brian C
Forde, Brian J
Forde, Greg P
Forde, Patrick J
Freeman, Seamus
Gaffney, Anthony
Gaffney, Tony
Gallagher, Conor
Gallagher, Patrick K
Galvin, Barry
Galvin, Conor
Galvin, Daniel F

Galvin, John
Galvin, Leo P, Dr
Galvin, Roddy, Dr
Galvin, Stephen
Geoghegan, Ruarai
Gibney, Jim
Giltinan, Frank
Gleeson, Edward A
Gosnell, Tony
Graham, Laurence A M, Revd.
Griffith, Brendan
Guerin, Dennis
Hallihan, Denis
Hallihan, Niall
Hanley, Seán
Hanley, Tony
Harkin, Hugh B, Revd. Fr
Harrington, Anthony
Harrington, David J
Harrington, Eamon G
Harrington, Jeremiah
Harrington, Jesse P
Harrington, John
Harris, Billy
Harris, Eoin
Hartnett, Geoffrey
Hartnett, Shane
Harvey, Joe
Hastings, Kieran
Hayes, Andrew
Hayes, Martin T
Hayes, Paddy, Dr
Hayes, Tom
Hedigan, Geoffrey V
Heffernan, Bryan
Heffernan, David
Heffernan, Gerald
Heffernan, John L
Heffernan, Mark
Hegarty, Patrick
Hegarty, Patrick
Hennessy, Patrick
Herbert, Andrew
Herlihy, Brian
Herlihy, Diarmuid
Herlihy, Patrick B
Herlihy, Paul F
Hickey, Brian G
Higgins, Diarmuid
Higgins, John G
Hill, Tony
Hodgins, Richard J
Hogan, John A
Hogan, John P
Hogan, Niall

Horan, Eamon C
Horgan, Declan
Horgan, Eoghan
Horgan, Leonard
Horgan, Michael K
Hourihan, P J Noel
Howell, Barry
Howell, Conor
Howell, Edward Noel
Hubbard, Tom
Hughes, John Paul
Humphries, Barry
Humphries, Ian
Hurley CC, Richard, Revd. Fr
Hurley, Con P
Hurley, Dan
Hurley, Denis
Hurley, Donal A
Hurley, Feargal M
Hurley, Jack
Hurley, John M
Hurley, Kieran
Hurley, Liam I
Hurley, Ronnie
Jackson, Brian
Jackson, Daniel J
Jackson, Ken
Jermyn, John C
Jermyn, John L
Jordan, Aidan
Jordan, Kieran
Kavanagh, Michael
Kavanagh, Ned
Kavanagh, Paul
Keane, Seán
Keane, Shane
Keane, Tim B
Keating, Anthony
Keating, Frank
Keating, John
Keating, Paddy, Revd. Fr
Keelan, Simon
Keenaghan, Oliver
Kelleher, Ian
Kelleher, John
Kelleher, Martin
Kelleher, Patrick
Kelleher, William
Kelly, Mortimer
Kelly, Seán F
Kemery, Keith
Kenefick, Richard M, Dr
Kenneally, Brian
Kennedy, Seán
Kennedy jun., Seán

Kenny jun., Michael J
Kenny, Barrie J
Kenny, Bart F
Kenny, Bryan
Kenny, David
Kenny, Edmund
Kenny, Edward P
Kenny, Jack
Kenny, James
Kenny, John
Kenny, John C
Kenny, Ken
Kenny, Michael C
Kenny, Paul
Kenny, Ray
Kenny, Richard
Kenny, Ronan C
Kenny, Tony
Kerins, John
Keyes, Michael
Keyes, Ralph P
Kiely, Eamonn A
Kiernan, Cameron
Kiernan jun., Thomas
Kohli, Sam
Lane, Billy
Lane, David
Lane, Eoin
Lane, Hugh
Lane, Joseph
Lane, Kevin J
Lane, Richard A
Lane, Richard J
Lane, Robert
Langford, Conor R
Langford, Dick
Langford, Joseph A
Langford, Richard F
Leahy, Daire
Leahy, Tom
Leen, Colm
Lehane, Jack
Lehane, Rory, Dr
Lenihan, David
Lenihan, Donal G
Leopold, Ivan
Lester, Tomás
Lester jun., Tomás
Linehan, Dan P
Linehan, Patrick
Linehan, Thomas
Lonergan, Darragh
Lonergan, Gerard
Lonergan, Richard G
Long, Philip

Loughnane, Ciaran
Loughnane, John P
Lucey, Michael
Lynch, Cornelius F
Lynch, Denis C
Lynch, Francis
Lynch, John F
Lynch, Kristian
Lynch, Liam F
Lynch, William
Lyons, John
Lyons, John B
Lyons, Michael J
MacCurtain McGrath, Tomás
Macken, John D
Mackey, Donal
Mackey, Frank R
Mackey, Jack
Mackey, John
Madden, Alf
Madden, Conor
Madden, David
Madden, Michael N
Magnier, Owen
Maguire, Derek
Maguire, Kevin
Maguire, Stephen
Mahalingam, Karuppiah, Dr
Maher, Frank
Mahon, Stephen
Mahony, David
Mahony, Paul
Malone, John
Mansfield, Hugh R
Mansfield, Mark
Marshall, Ger
Martin, Emmett
Martin, Michael
Martin, Michael
Martin, Ruaidhrí J
McAuliffe, Ben
McAuliffe, Matthew
McAuliffe, Michael
McAuliffe, Noel
McCann, Richard
McCarthy, Colin
McCarthy, Donal J
McCarthy, James
McCarthy, Jamie
McCarthy, Joe
McCarthy, John W
McCarthy, Kieran
McCarthy, Paul
McCarthy jun., Paul
McCarthy, Pearse

McCarthy, Seán R
McCarthy, Thomas
McCarthy, Thomas G
McDaid, Anthony
McDaid, Kevin P
McDonald, Philip
McGinley, Myles
McGrath, Frank C
McGrath, John (Jack) B
McGrath, John A
McGrath jun., John
McGrath, Ross
McHenry, Jack
McHenry, Kevin F
McHenry, Seán
McHugh jun., David
McHugh, David T
McHugh, Dermot
McHugh, Shane
McMahon, Frank
McMullen, William J
McQuillan, Finian A
McSweeney, Eamonn
Mescal, Michael
Meyler, David J
Mills, Colin
Mills, Eamonn K
Mills, Eoin R
Mills, George
Mills, Gerard
Moloney, Edmund
Moloney, Tony
Monaghan, John F
Mooney, Ricky
Moore, Gerard
Moran, Eddie
Moran, John
Morris, Christopher
Morris, John C
Morris, Peter
Morton, Geoffrey
Moynihan, John
Mulcahy, Brian
Mulcahy, Daniel
Mulcahy, Denis
Mulcahy, Frank
Mulcahy, Kevin
Mulcahy, Rory
Mullin, Michael F
Mullins, Joe
Murphy, Denis F
Murphy, Dom
Murphy, Donal
Murphy, Frank
Murphy, Frank J

Murphy, Gavin	O'Connor, Michael	O'Keeffe, Peter
Murphy, Gerard	O'Connor, Stephen	O'Leary, Denis
Murphy, John P	O'Connor, Thomas P	O'Leary, Denis, Revd.
Murphy, John Paul	O'Connor, Thomas PF	O'Leary, Edward
Murphy, Mark	O'Connor, Tom F	O'Leary, Flor A
Murphy, Maurice A	O'Donnell, Bryan B	O'Leary, Flor J
Murphy, Michael	O'Donnell, Jerry	O'Leary, Jamie
Murphy, Peter D	O'Donnell, Myles	O'Mahony, Darragh
Murphy, Raymond (Ray)	O'Donoghue, Brendan N	O'Mahony, Declan
Murphy jun., Raymond	O'Donoghue, Finbarr J	O'Mahony, Denis
Murphy, Seán	O'Donoghue, Jim	O'Mahony, Ger
Murphy, Stephen	O'Donoghue, John M	O'Mahony, John C
Murphy, Tadgh Og	O'Donoghue, Kieran	O'Mahony, Michael
Murphy, Will	O'Donoghue, Patrick (Paddy)	O'Mahony, Val
Murray, Darragh	O'Donoghue, Peter	O'Mahony, Val D
Murray, David J	O'Donova jun., Teddy	O'Mara, Alex
Murray, David T	O'Donovan, Conor	O'Mara, Colin
Murray, Donal B	O'Donovan, Denis	O'Mara, Patrick J
Murray jun., Donal	O'Donovan, Denis J	O'Neill, Brian, Dr
Murray, Kieran	O'Donovan, Donal J	O'Neill, Denis
Murray, Tom	O'Donovan, Eamon	O'Neill, Frank
Murray, Traolach	O'Donovan, Michael	O'Neill, Liam A
Musgrave, David	O'Donovan, Michael J	O'Neill, Michael, Dr
Mythen, Mark	O'Donovan jun., Michael J	O'Neill, Michael
Nagle, John	O'Donovan, Noel	O'Neill, Noel
Nagle, William	O'Donovan, Pat	O'Neill, Paddy A
Neligan, Paul	O'Donovan, Pat A	O'Neill, Ronan
Nestor, Dermot	O'Donovan, Patrick D	O'Neill, Steven
Nicholson, Ciaran W	O'Donovan, Rory	O'Regan, Alex
Nicholson, Garry S	O'Donovan, Seán	O'Regan, Andrew
Nicholson, Seán K	O'Donovan, Shane	O'Regan, Billy
Noonan, Edward	O'Donovan, Ted P	O'Regan, Brendan, Dr
Noonan, Robin	O'Dowling, Ryan	O'Regan, Charlie
Norton, Liam, Dr	O'Driscoll, Alan	O'Regan, Liam, Revd.
O'Brien, Brian D	O'Driscoll, Brendan	O'Reilly, Stephen
O'Brien, Colum P	O'Driscoll, Michael	O'Riordan, David R
O'Brien, Conor	O'Driscoll, Philip	O'Riordan, Don J
O'Brien, Donal A, Revd.	O'Flaherty, Dermot F	O'Riordan, James
O'Brien, Parie L	O'Flynn, Ian	O'Riordan, Jeremiah (Jerry)
O'Brien, Pat	O'Halloran, Ian	O'Riordan, Niall
O'Brien, Patrick J	O'Halloran, James	O'Riordan, Thomas F
O'Callaghan, Aaron	O'Halloran, Michael F, Dr	O'Riordan, Tom J
O'Callaghan, Bernard	O'Halloran, Michael P	O'Shaughnessy, Bernard D
O'Callaghan, John C	O'Halloran, Tadgh	O'Shaughnessy jun., Bernard R
O'Callaghan, Kevin, Msgr.	O'Hanlon, Noel E	O'Shaughnessy, Eoin
O'Caoimh, Seán	O'Hanlon, Roy	O'Shaughnessy, James B
O'Connell, Barry	O'Hara, Rory	O'Shaughnessy, John
O'Connell, David	O'Herlihy jun., Maurice	O'Shaughnessy, Michael J
O'Connell, Declan G	O'Herlihy, Daniel (Donal) A	O'Shea, Cornelius (Con)
O'Connell, Kieran	O'Herlihy, Gareth (Gary) D	O'Shea, Diarmuid
O'Connell, Pat	O'Herlihy, Maurice J	O'Shea, Niall
O'Connell, Tom	O'Herlihy, Pat J Fr	O'Sullivan PP, Teddy, Revd.
O'Connor, Bill	O'Herlihy, Stephen E	O'Sullivan, Charles A
O'Connor, Colm	O'Keeffe, Anthony, Revd.	O'Sullivan, Colin J
O'Connor, Jack	O'Keeffe, Cormac	O'Sullivan, Dan

O'Sullivan, Derek
O'Sullivan, Donal F
O'Sullivan, Felix D
O'Sullivan, Gary D
O'Sullivan, Gerard P
O'Sullivan, Jack
O'Sullivan, Jerome
O'Sullivan, Joe
O'Sullivan, John F
O'Sullivan, John M
O'Sullivan, John R
O'Sullivan, Kevin J
O'Sullivan, Kevin N
O'Sullivan, Kevin T
O'Sullivan, Killian
O'Sullivan, Mark
O'Sullivan, Mark J
O'Sullivan, Michael T
O'Sullivan, Nigel
O'Sullivan, Patrick A
O'Sullivan, Seán
O'Sullivan, Tadhg, Dr
O'Sullivan, Timothy J
O'Sullivan, William H
O'Tuama, Barra
Olden, Brian
Olden, Dan
Olden, Niall
Oliver, Barry, Dr
Oliver, John
Owens, Gerard
Owens, Richard
Pierce, Kevin
Poland, Don
Poland, James
Poland, John
Poland, Mark
Poland, Vincent
Power, James
Power, Tony
Prenderville, Michael
Quinlan, John Frank
Quinlan, John M
Quinn, Philip J
Quinn, Ray
Quinn, Tom
Ratcliffe, Thomas P
Reardon, Gerry J
Reardon, Robert
Reardon, Tim
Redmond, Shane
Revd. Bursor, The
Riordan, J Cashel
Riordan, Patrick J
Ronan, Jack F

Ronan, Seán
Ronayne, Dave
Rose, Vincent
Ryan, Daniel J
Ryan, Gerry
Ryan, John G
Ryan, John P
Ryan, Peter C, Dr
Ryan, Shane
Ryan, Tony
Santry, Michael
Scanlan, Andrew J
Scanlan, Eamon G
Scanlan, Frank
Scanlan, Shane
Scannell, Billy
Scannell, John
Scannell, Niall
Scannell, Rory
Scott, Conor
Scully, Paul
Shannon, Brendan F
Sheehan, Eddie
Sheehan, Fintan
Sheehan, Frank
Sheehan, James T
Sheehan, John C
Sheehan, John F
Sheehan, Michael V
Sheehan, Niall
Sheill, Jack
Sheridan, Noel P
Shinkwin, Charles A
Silke, Ian K
Sinnott, Declan
Smith, Ray
Spillane, Brian
Stack, Eoin
Stack, Peter
Stokes, Dylan
Stokes, Glen
Sugrue, Kevin
Sugrue, Tadhg
Synnott, Edward C Prof.
Thomas, Andrew
Thomas, Benjamin A
Thomas, David
Thomas, Ian A
Thomas, Matthew R
Thompson, Geoffrey F
Thompson, Gerard
Thompson, Sam
Tingle, Paul
Treacy, Byron
Treacy, James

Treacy, John
Treacy, Paul
Treacy, Seán
Troy, Dermot
Troy, Frank Capt.
Twomey, Barry
Twomey, Cillian, Dr
Twomey, Colman
Twomey, David A
Twomey, Feargal, Dr
Tyrrell, Malcolm
Uniacke, Aidan
Uniacke, Bernard D
Wain, Barry
Wain, Brian
Wall, Liam
Walsh, Frank
Walsh, Michael
Walsh, Michael J
Walsh, Pat
Walsh, Paul
Waters, Eoin, Dr
Watson, Brendan J, Dr
Watson, Daragh J
West, Eoin
West, Leo
Whelan, Bryan K
Whelan, David, Dr
Whelan, David
Whelan, James
Whelan, Richard
Whelehan, Bernard
Whelehan, Richard Marcus
Whelton, Michael, Dr
Whooley, Brian
Wilkins, Jack
Wilkinson, Adrian, Revd.
Williams, Barry

Members: Female

Ahern, Maura
Arthurs, Christine
Arthurs, Theresa
Attridge, Margaret
Baker, Shivaun
Barber, Frances M
Barber, Louise
Barrett, Joan M
Barrett, Mary
Barriscale, Terry
Barry, Anne
Barry, Bernadette
Barry, Gillian
Barry, Helen
Barry, Irene
Barry, Kay
Barry, Lynda
Barry, Margaret
Barry, Marguerite
Barry, Susan
Barry, Una
Bayliss, Veronica P
Beechinor-Collins, Alice
Bergin, Sarah
Bohan, Jane
Boland, Mairin M
Boland, Maura
Buckley, Deirdre D
Buckley, Eucharia
Buckley, Fiona
Buckley, Fiona
Buckley, Frances
Buckley, Grace
Buckley, Grace C
Buckley, Maeve C
Buckley, Mary T
Burke, Betty
Burns, Ali
Burns, Veronica
Buttimer, Geralyn
Byrne, Ann M
Byrne, Gretta
Canniffe, Patricia
Canton, Noelle
Canty, Mary Veronica V
Canty, Pauline
Carmody, Rhona Dr
Carrigy, Clare M
Carrigy, Niamh
Casey, Deirdre M
Cawley, Kay
Clancy, Roisin
Clune, Deirdre

Clune, Elizabeth
Clune, Patricia
Clune, Sarah
Coakley, Maeve
Cody, Mary M
Cogan, Clio
Cogan, Jackie
Cogan, Laura
Coleman, Alice
Collins, Mary
Collins, Mary B
Conlon, Kitty
Connolly, Louise
Connolly, Patricia
Conway, Amy
Conway, Jean
Conway, Myrtle
Conway, Susan
Costello, Mary
Coughlan, Joan
Coughlan, Leah
Coughlan, Veronica
Crofts, Yvonne
Cronin, Jakki
Cronin, Liz
Cronin, Margaret
Cronin, Mary F
Crowley, Kathleen
Cullen, Valery
Cullen-Hayes, Mary
Cullinane, Valerie
Daly, Emma
Daly, Pippa
Daly, Wendy A
Deasy, Sarah
Deegan, Ann
Dennehy, Val
Desmond, Margaret
Desmond, Pat
Dillon, Judy
Dillon, Kitty
Dillon, Patricia
Donovan, Valerie
Doolan, Lia
Dorgan, Ann F
Dromey, Mary
Dudley, Imelda
Duffy, Mary
Duggan, Amy
Dullea, Eileen
Dwyer, Suzanne
Dwyer, Sylvia
Edwards, Catherine

Egan, Mary
Elwood, Esther C
Elwood, Helen E
Farmer, Mary
Farmer, Rachel
Farmer, Ruth
Farry, Teresa
Fehily, Teresa
Fitzgerald, Ciara
Fitzgerald, Jill
Fleming, Lucy
Foley, Deirdre
Foley, Maureen
Forde, Freda B
Fox, Mary
Gaffney, Margot
Gaffney, Ruth
Gallagher, Mary J
Galvin, Eimar
Galvin, Maureen P, Dr
Gleeson, Anne C
Golden-Barry, Brenda
Griffith, Maura
Hanley, Ann
Harrington, Evelyn
Harrington, Mary B
Harrington, Patricia
Harrington, Phyllis
Harte, Mary
Hartnett, Anne
Harvey, Ann
Harvey, Grace
Harvey, Kate
Harvey, Susan
Hayes, Ellen
Hayes, Mary
Healy, Dara
Heffernan, Bernie
Heffernan, Biddy
Heffernan, Colette
Hegarty, Ann
Hegarty, Anne P
Hegarty, Cliodhna
Hegarty, Elizabeth
Hegarty, Patricia Anne
Hennessy, Helen
Hennessy, Tess
Herbert, Hilary
Herbert, Suzy E
Herlihy, Rian
Heskin, Mary
Hickey, Fiona
Higgins, Andrea

Higgins, Dylla
Higgins, Mary G
Higgins, May
Hodgins, Mary Pat
Hogan, Linda
Horan, Jennifer
Horan, Nuala
Horgan, Anne Marie
Horgan, Emily
Horgan, Maddie
Horgan, Marjorie
Horgan, Mary V
Horgan, Rachael
Hornibrook, Jill
Hughes, Ann M
Hurley, Ethel M
Hurley, Mary
Hurley, Niamh
Hurley, Patsy
Hurley, Sinead A
Hurley, Susan P
Hutchinson, Ann
Jermyn, Mary
Jordan, Rena
Judge Casey, Martyna
Kavanagh, Orna
Kearney, Patricia
Keary, Marian
Keating, Clare
Keating, Nuala
Kelleher Moloney, Mary E
Kelleher, Cecily
Kelleher, Esther
Kelleher, Jill
Kelleher, Maeliosa
Kelly, Helen
Kenny, Ann Marie
Kenny, Anne M
Kenny, Mary
Kidd, Breda
Kiernan, Maree
Kiernan, Valerie
Kindlon, Una
Kirwan, Ita
Lane, Angela
Lane, Aoife
Lane, Eileen
Lane, Grace
Lane, Hilary
Lane, Jane A
Lane, Niamh
Lane, Sheila
Langford, Nuala
Lavelle, Maria Bernadette
Leader, Mary P

Leahy, Joan
Leahy, Mary
Lehane, Holly
Lehane, Tara
Lonergan, Patricia
Long, Claire
Lynch, Hilda
Lynch, Pamela
Lynch-Healy, Mary
Lyne, Maureen
Lyons, Sally
Mac Cann, Kate
MacCurtain Mc Grath, F
MacCurtain, Mai
Mackessy, Mary
Mackey, Anna G
Mackey, Katie
Mackey, Margaret
Mackey, Mary
Mackey, Patricia
Madden, Ann
Mansfield, Alethea
Martin, Máirín T
Martin, Phyllis
McCann, Carmel
McCarthy, Helen
McCarthy, Pauline
McD Murphy, Ursula
McDaid, Una B
McGrath, Maura
McGrath, Ruth N
McHenry, Patricia A
McHugh, Kay
McNicholl, Sheila
Mee, Claire G
Meyler, Stella
Mills, Bernie
Mills, Greta
Mills, Sarah
Molloy, Catherine, Dr
Moloney, Constance
Monaghan, Lisa
Monaghan, Phyllis
Moran, Frances
Morris, Ciara
Morris, Jill
Morris, Ursula
Mulcahy, Norma
Murphy, Alice
Murphy, Carmel
Murphy, Catherine
Murphy, Claire
Murphy, Della
Murphy, Emer
Murphy, Grace

Murphy, Jean
Murphy, Julie
Murphy, Linda
Murphy, Margot
Murphy, Marjorie
Murphy, Mary
Murphy, Mary E
Murphy, Vivienne
Murray, Marion
Murray, Siobhan
Musgrave, Avril
Nagle, Breda
Nagle, Helen
Nagle, Sabina M
Nash, Claire D
Nation, Fiona
Noonan, Chelsea
Norton, Dara
O'Brien Scanlan, Muriel
O'Brien, Eileen M
O'Brien, Evelyn
O'Brien, Gillian B
O'Brien, Kate
O'Brien, Peggy
O'Connell, Aileen P
O'Connell, Rosemary
O'Connell, Susan
O'Connor, Claire
O'Connor, Eleanor M
O'Connor, Jennifer
O'Connor, Mary
O'Connor, Nuala, Dr
O'Connor, Valerie
O'Donnell, Elizabeth V
O'Donoghue, (Mary) Patricia
O'Donoghue, Bonnie T
O'Donoghue, Noelle
O'Donoghue, Patricia
O'Donovan, Deirdre
O'Donovan, Eileen
O'Donovan, Elaine
O'Dowling, Brenda M
O'Driscoll, Eileen
O'Driscoll, Geraldine
O'Farrell, Aoife
O'Flynn, Stephanie
O'Halloran, Ber
O'Halloran, Elaine
O'Halloran, Gillian M
O'Halloran, Grace
O'Halloran, Lisa
O'Hanlon, Alice Maude
O'Hanlon, Ciara
O'Hanlon, Deirdre
O'Hanlon, Deirdre M

O'Hanlon, Rachael
O'Hara, Catherine
O'Hara, Claire
O'Hara, Kate
O'Hara, Maeve
O'Herlihy, Brigid Marieann
O'Herlihy, Christine A
O'Herlihy, Ciara C
O'Keeffe, Kay
O'Keeffe, Norma
O'Keeffe, Saerlaith
O'Kennedy, Isobel
O'Kennedy, Laura
O'Leary Cooney, Mary
O'Leary, Aisling
O'Leary, Eileen
O'Leary, Eileen M
O'Leary, Jackie
O'Leary, Susan
O'Mahony, Margaret
O'Mahony, Noreen
O'Neill, Eileen
O'Neill, Karen
O'Neill, Maureen
O'Regan, Rosemarie
O'Riordan, Aine
O'Riordan, Sally
O'Shaughnessy, Meg
O'Shaughnessy, Teresa
O'Shea, Patricia
O'Sullivan, Ann P
O'Sullivan, Anne M
O'Sullivan, Claire
O'Sullivan, Deirdre A

O'Sullivan, Gwen, Dr
O'Sullivan, Helen
O'Sullivan, Kathleen
O'Sullivan, Mary
O'Sullivan, Michelle
O'Sullivan, Sinead
O'Sullivan, Susan
O'Toole, Ciara
Pearce, Catherine
Poland, Bretha
Poland, Cathy
Poland, Kay
Powell, Claire
Quinn, Renee
Quinn, Rhona
Redmond, Rose
Ringrose, Ann
Ronan, Deirdre M
Ronayne, Jayne
Ronayne, Kaye
Rose, Ann
Rose, Marion
Rosingrave, Clare
Ruby, Mary
Russell, Deirdre
Ryan, Carmel
Ryan, Rosaleen
Ryan, Sarah
Ryan, Siobhan E
Scanlan, Noreen
Scanlan, Nuala
Scanlan, Rose
Scanlon, Margaret B
Scannell, Edie

Scannell, Kate
Shannon, Valerie
Sheehan, Clodagh
Sheehan, Fiona
Sheehan, Helen
Sheehan, Judy
Sheehan, Laura
Sheehan, Mary
Sheehan, Yvonne
Slattery, Joan
Smith, Joan
Sugrue, Mary
Sullivan, Kathleen
Tassie, Betty
Thompson, Ailish
Thompson, Margaret
Toner, Mary
Troy, Joan M
Twomey, Bridie
Twomey, Maggie
Tyrrell, Lucy
Walsh, Lisa
Walsh, Niamh
Walsh, Róisín
Warren, Ann
Watson, Bernie
Whelan, Mary
Whelan, Una
Whelan, Valerie
Whelehan, Hilda M
Whooley, Patricia
Wilkins, Karen K
Withrington, Jean

Members of Douglas Golf Club committees celebrate centenary year.

Endnotes

Chapter 1: Origins

1. C O'Rahilly (ed.), *Táin Bó Cúalnge from the Book of Leinster* (Dublin, 1970), 160.
2. Quoted in William Gibson, *Early Irish Golf: The First Courses, Clubs and Pioneers* (Naas, 1988), 5.
3. Ibid. 9.
4. G Cousins, *Golf in Britain: A Social History from the Beginnings to the Present Day* (London, 1975), 4.
5. Ibid. 51–2.
6. Gibson, *Early Irish Golf*, op. cit., 87.
7. Quoted in Gibson, *Early Irish Golf*, op. cit., 41.
8. Tim O'Brien, *Golf in Cork* (2006, unpublished), 1.
9. Quoted in Gibson, *Early Irish Golf*, op. cit., 44.
10. O'Brien, *Golf in Cork*, op. cit., 1.
11. M Heffernan, *Kinsale Golf Club, 1912–1987* (no place or date of publication given), 3–5.
12. Quoted in O'Brien, *Golf in Cork*, op. cit., 5.
13. *Fermoy Golf Club: 100 Years of Golf, 1892–1992* (no author or place of publication given).
14. O'Brien, *Golf in Cork*, op. cit., 7.
15. Ibid. 12, 14–15.
16. Ibid. 15, 17; Gibson, *Early Irish Golf*, op. cit., 154, 217.
17. O'Brien, *Golf in Cork*, op. cit., 13–14, 19.
18. D S Duncan (ed.), *Golfing Annual, 1895–96*, 228.
19. W Menton, *Golfing Union of Ireland, 1891–1991* (Dublin, 1991), 17.

Chapter 2: Beginnings: 1909–1911

1. Copies of these documents were kindly lent by Liam Connolly of Douglas Golf Club.
2. *Irish Times*, 20 Nov. 1909.
3. *Cork Examiner*, 24 July 1909.
4. Ibid. 21 July 1909.
5. Ibid. 22 July 1909.
6. Though attributed to the *Cork Examiner* of 7 Jan. 1910, this author has not been able to locate the account.
7. *Cork Examiner*, 5 Feb. 1910.
8. *Irish Field*, 27 Nov. 1909.
9. Ibid. 18 Dec. 1909.
10. *Muskerry Golf Club, 1907–2007* (no author or place of publication given), 36.
11. T M Healy, *Portmarnock Golf Club, 1894–1994: A Centenary History* (Dublin, 1993), 9.
12. *Cork Examiner*, 22 Mar. 1910.
13. Quoted in *Cork Examiner*, 20 Mar. 1911.
14. *Cork Examiner*, 23 Apr. 1910. Charlie Mulqueen, *Douglas Golf Club, 1910–1985* (Cork, 1985), incorrectly states that this competition took place on 23 April.
15. *Cork Examiner*, 3 May 1910.
16. On page 17 of Mulqueen, *Douglas Golf Club, 1910–1985*, op. cit., it is incorrectly stated that this competition took place on 5 May.
17. On page 17 of Mulqueen, *Douglas Golf Club, 1910–1985*, op. cit., it is incorrectly stated that this round was played on 22 Oct.; J J McLure's score is incorrectly given as 79.
18. *Cork Examiner*, 4 Nov. 1910.
19. Ibid. 3 Oct. 1910.
20. Ibid. 1 Nov. 1910.
21. Ibid. 5 Nov. 1910.
22. *Cork Sportsman*, 15 July 1911.

Chapter 3: War, Turbulence & Change: 1912–1920

1. Gibson, *Early Irish Golf*, op. cit., 86.
2. Ibid. 87.
3. A St Leger, *Monkstown Golf Club: A Centenary History, 1908–2008* (Monkstown, 2008), 29.
4. Gibson, *Early Irish Golf*, op. cit., 89.
5. D Gilleece and J Redmond, *Irish Ladies' Golf Union: An Illustrated Centenary History, 1893–1993* (Dublin, 1993), 10.
6. The information regarding the failure of Douglas Golf Links Ltd and the formation of the new entity Douglas Golf Club comes from a short history of the club apparently compiled by Jim Cullen in the late 1960s, a typescript of which was kindly lent by Liam Connolly. A serialised version of this was published in *Douglas Golf Club Newsletters* in 1977. Much of the information was originally given by Fr Matt McSwiney, a former president of the club.
7. Quoted in Gibson, *Early Irish Golf*, op. cit., 91.

Chapter 4: Fire! May 1921

1. *Cork Examiner*, 27, 28 May 1921; *Cork Constitution*, 28 May 1921.
2. J Borgonovo, *Spies, Informers and the 'Anti-Sinn Féin Society'* (Dublin, 2007), 93.
3. Donal Ó Drisceoil, 'Conflict and War, 1914–1923' in J Crowley et al (eds.), *Atlas of Cork City* (Cork, 2005), 260.
4. Gibson, *Early Irish Golf*, op. cit., 92, 94.
5. Minute book of general and green committee meetings (hereafter, Minutes), 27 May 1921.
6. Ibid. 31 May 1921, 4, 8 July 1921, 9, 18 Aug. 1921, 5 Jan. 1922.

7. Ibid. 29 Nov. 1921.
8. Account ledger, 1921–29.
9. Minutes, 4, 8 July 1921.
10. Ibid. 31 May 1921.
11. Ibid. 14 Oct. 1921.
12. Ibid. 9 Sept. 1921.
13. Ibid. 8 Nov. 1921.

Chapter 5: The Phoenix Rises: 1920s

1. Minutes, 30 Nov. 1923.
2. *Douglas Golf Club Newsletter* (1977).
3. Minutes, 8 Oct. 1922.
4. Ibid. 5 Feb. 1924.
5. Ibid. 15 Jan. 1925.
6. Ibid. 19 Feb. 1924.
7. Ibid. 5 Dec. 1924.
8. Account ledger, 1921–29, 26 Jan., 11 Mar. 1925.
9. A copy of this agreement with the Munster & Leinster Bank was kindly lent by Liam Connolly of Douglas Golf Club.
10. Minutes, 22, 28 May 1925, 10 Nov. 1925, 12 Jan. 1926, 13 Apr. 1926.
11. Ibid. 22 Jan. 1926.
12. Ibid. 13 Apr., 13 July 1926.
13. Ibid. 23 Oct. 1924.
14. Ibid. 8 Oct. 1924.
15. Ibid. 14 Nov. 1924.
16. Ibid. 1 Dec. 1925.
17. From an interview with Fr Daniel P Fitzgerald, 8 Apr. 2008.
18. *Irish Golf*, June 1925.
19. Ibid.
20. *Cork Examiner*, 27 Sept. 1926.
21. Ibid.
22. Menton, *Golfing Union of Ireland, 1891–1991*, op. cit., 79.
23. *Cork Examiner*, 7 Oct. 1926.
24. Ibid. 14 Aug. 1926.
25. Menton, *Golfing Union of Ireland, 1891–1991*, op. cit., 76–7.
26. St Leger, *Monkstown Golf Club: A Centenary History, 1908–2008*, op. cit., 30.
27. The figures on membership are based on counts of the subscriptions paid by members as recorded in the account ledger, 1921–29. The figures are not entirely accurate as a relatively small number of members sometimes paid their subscriptions a year in arrears, and were then not recorded as members for the previous year.
28. Minutes, 1 May 1925.
29. Ibid. 11 Aug. 1925.
30. Account ledger, 1921–29.

Chapter 6: Testing Years: 1930s & 1940s

1. *Cork Examiner*, 7 June 1930.
2. *Irish Golf*, July 1939.
3. Ibid. Aug. 1934.
4. Ibid. May 1942.
5. Ibid.
6. Minutes, 13 July 1937.
7. Ibid. 12 Oct., 9 Nov. 1937.
8. Ibid. 15 Feb. 1930.
9. Ibid. 12 Feb. 1935.
10. Ibid. 9 Nov. 1937.
11. Ibid. 9 Sept. 1941.
12. Ibid. 9 Mar. 1943.
13. Ibid. 8 Mar. 1945.
14. Ibid. 10 Dec. 1946.
15. Ibid. 10 Mar. 1949.
16. Ibid. 15 Mar. 1938.
17. Ibid. 11 May 1943, 10 July 1945, 13 Nov. 1945.
18. Ibid. 10 Nov. 1936.
19. Ibid. 19 Oct. 1943.
20. Ibid. 20 Feb. 1946.
21. Ibid. 28 Nov., 10 Dec. 1947.
22. *Irish Golf*, Dec. 1939.
23. Minutes, 9 July 1940.
24. Ibid. 13 Jan. 1942.
25. Quoted in Menton, *Golfing Union of Ireland, 1891–1991*, op. cit., 102.
26. Minutes, 12 May 1942.
27. Ibid. 9 June 1942.
28. Menton, *Golfing Union of Ireland, 1891–1991*, op. cit., 102.
29. Minutes, 11 Feb. 1942.
30. Ibid. 10 Apr. 1945.
31. Ibid. 12 Mar., 14 May, 11 June, 28 June 1935.
32. Ibid. 10 May, 14 May, 12 July 1938.
33. Ibid. 11 Sept., 9 Oct. 1945, 10 Dec. 1946.
34. Ibid. 29 July, 18 Nov., 28 Nov., 10 Dec. 1947.
35. Ibid. 20 May 1949.
36. Ibid. 12 Oct. 1950.
37. Ibid. 26 Sept. 1933.
38. Ibid. 12 Dec. 1933.
39. Ibid. 14 Jan. 1934.
40. Ibid. 15 May 1934.
41. Ibid. 13 Jan. 1949.
42. Ibid. 12, 20 May 1949.
43. Ibid. 12 Apr. 1951.

Chapter 7: Middle Years: 1950s

1. *Irish Golf*, May 1948.
2. Ibid. Mar. 1943.
3. Interview with Éamonn McSweeney, 9 Oct. 2007.
4. *Irish Golf*, June 1952.

5. Ibid.
6. Ibid. Nov. 1955.
7. Ibid. Jan. 1956.
8. Ibid. July 1955.
9. Ibid.
10. Minutes, 5 June 1963.
11. *Irish Golf,* June 1953.
12. Minutes, 12 Nov. 1953.
13. Ibid. 8 Oct. 1954.
14. Ibid. 12 Nov., 8 Dec. 1953.
15. Ibid. 21 Jan. 1955.
16. Ibid. 12 Oct., 26 Nov. 1956.
17. Ibid. 18 Oct., 16 Dec. 1957.

Chapter 8: Swinging Sixties

1. *Irish Golf,* Mar. 1965.
2. Menton, *Golfing Union of Ireland, 1891–1991,* op. cit., 127–36.
3. Minutes, 25 Feb. 1960.
4. Ibid. 26 Aug. 1960.
5. Ibid. 9 Sept. 1960.
6. Ibid. 14 Oct. 1960.
7. Ibid. 21 Oct. 1960.
8. Ibid. 31 Oct. 1960.
9. Ibid. 25 Nov. 1960.
10. Ibid. 28 July 1961.
11. *Irish Golf,* Dec. 1960.
12. Minutes, 17 July, 3 Oct. 1962.
13. Ibid. 17, 20 Dec. 1962, 25 Feb., 4 Mar. 1963.
14. *Irish Golf,* Aug. 1963.
15. Minutes, 13 Dec. 1965.
16. Ibid. 19 June 1966.
17. Ibid. 23 Feb. 1968.
18. *Cork Examiner,* 16 Sept. 1963.
19. *Irish Golf,* Oct. 1963.
20. *Cork Examiner,* 16 Sept. 1963.
21. Ibid. 4 May 1962.
22. Ibid. 25 July 1962.
23. *Irish Golf,* Nov.–Dec. 1963.
24. Minutes, 16 Apr., 15 June, 17 July, 3 Oct. 1962; *Irish Golf,* Aug. 1963.
25. Minutes, 7 July 1962.
26. Ibid. 29 Oct., 21 Nov., 3 Dec. 1962.
27. *Irish Golf,* Nov.–Dec. 1964.
28. Minutes, 29 Apr. 1974, 31 July 1978.
29. Ibid. 28 Feb. 1964.
30. Ibid. 29 Oct. 1962.
31. Ibid. 28 Jan. 1963.
32. Ibid. 27 Jan. 1964.
33. Ibid. 14, 18 Dec. 1964.
34. Ibid. 18 Dec. 1964.
35. Ibid. 28 Feb. 1966.
36. Ibid. 27 May 1960.

37. Ibid. 21 Nov. 1962.
38. Ibid. 2 Dec. 1966.
39. Ibid. 23 Feb. 1968.
40. Ibid. 23 Mar. 1970.
41. Ibid. 7 Sept., 24 Oct., 15 Nov. 1961.
42. Ibid. 26 Feb., 14 Mar. 1962.
43. Ibid. 3 Oct. 1962.
44. Ibid. 20 Dec. 1962.
45. Ibid. 17 Dec. 1962.
46. Ibid. 28 Feb. 1964.
47. Ibid. 3 Dec. 1962.
48. Ibid. 25 Feb. 1963.
49. Ibid. 26 May 1967.
50. Ibid. 16 July, 28 Aug. 1964.
51. Ibid. 27 Sept. 1968.
52. Ibid. 17 Oct. 1969.
53. Ibid. 25 Mar. 1968.

Chapter 9: 1970s

1. *Cork Examiner,* 27 Oct. 1972.
2. Ibid. 30 Oct. 1972.
3. Minutes of committee meetings of the Ladies' Branch (hereafter, Ladies' minutes), 12 Sept., 10 Oct. 1977.
4. Minutes, 21 June, 31 July 1967.
5. Ibid. 18 Nov., 16 Dec. 1968.
6. Ibid. 10 Feb., 21 Mar. 1969.
7. Ibid. 27 May, 12 Sept., 24 Nov. 1969.
8. Ibid. 16 Feb. 1970.
9. Ibid. 2 June 1970.
10. Ibid. 18 Jan., 28 June, 30 Aug. 1971.
11. Ibid. 16 Apr., 27 Apr., 14 May, 30 July 1973.
12. Ibid 25 Oct. 1976.
13. Ibid. 18 Feb. 1977.
14. Ibid. 27 Apr. 1978.
15. Ibid. 21 Oct. 1974.
16. Ibid. 28 Aug. 1978.
17. Ibid. 29 Sept. 1975.
18. Ibid 27 Feb. 1976.
19. Ibid. 1 May, 11 May, 1 Dec. 1925, 13 Jan. 1926.
20. Ibid. 20 Feb. 1950.
21. Ibid. 18 Oct., 26 Nov. 1956, 10 Jan. 1966.
22. Ibid. 21 Mar. 1974.
23. Ibid. 1 Apr. 1974.

Chapter 10: 1980s & 1990s

1. *Cork Examiner,* 20 Sept. 1986.
2. Minutes, 22 Jan. 1987.
3. *Cork Examiner,* 20 Sept. 1991.
4. Ladies' minutes, 17 Feb. 1986.
5. Minutes, 26 Sept. 1991.
6. Ibid. 24 Jan. 1992.
7. *Cork Examiner,* 17 Sept. 1999.

8. Ibid. 18 Sept. 1999.
9. Ibid.
10. Ladies' minutes, 17 Feb. 1986.
11. Minutes, 19 Feb. 1973, 22 July 1974, 18 Feb. 1977.
12. Ibid. 21 Nov. 1988.
13. Ibid. 9 Dec. 1988.
14. Ibid. 12 Dec. 1985.
15. Ibid. 29 May, 25 Sept. 1989.
16. Ibid. 28 Apr. 1992.
17. Ibid. 12 Oct. 1981.
18. Ibid. 25 Apr. 1988.
19. Ibid. 22 Nov. 1993.
20. Ibid. 23 Apr., 21 May 1990.
21. Ibid. 16 Aug. 1990.
22. Ibid. 18 Nov. 1991.
23. Ibid. 17 Dec. 1991.
24. Ibid. 29 May 1995.
25. Ibid. 24 July 1995.
26. Ibid.
27. Ibid. 28 June 1999.
28. Ibid. 15 Jan. 1992.
29. Ibid. 17, 25 Nov. 1996.
30. Ibid. 3 Jan. 1997.
31. Ibid. 13 Jan. 1997.
32. Ibid. 5 Apr., 16 June 1997.
33. Ibid. 17 Apr. 1997.
34. Ibid. 16 June 1997.

Chapter 11: Towards a New Century

1. Minutes, 25 Feb. 1991.
2. Ibid. 22 Apr. 1996.
3. Ibid. 22 Apr. 1996.
4. Ladies' minutes, 16 Sept., 12 Oct. 1998.
5. Ibid. 10 Mar. 19 July, 13 Sept., 6 Dec. 1999; Minutes, 29 Mar., 30 Aug. 1999.
6. Ladies' minutes, 31 Jan. 2000.
7. Minutes, 21 Feb. 2000.
8. Ibid.
9. Ladies' minutes, 3 Feb. 2003.

Caddies

1. Minutes, 28 May 1931.
2. Ibid. 28 Jan. 1936.
3. Ibid. 26 July 1923.
4. Ibid. 14 May 1929.
5. Ibid. 3 Sept. 1929.
6. Ibid. 15 Jan. 1931.
7. Ibid. 7 Mar. 1922.
8. Ibid. 10 Sept. 1922.
9. Ibid. 9 Nov. 1926.
10. Ibid. 10 Apr. 1945.
11. Ibid. 3 Sept. 1929.

12. Ibid. 29 July 1940.
13. Ibid. 8 Oct. 1946.
14. Ibid. 13 Nov. 1952.
15. Ibid. 28 May 1931.
16. Ibid. 8 Dec. 1931.
17. *Irish Golf*, Mar. 1953.
18. Cousins, *Golf in Britain*, op. cit., 102.

Fr Daniel Fitzgerald

1. *Evening Echo*, 15 Dec. 1984.
2. Minutes, 12 May 1947

Professionals at Douglas

1. Cousins, *Golf in Britain*, op. cit., 63.
2. A F Jackson, *The British Professional Golfers 1887–1930: A Register* (Worcestershire, 1994).

John McKenna

1. *Irish Golf*, Aug. 1935.
2. Minutes, 9 Nov., 22 Dec. 1937.
3. From a profile of John McKenna by D Russell in the programme for the 1971 Dunlop Irish Professional Golf Tournament.
4. *Irish Golf*, July 1947.
5. From a profile of John McKenna by D Russell in the programme for the 1971 Dunlop Irish Professional Golf Tournament.
6. Ibid.
7. *Evening Echo*, 15 Dec. 1984.
8. *Irish Golf*, Sept. 1945.
9. Ibid, July 1947.
10. Interview with Ann Heskin and Oonagh Fitzpatrick (Heskin), 8 Nov. 2007.
11. *Irish Golf*, July 1951.
12. From a profile of John McKenna by D Russell in the programme for the 1971 Dunlop Irish Professional Golf Tournament.
13. www.irishgolfarchive.com

Bill Kelleher

1. *Irish Golf*, Feb. 1960.
2. Ibid. Aug. 1964.
3. Ibid. Aug. 1961.
4. *Country Life*, 20 Sept. 1962.
5. *Irish Independent*, 14 Sept. 1962.
6. *Cork Examiner*, 14 Sept. 1962.
7. *Evening Echo*, 4 June 1997.
8. *Irish Golf*, Aug. 1964.
9. Ibid. Mar. 1965.

Douglas Golf Club Ladies' Branch

1. Gibson, *Early Irish Golf*, op. cit., 105.
2. M Hezlet, *Ladies' Golf* (London, 1904), 3.
3. *Cork Examiner*, 29 May 1911.
4. Hezlet, *Ladies' Golf*, op. cit., 234–5.
5. Cousins, *Golf in Britain*, op. cit., 79.
6. Hezlet, *Ladies' Golf*, op. cit., 6.
7. Cousins, *Golf in Britain*, op. cit., 79.
8. Ladies' minutes, 11 July 1940.
9. Ibid. 14 Apr. 1942.
10. Ibid. 12 Jan. 1944.
11. Ibid. 23 Aug. 1982.
12. Ibid. 8 Nov. 1982, 21 Feb. 1983.
13. Ibid. 24 Jan. 1983.
14. Ibid. 20 Jan. 1986.
15. Ibid. 9 Jan. 1942.
16. Ibid. 3 Feb. 1942.
17. Ibid. 23 Feb. 1942.
18. Ibid. 18 May 1987.
19. Ibid. 22 June, 20 July 1987.
20. Ibid. 19 Sept., 19 Oct. 1992.
21. Ibid. 17 Jan. 1994.
22. *Irish Golf*, May 1952.

Eavan Higgins

1. D Gilleece and J Redmond, *Irish Ladies' Golf Union: An Illustrated Centenary History, 1893–1993* (Dublin, 1993), 54.

Bibliography

Archive Material

The Douglas Golf Club archive is held by the club and contains the minute books of general committee meetings from 1921 to 2000. The minute books of the committee meetings of the Ladies' Branch run from 1939 to 2000. In 2000 a new management structure was introduced in the club, and since then the meetings of the management committee and of the committees of the Men's and Ladies' Clubs are minuted. The archive also contains an incomplete set of account ledgers, some membership books, minute books of the greens committee, competition books and miscellaneous other items.

Newspapers and Magazines

Cork Constitution

Irish Examiner (formerly the *Examiner* and the *Cork Examiner*)

Irish Field

Irish Times

Irish Golf, published as a monthly magazine from May 1924 to the end of 1965, was an invaluable source, but was available to this author only from January 1934, apart from the June 1925 edition; the 1934–65 editions were accessed at the British Newspapers Library at Collindale, London

Books and Articles

Beale, E, Gilleece, D and Redmond, J, *Milltown Golf Club: An Illustrated Centenary History, 1907–2007* (Dublin, 2007).

Borgonovo, J, *Spies, Informers and the 'Anti-Sinn Féin Society'* (Dublin, 2007).

Brennan, D, *Tramore Golf Club, 1894–1994* (Tramore, 1994).

Clark, R (ed.), *Golf: A Royal and Ancient Game* (Edinburgh, 1875).

Cousins, G,. *Golf in Britain: A Social History from the Beginnings to the Present Day* (London, 1975).

Darwin, B, *Historic Golf Courses of the British Isles* (London, 1987, first published in 1910 as *The Golf Courses of the British Isles*).

Doak, T, Scott, Dr J S and Haddock, R M, *The Life and Work of Dr Alister Mackenzie* (Chelsea, MI, US, 2001).

Duncan, D S (ed.), *Golfing Annual* (London, 1895–1910, 15 vols.).

Fermoy Golf Club: 100 Years of Golf, 1892–1992 (Fermoy, 1992).

Flannery, M, and Leech, R, *Golf Through the Ages* (Fairfield, IA, US, 2004).

Guy's Cork Almanac and Directory (Cork, 1895–1924, 30 vols.).

Gibson, W H, *Early Irish Golf: The First Courses, Clubs and Pioneers* (Naas, 1988).

Gilleece, D and Redmond, J, *Irish Ladies' Golf Union: An Illustrated Centenary History 1893–1993* (Dublin, 1993).

Glynn, E, *A Century of Golf at Lahinch 1892–1992* (Lahinch, 1992).

Golfing Union of Ireland year books.

Healy, T M, *Portmarnock Golf Club, 1894–1994: A Centenary History* (Dublin, 1994).

Heffernan, M, *Kinsale Golf Club, 1912–1987* (Kinsale, 1987).

Hewson, L (ed.), *The Irish Golfer's Guide* (Dublin, 1910 and 1911).

Hewson, L (ed.), *The Irish Golfing Guide* (Dublin, 1912–16, 5 vols.).

Hickey, D, *Queen of Them All: A History of Killarney Golf and Fishing Club, 1893–1993* (Killarney, 1993).

Hobbs, M, *British Open Champions* (London, 1991).

Jackson, A F, *The British Professional Golfers, 1887–1930: A Register* (Worcestershire, 1994).

Lane, V (ed.), *Royal Tara Golf Club, 1906–2006* (2006).

McGrath, W, *Tram Tracks Through Cork* (Cork, 1981).

Menton, W, *The Golfing Union of Ireland, 1891–1991* (Dublin, 1991).

Mulhall, D, '"A Gift from Scotland": Golf's Early Days in Ireland', in *History Ireland*, September/October 2006.

Mulqueen, C, *Douglas Golf Club, 1910–1985* (Cork, 1985).

Muskerry Golf Club, 1907–2007 (Cork, 2007, no author given).

O'Brien, T, *Golf in Cork* (unpublished, 2006).

Ó Drisceoil, D, 'Conflict and War 1914–1923', in Crowley, J, Devoy, R J N, Linehan, D and O'Flanagan, P (eds.), *Atlas of Cork City* (Cork, 2005).

O'Rahilly, C (ed.), *Táin Bó Cúalnge from the Book of Leinster* (Dublin, 1970).

O'Riordan, D, *St Anne's Golf Club, 1921–1996: A History of the First Seventy-Five Years* (Dublin, 1996).

Redmond, J, *The Book of Irish Golf* (Dublin, 1997).

Rooney, J P (ed.), *Irish Golfer's Blue Book* (Dublin, 1939).

Quinlan, A, *'South of Ireland': Centennial Memories* (Lahinch, 2001).

Russell, D J, *Cork Golf Club, 1888–1988* (Cork, 1988).

Ryde, P (ed.), *Royal and Ancient Championship Records, 1860–1980* (St Andrews, 1981).

Spillane, M, *Adare Manor Golf Club, 1900–2000: A Centurial Record* (Adare, 2000).

St Leger, A, *Monkstown Golf Club, 1908–1983* (Cork, 1983).

St Leger, A, *Monkstown Golf Club: A Centenary History, 1908–2008* (Monkstown, 2008).

Afterword

No doubt these pages have raised an eyebrow, drawn a smile, or brought a tear to the eye, but I am sure you have enjoyed this book. Many thanks to all involved in its production, especially to Diarmuid, the author.

As can be seen from reading this history, the fortunes of the club have ebbed and flowed over the years. Whatever difficulty arose it was overcome. I am sure that no matter what the future holds for Douglas Golf Club, we would all be confident that in 2109 the second volume of our history will be published!

Tar éis an leabhar seo a léamh, táim cinnte gur bhain tú, a léitheoir, taitneamh as agus b'fhéidir gur shil tú deoir nó gur dhein tú gáire faoi rud éigin a léigh tú. Buíochas le gach duine a raibh baint acu leis an obair seo, go mór mhór le Diarmuid, an t-údar.

Tá sé soiléir ón stair seo gur sháraigh an club na constaicí agus na dúshláin a tháinig os a chomhair thar na blianta. Pé deacrachtaí atá i ndán don chlub amach anseo, táim cinnte go sárófar iad leis agus go bhfeicfear an dara imleabhar d'ár stair sa bhliain 2109!

Paul Clune
Chairman 2009

Index